ONE WORLD,
MANY NEIGHBORS

ONE WORLD, MANY NEIGHBORS

A Christian Perspective on Worldviews

Perry C. Cotham

Abilene Christian University Press

Abilene, Texas

ONE WORLD, MANY NEIGHBORS
A Christian Perspective on Worldviews

Copyright 2008 by Perry C. Cotham

ISBN 978-0-89112-522-8

Printed in the United States of America

Cover design by Marc Whitaker
Interior text design by Sandy Armstrong

For information contact:
Abilene Christian University Press
1648 Campus Court
Abilene, Texas 79601

1-877-816-4455 toll free
www.abilenechristianuniversitypress.com

Contents

Outside the Box

Whether you are aware of it or not, you already have a worldview. And each typical day you are involved in the process of being influenced by that worldview, perceiving the unfolding of history by this worldview, and/or refining and reshaping that worldview. And, to further complicate matters, your present worldview and sense of security influence how much you are willing to examine your deepest convictions and most cherished values. How fascinating that you may currently think in such a way that prevents enriching your thinking and enjoying the fruit of an examined life! Having lived over a half century of study, travel, multiple careers, and other life experiences, I cannot pretend to possess all the answers to the limitless questions that abound in life. The specifications for a fulfilling life cannot be neatly packed into a neat box, wrapped with colorful paper, and tied with bright ribbon and bow.

Life situations often remain deeply complicated. We can be at a loss to understand the passions and values that drive people's behavior. How do we explain why some cruel and traumatizing violence committed by one activist brings the label of "terrorist" within one worldview and within another worldview the same activist might be called a "freedom fighter"? In Tel Aviv or Jerusalem, one angry young man may enter a restaurant or nightclub filled with customers and set off a bomb strapped around his waist in the expectation of killing a number of Jewish citizens, thus terminating his life for the cause of Palestinian liberation. In the heart of Africa, another young man may have left a comfortable home on another continent and offer his life as a "living sacrifice," risking his body's contracting malaria or some other tropical disease, in order to bring good news and healing to a community of impoverished natives.

How could each of these persons possess a worldview that reinforces such radically nontraditional behavior by equating it with honor and service to God? One may expect an immediate reward as a welcomed martyr in paradise and a financial payoff for his immediate family whom he hopes will remember him as a man of courage and honor. The other may imagine no precise blueprint for the afterlife and in fact may not be a believer in any divine being, but seeks only the reward of inner joy and satisfaction for a life fulfilled in sacrificial service to "the least of these" among us.

One woman is convinced there is a personal, benevolent, providential Creator God who cares about her and guides even the smallest of her personal choices, yet also holds her accountable for every personal thought, decision, and action. Another woman concedes only that there might be some vague, impersonal higher power that somehow permeates all living entities but makes no real difference in her life and certainly could not lead her to think in terms of guilt and forgiveness. What makes the difference in the worldviews that espouse such contrasting conceptions of Ultimate Reality?

Why do some individuals in American society resort to the practice of witchcraft or attunement to the sacred powers of nature, claiming an intimate connection with a European pre-Christian religion called *Wicca*, while the majority does not? Why do billions read sacred texts and consider the vast world around them and believe in one great God, while billions of others consider the vast world about them and believe in many gods (and a few, of course, believe in no god at all)? Why do some young people seem to be "carbon copies" of their parents' Christian faith commitment and others defect from the Christian faith and embrace Buddhism? Why are more students declaring they are agnostic about the existence of a Supreme Being? And why the renewed interest in atheism in this nation? The fact that such questions are not easily answered does not render the questions any less important.

As Christians we do not enjoy the option of picking the times in which we live. We are challenged, however, to make sense of what is happening all around us, and we are definitely summoned to engage the culture for the noble cause of our Lord's will for humankind. We must not retreat. Our religious commitment needs a strong dose of humility, but it need not be timid.

This book confronts life's greatest questions and its most significant issues and how they are answered in a wide variety of worldviews and world contexts. The following discussion is certainly not intended to be a comprehensive textbook, though you will find its pages touching on a variety of subject areas, especially theology, philosophy, history, apologetics, and biography. The attempt here is to provide fresh thinking and to integrate Christian faith and contemporary culture.

I hope that as you read you will learn a great deal. You may be a bright student in a university, perhaps even a graduate program, or maybe even in high school. You may feel that your faith is "rock solid," or you may be one of a growing number of young people who think and live on the fringes of religious faith. You, like many university students I know, may be a seeker; or you may be a person who considers yourself to be spiritual but not "religious."

On the other hand, you may be a serious and intelligent Christian man or woman of mature faith and spiritual security, yet willing to think "outside the box" of the traditional Christian doctrine that safeguards all the ideas, propositions, and admonitions you were taught early in life. Actually, Christians should always remain seekers, too. Typically, seekers rely on a clue or organizing principle in their search. The difference between Christian seekers and non-Christian seekers is that Christians believe the decisive clue or organizing principle is revealed in Jesus the Christ.

Sharing new facts is not the most important purpose of this writing, of course. My hope is that you will come to a better understanding of your own worldview, as well as to understand the worldviews held by many other people whose backgrounds are different from your own, and then come to evaluate and re-shape your own worldview. No matter your background, you will be introduced to a diversity of ideas, thinkers, and personalities. Diversity should be welcomed, not because it is politically correct but because diversity provides the context for learning new ideas, developing empathy for others, discovering new insights, and exploring mysteries of life.

While religious pluralism has always been around, the world almost seems too populous, too dangerous, and too tragic for us not to see reality from others' point of view. Though the 9/11 attacks on the USA compelled most Americans to take their first serious look at Islam, surely mayhem, violence, and fear must not be prerequisites for a religion or worldview to merit serious attention and understanding!

For Christian readers, my hope is that your faith can be deepened, refined, and rendered more realistic. This book attempts to find some answers, draw some analogies, make comparisons, and offer some counsel to readers seeking to understand or deepen personal faith. For non-Christian readers and others who seek knowledge and insight, my hope is that this dialogue is both fair and honest as I place the major worldviews side by side and as I state the unique claims both of Christianity and of some other religions, too.

So I approach this study with a deep measure of both respect for the sincerity and devotion of adherents to other faiths and humility about my own perceptions and conclusions. Still, the plan here is not simply to structure logical arguments and marshal evidence on behalf of Christian doctrine and claims. How much more respectful to invite you to think like a mature Christian or sincere seeker, to read some stories of other sincere men and women who "fleshed out" their worldview convictions in their own time and culture, to draw your own conclusions honestly and independently, and to act decisively and courageously!

Additionally, because the lives of so many of the people discussed here have been inspiring to so many people over the centuries, I feel compelled to lead you in some devotional reflections at the end of each chapter. For my Christian readers, this is not intended to be the typical devotional book that offers brief inspirational readings. Too often Christianity has been taught like a math formula employing the "If..., then..." equation. "If you do this, then you will please God and go to heaven. If you don't, your sad destination will be eternal punishment." It seems all too tempting and oddly reassuring for some to reduce the Christian faith to a set of memorizable rules and equations and to imprison God in a box of our own parochial conceptions and expectations. Only occasionally will these devotional thoughts dare to make application to your life, though generally you are trusted to be intelligent and resourceful enough to make your own applications.

The Japanese word *shin-ken* draws meaning from both the Shinto and Buddhist worldviews. *Shin-ken* literally means "real sword," but its practical meaning is "to do with utmost earnestness" or "to be deadly serious." Buddhism teaches the value of seriousness of mind, of being single-minded and undistracted while grappling with weighty matters. As a reader, please join me in *shin-ken,* being deadly serious about these subjects and issues raised. The only two additional prerequisites I ask that you bring to these pages are an open, seeking mind and a humble, loving heart.

We live in one world. On one hand, we share the common virtues and frailties, the common hopes and dreams, of all humanity, past and present. So we proceed on the reasonable assumption that there are positive lessons and rich insights to be garnered from various faith traditions that have been followed for centuries. On the other hand, a Christian perspective clearly and unapologetically pervades every topic in this book. I could not avoid the Christian perspective even if I tried.

My prayer is that this material will stimulate your thinking in the direction of knowing Jesus Christ as the author and perfector of your worldview, to know Jesus as a Savior who promised to share the Spirit of God with you as an abiding presence for life's journey—every step, every day.

Identifying and acknowledging all the streams of influence that made some impact on this book—whether other authors, teachers, colleagues, students, and, most of all, valued friends—would most certainly be impossible. In classrooms and other venues for conversation, I'm sure that often I have learned as much or more from some friends and students as they have learned from me.

Some special acknowledgements, offered with much gratitude, are very much in order. First, to Dr. Leonard Allen, Director of ACU Press/Leafwood Publishers, I express appreciation for his confidence and support in general and, specifically, for highly professional editorial direction and counsel.

To Carolyn Wilson, Director of Beaman Library, Lipscomb University, and her excellent professional staff, I am grateful for the resource material made accessible for this study and for the comfortable research and writing environment this library provided for my frequent visits.

To Diane Kilmer, an excellent writer and editor, I am greatly appreciative for her professional assistance in copyediting and proofing the text in the last stage of this book's production and for her enthusiasm and encouragement in general.

And, finally, to my dear brothers and sisters in the fellowship of Owen Chapel, Brentwood, Tennessee, I am thankful for their willingness to provide copies of this book to a number of missionaries, mission families, and university students with a strong interest in missions. Many of these recipients will be engaging cultures where a Christian worldview clashes with other, more dominant worldviews.

Perry C. Cotham
January 2008

1

Lessons Learned in a Guatemalan Village

I t was around 2:30 A.M. A nurse from the little hospital across the walkway entered the unlocked room I shared with Marcos Diaz, a native Guatemalan and minister, and Dr. Kenneth Mitchell, a gynecological surgeon who practiced his medical specialty in Pensacola, Florida. The nurse whispered an urgent request in Ken's ears. Ken answered: "There's no way any of us can leave the hospital and barracks area and go into the darkness of the night to someone's home. That may create a real risk for someone here in our program. Tell the father to bring his daughter to us if he believes she is in real danger."

Less than an hour later, the nurse returned to our quiet room. "The father has gotten here with his sick daughter. They rode here in a neighbor's pickup truck. The man's wife is here, too." Ken arose immediately, pulled on some slacks, a shirt, and some shoes and headed across the way to the clinic at which 30 to 35 of us representing Health Talents International had come to devote a week of our September in 1999 to providing health care, diagnosis, surgery, and counseling to the residents of an impoverished village in Guatemala named Chocola.

I lay in bed for a few minutes wondering what I should do. "Obviously, there is some girl who is sick and her dad and mom brought her to the clinic," I reasoned, "but I had not been summoned to offer any spiritual assistance. I wonder how sick she really is." My role on this medical missions' journey was chaplain. I was expected to provide spiritual leadership for the full week, including the directing of worship services, nightly devotionals, teaching and answering questions for any who were interested. During the day

13

when the surgeons and nurses were performing operations, I learned as much about medical missions, surgery, and native Central Americans that I could assimilate.

Yet this night-time visit was both unusual and haunting. "Maybe I'm needed in some way at the clinic," I thought. I slipped out of my bed, which was only a thin mattress stretched over some small springs, and into some walking shorts, tennis shoes, and my orange U.T. tee shirt, a shirt I wore proudly since the Vols' football team had won the national championship a few months earlier, and walked the brief distance to the clinic.

The situation was much more grave than I dared to imagine. A panicked father and mother had watched their daughter grow suddenly gravely ill and lapse into a coma after 25 days of vomiting and diarrhea followed by nose bleeds, dehydration, and accompanying weakness. Ken later told me this was a simple case of salmonella or food poisoning, and the end stage of the ailment is characterized by peritonitis, overwhelming sepsis, and renal failure. Some of the terms were unfamiliar to me. When the patient was brought to the clinic, she had a temperature of 94 degrees, a weak pulse, and rigid abdomen. As it turns out, this patient was not a young girl but rather an 18 year-old young woman.

"There's nothing we can do for your daughter," Ken explained to the parents. "It is now too late to do anything for her physically." Within minutes after the young woman was placed on a gurney, her respiration became erratic and labored. Her helpless mother cradled the young woman's head and lifted it slightly to help her breathe. And so, Ken joined the stunned parents by placing hands on their daughter and we all prayed for a measure of grace to sustain this family during that terrible hour.

What followed was that deep, nauseating pain deep within one's gut and the broken heart cry that something grossly unfair had irreversibly occurred. There's no greater perversion in nature than parents having to say goodbye to one of their children. The eyelids of this young woman were lovingly and gently closed and I looked more closely upon her face—a stunningly beautiful face with rich brown skin. I, along with others who were gathering, lingered in silence beside her lifeless body. The awesomeness of a death which had just occurred, compounded by the tragedy that the disease could have been treated with antibiotics so easily only a few days earlier, left me speechless and tearful.

For what seemed like the longest time, several stood around in the room and later moved out on the sidewalk in front of the building. Connie Campbell, a nurse from Kentucky, and I wrapped our arms around a sobbing mother. There were few words uttered. My Spanish was inadequate. I kept trying to say something akin to "yo tengo siento," but I knew those words were inadequate. Connie and I maintained this hugging support for the sobbing mother for over half an hour. One by one, others of our group had been awakened and quietly joined the gathering outside the clinic and in hushed tones shared the news of what had happened and their reactions to the tragedy.

As the rays of the morning sun were scissoring their way between the eastern Guatemalan mountains, the dad, mom, and their neighbor who owned the old Japanese-vintage pickup truck in which they had delivered their patient began to gather themselves to journey home. A translator came to me with a message from this grieving family—a request that I come to the graveside service which would take place later in the day.

What I witnessed next once again tore at my heart, filling my eyes with tears. As the wife and their neighbor got inside the cab of the truck, the father slowly picked up the lifeless body of his daughter. Her remains had been wrapped in the ordinary blanket in which she had been wrapped when delivered to the clinic hours earlier. The father carried his precious cargo to the truck bed, lifting her over the wall, gently laid her in the back of the truck. He next slowly and silently climbed over the tailgate and took his seat next to the body as the truck slowly moved down the rocky road toward their home.

Unknown to us during this ordeal, the native cooks and servants had gathered outdoors to form a tight huddle, placing their young children in the middle of the protective circle. Hovering over their precious little ones as the truck slowly vanished down the road, they were offering prayers and incantations to prevent the wandering spirit of death which had departed the young woman upon her death from invading any of them, especially their children. We later learned that this numbing encounter with death is not uncommon, and it reminded us of what medical missions in a third world country is all about.

A Worldview—What Is It?

On that early morning in 1999 in the almost primitive village of Chocola, worldviews collided. Or at least they encountered each other. For you see, worldviews do not meet in the library. Religious truths do not encounter each other in the pages of a textbook. They meet in the minds and souls of men and women and get fleshed out in the crises and unexpected moments of real life.

On the one hand, during those early morning hours of darkness, there were well-educated doctors, nurses, and other medical staff. All but two of us were professing Christians and most were quite active in our local churches. All of us reflected sadly that the right antibiotic given at the right time would have been the agent of quick healing for this lovely young woman. None of us believed that the sick woman was possessed by an evil spirit that would leave her body upon its expiration and seek another body nearby to possess and devastate. On the other hand, there were the local villagers who surely hoped and prayed for healing and most surely plied their own home remedies and then in desperation turned to the "gringo" visitors from the U.S. for help.

In this book we will be dealing with philosophy, worldviews, and religions. The words are almost, though not quite, interchangeable. Philosophy begins with wonder. Though many of us may not be familiar with the history and jargon of philosophy, we have all been moved by the feelings of curiosity, longing, and wonder with which philosophy begins. And a worldview is something that everyone has, that no one can live without, a prism through which every important decision in life is made, and yet something that the vast majority of people do not even know they possess. Religion augments philosophy and worldview by adding a spiritual dimension.

No sane and intelligent person who has ever lived was without a worldview of some kind that informs his or her every decision. The American has a worldview. The Arab has a worldview. Asians and Africans have worldviews. Hitler had a worldview. The apostle Paul discussed his worldview in Athens' marketplace of ideas. Job had an ancient worldview. The young man Joseph while in Egypt had a worldview. Some people—analytical and conscientious men and women—have sifted through various worldviews in seeking answers to life's greatest questions. A function of a healthy worldview is helping people frame the right questions. Most people have simply and thoughtlessly accepted a worldview bequeathed by their ancestors, families, and the culture about them.

A worldview is a set of presuppositions (assumptions which may be true, partially true, or entirely false) which one holds about the world. A worldview is how one views or interprets reality. It has been called by several names: a road map; a cosmic picture (or "the big picture"); a meta-narrative; a philosophy of life; and, most simply, a lifestyle. The Germans had a long word for it: *weltanschauung*, meaning a "world and life" view or a "paradigm." Everything we experience, every event in which we participate or hear of, every striking declaration or claim that is made to us, must be placed in a context that makes it consistent with everything else we know. And this process may be conscious or unconscious, but it brings a sense of interpretation and integration to life.

Many of us wear eyeglasses or contact lenses. We may try to read a road sign or the listings in the phone book and find ourselves facing a big blur unless we put on the glasses. Events in the world can seem like a big blur, and some can even "blow our mind," unless we place them in the sharp focus of the proper worldview. If the world never seems to make sense to a rational person, the problem is likely that this person has adopted the wrong worldview.

Few concepts are more important in our lives than the worldview by which we think and act. A realistic worldview is a vital component of good mental health. It serves as an integrating force that brings all the diversity and perplexity of our lives together. Our worldview is comprised of our individual collections of presuppositions, convictions, and values from which each of us attempts to understand and make sense of the world and life. If we think of the major events and experiences in our lives, whether personal or national, as a series of dots on the radar screen of our minds, then our worldview enables us to connect the dots in some meaningful pattern. Indeed, our worldview is also our "life-view" and our "faith-view."

Your worldview is shaped by many factors that influence you over an entire lifetime. The contributions made by your family to your worldview could hardly be measured. Your race, your gender, your nationality, your training and education, your life experiences, your peers, whether friends or enemies, all shape the mindset into which all new experiences are filtered and interpreted. And because people are unique individuals and the fingerprint of one's mind is more complicated than any pattern or design of one's physical body, everyone's worldview is at least slightly different from everyone else's worldview. In fact, it is probably rare when the worldviews of two people match in every important detail.

In our contemporary age that seeks to be fair-minded, inclusive, and all-embracing, there is a stark reality: no one can consistently believe in more than one over-arching worldview. And why? Because several core premises of each clash in irreconcilable opposition. Yes, of course, various worldviews can agree in many important issues and subjects, but there cannot be two radically different yet correct maps of reality. There is absolute truth and there is absolute falsehood; there is absolute goodness and there is absolute evil. These distinctions remain realities despite complexities of life and relationships as well as the mixture of motives and consequences for moral decisions. To state an obvious illustration: the worldviews of the atheist and of the theist cannot be harmonized. And a false worldview that is tenaciously held serves like blinders on a horse that prevent a wider vision of reality.

This is not to say that one's worldview can avoid all problems and answer all questions. Would that life were so simple! Every worldview poses questions and difficulties it appears unable to answer satisfactorily and convincingly. Yet all of us live our lives on the basis of unverifiable premises. Thus, the role of faith is certainly indispensable. It is far better to ask the right questions and not be certain of the answers than to find absolutely clear answers for the wrong questions.

A Worldview Deals with the Most Vital Questions in Life

Human beings have a marvelous capacity for self-awareness and reflection. This means that we ponder certain fundamental and crucial questions about the nature of human life. For thinking persons, addressing ultimate questions is not a luxury—it is essential to our mental and emotional health. Life's most important questions are addressed, if not answered with total satisfaction, by one's worldview. In many cases, the biggest factor in one's worldview is one's religion. These great questions may be grouped under several broad headings:

(1) The Absolute

A child may wonder who is in charge of the schoolroom or playground. An adult may ask who is in charge of the world. An engineer may inquire about the physics of building a secure bridge or tall skyscraper. A scientist may ask what principles govern the universe. Most religions assure us that something or someone is in control. Why do humans throughout history seek to surrender control to something beyond themselves? Who or what is the Supreme Force that guides and governs the universe we experience? If there is a God, what is God like? Is God personal or impersonal? Does God have gender? Does God have absolute power or is God limited? And how is the universe governed? Most religions have something to say about the Absolute—the highest reality that precedes all else and on which everything else is dependent.

(2) The World

What is the nature of the world around us? Each religion has a view of the world: Is the world an orderly cosmos or is it a jungle? Is it a friendly or a hostile place? Is it a place that is pleasant or is it filled with suffering? Do we affirm its goodness or seek to escape its miseries? Does the world have design and meaning or is it all happenstance?

(3) Humans

What are humans? How did humans come into existence and what is their place in the order of all creatures in the world? Is it true, as the first book in the Bible declares, that humans are made in the image of God or is such a claim nonsense? Are humans simply "naked apes" that evolved through natural processes? Are they mere objects? Are they different and more valuable than other animals? Are they akin to the gods? How we answer these questions likely determines how we treat other human beings.

And how much freedom do humans really have? Are we simply puppets on a string held by some Supreme Being and all our behavior is pre-determined, or do we have genuine freedom and meaningful choices? And if we have freedom, what are our responsibilities? Does the human soul exist throughout eternity? Are humans by nature good or bad or capable of both good and bad? Or do we even possess a "human nature"?

(4) The Problem of Evil

Bad things happen to both bad people and good people. What is the source of evil? How do we account for the increase of violent acts among citizens? What is wrong with our world? How did it become that way? Is there such a thing as moral progress or is each generation as wicked and depraved as any other generation in history? Why does the question of determining a standard for good and evil continue to plague humankind? Why will pragmatism and logic not placate the longing of our hearts and souls?

And what is the basic problem with the human race? Christianity offers the idea that the problem is sin. Islam says it is the refusal to submit to God. Hinduism says it is some unfortunate rebirths and bad karma. Buddhists teach that our desires create our suffering. Secular humanism contends that we are still progressing toward some ideal society. There are almost as many answers to the question of evil as there are worldviews.

(5) The Better Life

Most people dream of a better life than the earthly existence plagued by pain, tragedy, and moral and spiritual discontent. What is the ideal? How is it reached? In Christianity, the answer is salvation from sin and the hope of eternal life with God and the saints. In Hinduism, it is reincarnation to a more noble existence. In Theravada Buddhism, liberation from suffering comes through the cessation of craving and longing, the cause of human pain and unease, and embracing the Eightfold Path leading to *nirvana*. The Islamic view of the "last things" is similar to the vision expressed in the New Testament with a trumpeter announcing Judgment Day, unbelievers and unrighteous ones cast into the eternal fire, and the righteous souls translated into Paradise.

In humanism, the answer is the enhancement of human reason. In a materialistic worldview, it is the accumulation of wealth and goods. The agnostic would likely claim there is not enough evidence to be decisive in answering questions about God and human destiny. And the nihilist would contend that nothing can be known or done meaningfully on this or any other ultimate question in life.

(6) Community and Ethics

How, then, should we live? In each religion, adherents accept responsibility for living by moral standards. All teach ethical standards. What is "right conduct"? What is valuable and what does not matter? What is the source of values? How do we know what is right and wrong? Do universal moral principles or moral absolutes exist? What should be the motivation for moral behavior? What do we owe to the people within our community? Who is our neighbor? Is what people do more important that what they believe? Is failure to perform moral duty worse than failure to perform religious duty?

(7) Interpretation of History

Humans are the only creatures who can reflect on their past and contemplate their future. Our worldview tackles some tough questions: How do you make sense of the past? Is there any value in studying history? Where is history moving? Should our view of history be cyclical or linear?

Other questions emerge, of course. These seven questions stagger us with their paramount importance in our lives. They are truly life's ultimate questions. Your faith may be so settled that you wonder how any rational person could raise these questions, or your faith may be so besieged that you wonder how anyone could ever answer them with any degree of certainty.

A BIBLICAL WORLDVIEW FOR TODAY

Many Christian preachers and teachers frequently urge their listeners to see life and make decisions from a "biblical worldview," yet that term can be ambiguous, even misleading. In our study we will typically employ the term "Christian worldview" (or maybe "Judeo-Christian worldview"), since these terms beg clarification.

Yes, of course, the Christian worldview is based on biblical teaching. If we urge the adoption of a "biblical worldview," then surely we do not see the physical world in the same lens as that world was viewed by the biblical characters. We certainly will not turn back the clock and cling to the pre-scientific, pre-Enlightenment view of science and medicine. We do not want to contend for a "biblical worldview" that accepts all the lifestyle patterns and all the moral positions of the nation of Israel (this would include acceptance of slavery and polygamy, for example, as well as justification for violent wars of conquest of territory in the Lord's name). Unlike the aim of many fundamentalist Islamists, and, to a lesser extent this nation's "religious right," most Christians would not contend for Israel's theocratic model of nationhood in today's world. The philosophy of criminal justice has changed dramatically from ancient times, and even the most conservative Christians would not advocate extending capital punishment for all the offenses punishable by death in ancient Israel. There is much commanded of ancient Israel in the Covenant Code to "flesh out" the Sinai Decalogue (see Exodus 21-24) that has long been archaic and senseless in contemporary culture. A generalized and simplistic admonition that contemporary Christians should adopt a "biblical worldview" seems embarrassingly unworkable at worst and poorly articulated at best.

Thus, when we speak of the Judeo-Christian worldview, we seek out the timeless wisdom and insight of God's Spirit intended for every generation. We see God as the unique source of all truth and all life. Within this worldview framework, we seek insights about God, who God is, the nature of God's moral character, and how we can know this God. And we seek insight into how we may communicate with this God as our Father and how we can maintain a loyal relationship with our heavenly Father.

And from this Christian worldview we seek insights about ourselves. We seek answers for how to get along with one another and how we should relate to those who do not share our faith commitment. From our Christian worldview we ask about ideal humanity, and we are pointed to Jesus. We may seek other moral examples for insight and inspiration. Common sense tells us there is a difference between emulating an Adolph Hitler or a Jim Jones and emulating a Dietrich Bonhoeffer or a Mother Teresa.

The very best within a Judeo-Christian worldview keeps us in touch with life-sustaining truths and practical wisdom. Such a worldview does not fragment our hearts and minds—it unifies. After our acceptance of Jesus as Lord and Savior, we can enhance our worldview by varied experiences and deeper study. A Christian worldview is rooted in Holy Scripture, but its development need not be limited to Bible study. Other sources include: Christian theology, Christian biography, historical studies, the wisdom of the ages as gleaned from all kinds of men and women who have struggled deeply with fundamental issues of human existence. Because we always need to re-think life issues and seek truth even from unlikely sources, we may employ the best non-Christian thinkers and writers as well as Christian philosophers and writers. Such a path may seem dangerously unwise to some, but it should lead to deeper understanding and greater wisdom.

ASKING QUESTIONS OF GOD

A final point: Your worldview not only determines how you answer life's ultimate questions, but also determines the kind of questions that you ask God. Each generation has its own set of questions that emerge from a unique social, historical, and cultural context. The questions that seem important in one context may seem trivial to people living in another setting. On the night that the Guatemalan villagers were convinced that the death angel had visited a local family they cared about, their questions included: "Why did a simple sickness suddenly turn deadly and take the life of someone we love?" or "God, can these doctors from the U. S. save my daughter?" or "God, will you please keep the free-floating, evil angel of death away from my child?" A black theologian named James Cone reminds us that if Martin Luther had been an African, kidnapped from his family and tribe, forced to travel to America and traded at the slave auction, he would not have been wrestling with the theology of salvation or the nature of communion service. Instead, "his first question would not have been whether Jesus was at the Lord's Table, but whether he was really present at the slave's cabin." Jewish citizens living in Europe during the 1930s and 1940s were likely not asking how God was present among ancient Israelites who transported the Ark of the Covenant, but they were surely asking whether God was present for them during the Holocaust. Those living in the center of violence in today's world, whether in the Middle East or in the African Sudan, are surely asking in their own language and dialect the same question.

People in different life situations with different worldviews and different histories will certainly see life in different ways and ask different questions. We ask different questions about the meaning of God and the meaning of life, depending on whether we find ourselves living in a free, democratic society or under a wicked tyrant's totalitarian rule; whether living in a spacious home in Beverly Hills or a small shack with a dirt floor and tin roof in Honduras; whether in an ivory tower writing books or in an oriental sweatshop producing piece goods to be shipped to a western market; whether considering candidates before entering an American polling booth or considering the act of strapping a bomb around the waist to blow up "enemies" riding a commuter bus. Yes, where we are, what we have been taught, what we value, and what we have experienced deeply affect who we think God is and what we are convinced God expects us to be.

---·-·---

Devotional Reflection

Through these eyes I see the world unfold;
Through these eyes my purpose in life is told.
Through these eyes my choices are instinctively made.
Through these eyes my plans for the future are laid.
Through these eyes I examine my fellow man.
Through these eyes I accept or reject a Creator's plan.
Through these eyes both pains and joys translate.
Through these eyes come responses that seal my fate.
Through these eyes other people I see.
Through these eyes I determine what my response should be.
Through these eyes I will face both death and life.
Through these eyes I wrestle with humanity's strife.
Through these eyes I discern what is false or true,
For these are the eyes of my worldview.

Prayer: Almighty God, please give your Spirit to me for shaping the worldview that you want me to formulate. I pray that my perception will never limit your power and work in my life. May I always strive to come to you with the right questions and be humble enough to listen to the right answers. Through Jesus. Amen.

2

The Stewardship
of the Mind

T he story is told of a devout church-going woman living around the turn of the
twentieth century. She had heard only a little of Darwin's theory of evolution,
but had been warned about how insidiously evil and dangerous the theory was.
When asked what she thought about Darwin's theory, she answered: "I just hope that
it is not true, but that if it is true it will not be widely known."

The story has the ring of truth, doesn't it? We may all have encountered Christian
men and women who quake upon hearing new ideas that seem to threaten comfortable ideas and prejudices cherished and sheltered for a lifetime. There is a certain
blind security and comfort in believing that everything we have ever been taught and
continue to believe is unassailably true. We tenaciously maintain our beliefs, and we
might hope that anyone who questions or scorns our belief system will harbor such
objections in silence or seclusion from us. And yet, ideas and realities do not cease to
exist just because they are ignored. Can one be afraid of new ideas and still lay claim
to being a mature Christian? Is living a life in fear that someone might validly disagree
with our most cherished beliefs any way to live?

Let's move into theology for a moment. God created human beings as very special creatures. Holy Scripture informs us that we bear the image of God. And while
the meaning of the phrase "image of God" is not transparently clear, we may point to
some possible dimensions of human existence that reflect the *imago Dei*.

Men and women have the capacity for self-awareness or self-transcendence. We
possess a highly developed brain and nervous system, with the intelligence to store

memories and knowledge, to reflect on the past, to live in the present, and to contemplate the future. We have developed a linguistic system that enables us to communicate with one another, to express ourselves artistically, and to record the past. We are not only free moral agents, but are able to place a moral judgment on all our thoughts and deeds, however flawed or even absent at times that judgment may be. We can either develop or neglect the conscience, that inner voice which reflects the way it has been educated. We can consider what we should be as moral beings and what we should think and do.

This special creation by God carries inherent moral responsibility. "It is man's glory to be the only intellectual animal on earth," writes Mortimer Adler in *Intellect: Mind Over Matter*. "That imposes upon human beings the moral obligation to lead intellectual lives. The slothful are blind to the glory and neglectful of the obligation." In his *Diary*, Danish philosopher Soren Kierkegaard (1813-1855) wrote, "If a person does not become what he understands, he does not really understand it."

Deeply woven into the nature of human beings is a concern with certain crucial and fundamental questions about the nature of human life—its ultimate meaning and final destiny. To be human in its highest sense means to wrestle with great questions: Is there really a supreme, personal God who cares about my life and my world? Where did I come from? Where am I going? What is my life? How shall I live? To whom am I accountable? If there is a God, does this God expect anything from me? Can I be at peace with this God? Thoughtful men and women from all cultures, all generations, and all ages have raised these questions—some openly and explicitly and others more implicitly and indirectly in the arts and literature. And these are life's ultimate questions. They are answered by one's worldview. And, as you'll see by reading through this book, there are several competing worldviews in contemporary Western society.

MORE THOUGHTS ON THINKING

We all want to think well. We want to think what is true. We believe that finding and knowing the truth is a grand experience. Truth is the point of all thinking. Whenever we think or say what we think, it is assumed that we want the thought we think to be true. Only when we encounter highly unpleasant truths do we pull out the old saw, "Ignorance is bliss!"

Thoughts are what we think. Thoughts are all the ways we are conscious of the varied realities in our lives, including ideas, memories, attitudes, beliefs, perceptions, and observations. Critical thinking is *metacognitive*; that is, it is thinking about thinking. Such thinking is the mental process of searching out what must be true and separating it from what is either false or at least less likely to be true in light of given facts and valid assumptions. Critical thinking begins when we ask questions that need to be asked, questions that get to the heart of the matter. As a basic source of life, thoughts provide a map of our world and motivate our actions. Theologian Dallas Willard draws an apt analogy between the role of our senses in presenting a landscape for our bodies and our thoughts which present a "life-scape" for our intellects, our wills, and our lives as a whole.

We can express and discuss thoughts in sentences, but the thoughts are not the sentences any more than you are your name. After all, the same thought can be expressed in different words and different languages. That God would endow human beings with the capacity for both specific and abstract thinking is both a blessing and a sign of the divine image within us. As Willard puts it, "Thought is that which enables our will (or spirit) to range far beyond the immediate boundaries of our environment and the perceptions of our senses."

The ultimate freedom we have as human beings is the power to select our thoughts and develop attitudes toward God, one another, and indeed toward all of life. Some philosophers would contend that we are not totally free herein, because we cannot think of people or ideas that we've never encountered. And yet, we do possess a freedom that seems almost unbounded. The one inexhaustible source of ideas for today's world is the human mind, and the human mind is capable of rich imagination. Responsible use of our minds is the starting point for growth and renewal of the Christian life. And of all the varied dimensions of our stewardship as followers of Jesus, the discipleship of the mind is perhaps the most important and, sadly, perhaps the most neglected of all callings.

Stewardship of the Mind—Does the Concept Exist?

Church-going Christians are quite accustomed to hearing sermons and lessons on the stewardship of their time, their talents and gifts, and, most of all, their money. They are admonished not to squander these precious resources, and the advice is excellent. But is there a God-ordained stewardship of one's mind? Does God care about what we do with our brains? And if the answers are affirmative, then why do we hear so little about this dimension of discipleship?

Most of us know some facts about our bodies. We know our height, our weight, and our physical capacities. We know lifestyle habits good for our bodies and we know habits that are harmful. And yet it is not in our bodies that we are made in God's image. Human beings are uniquely separate from all other life forms in the creation by being custom-designed in the image of God through our capacity to think profoundly and order our thoughts and behavior wisely. Think about the brain God gave you. That brain weighs about three pounds. It comprises one hundred billion neurons and handles ten thousand thoughts daily, regulates over 103,000 heartbeats every 24 hours, coordinates over 23,000 breaths a day, and controls over 600 muscles—indeed, the brain is one giant control center regulating our human existence. The brain is also the command center for all our thoughts and decisions. "For those who live according to the flesh set their minds on the things of the flesh," the apostle Paul told the Roman Christians, "but those who live according to the Spirit set their minds on the things of the Spirit" (8:5).

The Scriptures speak pointedly about a person's mind. Jesus commanded his disciples to love God "...with all your *mind*" (Mt. 22:37). On several occasions Jesus employed critical thinking skills in order to handle the accusations, loaded questions, and false dilemmas posed by some Pharisee critics. And surely he intended for his disciples to use their reasoning skills. By using the device of rhetorical questioning, Jesus evoked his listeners' independent thinking. For example, he asked what man building a tower would not first sit down to calculate the costs and determine if he had adequate funding to complete the project; and also asked if a king intending to go to war would not first sit down and determine if he had adequate military strength or if he needed to use a negotiating strategy (Lk. 14:28-33). Jesus also used an analogy in home construction to contrast different kinds of listeners (Mt. 7:24-27).

Typically, Jesus did not offer simple, direct answers to seekers or to his critics; instead he resorted to penetrating questions or paradoxical assertions to stimulate thinking. He compared the closed mind to three kinds of impacted soil in his familiar parable of the sower (Mt. 13). The apostle Paul defined discipleship as "the renewing [or transforming] of your mind" (Rom. 12: 2) and called for "destroying speculations...taking every thought captive to the obedience of Christ" (2 Cor. 10:5). He also commanded disciples at Philippi: "Have this mind among yourselves, which you have in Christ Jesus...Whatever is true...think on these things" (Phil. 2:5; 4:8).

We speak of the Christian life as a journey. Surely, the metaphor "journey" means traveling with others along a certain road, sharing experiences, facing both joys and hardships, and deepening our commitment to God and eternal values. And yet, is there a journey of the mind? Abraham Lincoln is quoted as saying, "I do not think much of a man who is not wiser today than he was yesterday." Most of us have faced emotional upheavals and significant turns of events that taught valuable lessons, but many of us find that the most liberating experiences have been intellectual transformations. Our liberation from old, dysfunctional, and unhealthy ways of thinking may come in special "aha" moments while listening to a great teacher or may be the product of years spent in study, dialogue, and reflection that constitute a gradual awakening. The literal meaning of repentance is to "think again" or "rethink," and perhaps the most difficult challenge in any major conversion is the "rethinking" process.

A Call to Higher Learning

God calls you and me to higher learning and to set our affections and minds "on things above, not on earthly things" (Col. 3:1-2). We typically think of "higher learning" as education at the post-secondary levels, such as college or post-graduate studies. "Higher learning" might also mean an effort to learn about issues and concerns that have the highest priority and significance for our lives—the realities beyond mere human existence and income-earning potential, concerns that carry enduring, utmost value.

Educating the mind does not mean finding all the answers to life's most profound questions. Do not be discouraged when sincere seeking and genuine openness produce no clear knowledge or understanding. Someone has defined education as "a continuing journey from cocksure ignorance to thoughtful uncertainty." In fact, education may open the door to even more uninvited questions. Sooner or later on our journey we must decide if our security and peace of mind rest in knowing all the answers to life's ultimate questions or in trusting the God who designed our lives and our habitat and whose ways and thoughts are far above our own (Isa. 55: 8-9).

Do you recall the old slogan, typically associated with the NAACP, "A mind is a terrible thing to waste"? The Bible clearly informs us that our thinking processes can be corrupted and wasted. The apostle Paul, clearly the best thinker and logician of biblical writers, used a number of negative words to describe the distortion and waste of a person's intellectual capacity: "debased" (Rom. 1:28); "hardened" (2 Cor. 3:14); "blinded" (2 Cor. 4:4); futility (Eph. 4:17); "darkened" (Eph. 4:18); "hostile" (Col. 1: 21); "deluded" (Col. 2:4); "deceived" (Col. 2:8); "depraved" (1 Tim. 6:5); "corrupted" (2 Tim. 3:8); and "defiled" (Tit. 1:15). The wasted mind might be "always learning and never able to arrive at a knowledge of the truth" (2 Tim. 3:7). And we all know people similar to many Jews of Paul's time, perhaps people engaged in a great deal of frenzied religious activity or who do much "God-talk," who possess "a zeal for God, but not according to knowledge" (Rom. 10:2).

Some people take an "extended intellectual vacation" when discussing the most important political and religious issues. Some make up their minds on the most important issues that affect their lives on preposterous premises and the flimsiest evidence. Despite abundant evidence of intellectual achievement and technical experience, we constantly come face to face with examples of irrelevancy, misunderstanding, human error, ignorance, oversight, and misjudgment. Self-deception is a universal disease.

Sometimes such mental dysfunction is knocked out by one powerful dose of reality; for most, overcoming it is a life-long struggle.

Stated boldly and bluntly: God has given us a mind. Thinking has always been crucially important, and it is no less so in our current age. One might contend that American citizens face an intellectual crisis of sorts. After 9/11 and all that this date in history represents, motives and information are questioned on all fronts. The cost of ignorance is always high, but especially costly is religious and historical ignorance. As Stephen Prothero, religion professor at Boston University, cautions: "The costs of perpetuating religious ignorance are too high in a world in which faith moves, if not mountains, then at least elections and armies....In debates about life and death and war and peace, the stakes are too high to defer to politicians and pundits."

Sure, thinking can be a tiring process, especially for those content with a nonreflective faith. How much easier it is to accept doctrine and beliefs passively, rather than rigorously questioning their foundations and the consequences of accepting them. And yet, if we are not thinking critically and skillfully, we do not honor God. God's purposes on planet Earth depend on people thinking well and acting courageously. To serve God effectively we must think straight—thoughtlessness, crooked thinking, deliberate distortion and sloppy reasoning are all insults to our Creator God!

CHRISTIANS, THINK!

The same apostle who summoned us to intellectual transformation, when defending his faith in a personal God in Athens, demonstrated considerable knowledge of his skeptics' philosophy and beliefs, and he quotes from Greek sources in buttressing his own case (Acts 17:28b). Can you imagine Paul telling the Athenian intellectuals, "Hey, fellows, I'm certainly willing to tell you about the God I worship and serve, but, quite frankly, I'm not interested in hearing your 'take' on Plato's or Aristotle's views on ultimate reality. None of those secular Greek philosophers does anything for me and I find them totally irrelevant to my personal reality, so let's just remove that topic from the table for today during my visit. Now, please, I want you to listen to me."

At his trial Socrates maintained that "the unexamined life is not worth living" and soon sealed this conviction with his tragic execution. Socrates believed that some principles are worth dying for. Let's adapt Socrates' words for our purposes here. Might we say, in light of Jesus' conquest of death, that Christians should demonstrate with moral integrity and intellectual discipline that *the unexamined faith is not worth believing*? Can people truly consider themselves Christians who have only been spoon-fed some doctrine by parents or grandparents but who have never examined that faith for themselves? (Surely that is what is meant by the saying, "God has children, but he has no grandchildren?")

GOD AS A LEARNING PARTNER AND TEACHING ASSISTANT

If you are currently a college student, you surely appreciate those professors who offer special assistance to you outside the classroom in order to make learning easier. Likely there are certain subjects in which each of us needs special guidance even to get started effectively. With competing worldviews all about you, you live and work in the middle of a war zone. The gunfire of random and wild ideas is flying about your head and you are called to arm yourself for the battle (Eph. 6:10-17). The education process is an integral part of preparing for this battle of ideas.

While God holds each individual responsible for learning, he also provides special assistance for this crucial process. God partners with Christians through his own indwelling presence in the person of his Holy Spirit. This is especially true in our search to understand spiritual truth, as Paul declares in 1 Corinthians 2:1-16. There are bold claims for the Holy Spirit of God as our partner: the Holy Spirit reveals the deep things of God (vs. 10); by virtue of his presence we have the mind of Christ (vs. 16). The apostle John quotes Jesus as calling the Holy Spirit the "Spirit of truth" (Jn. 14:17; 15:26; and 16:13). Paul reminded Timothy that "God gave us a spirit not of fear but of power and love and self-control" (2 Tim. 1:7), and consider that the Greek term translated "self-control" is sometimes translated "a sound mind" (NKJV). Thus, God is our partner in disciplined, logical thinking. We may not understand the process, but there are those moments of sudden inspiration in which we sense this phenomenon is real.

Devotional Reflection

An ancient sage once declared, "As a man thinks in his heart, so is he" (Prov. 23:7). As thoughts are the wellspring of action, then surely God cares immensely about how you use that marvelous and complex gift you call your mind. And why? Consider the old proverb from American folklore: "Sow a thought and reap an act. Sow an act and reap a habit. Sow a habit and reap a character." Others far wiser than ourselves may stir good thoughts, thus "let everyone be swift to hear" (Jas. 1:19).

Let's reflect for a moment on each of the three members of the Trinity. First, there is the Creator God who designed a human brain with more complexity than the most advanced Dell computer. So, clearly, God is a thinker. God is, of course, more than pure rationality. God is our Father whose dominant trait is love and whose goal is to establish a meaningful relationship with you and me. And yet, surely the principles of sound logic and good reason flow from his nature.

And, then, Jesus engaged both his followers and critics intellectually. His probing questions were intended to slice through layers of prejudice and useless tradition, and his heartwarming stories challenged listeners to make an intellectual connection between simple plot and the Kingdom of Heaven. When he commissioned and dispatched his disciples for mission work among their own people, he gave practical instructions, one of which was for them to be "wise as serpents and harmless as doves." Jesus is surely instructing us, as contemporary Christians: "Have a tough mind and a tender heart." Neither mind nor heart, of course, can be neglected. To have serpent-like qualities devoid of dove-like qualities is to be mean, selfish, and passionless; to have dove-like qualities devoid of serpent-like qualities is to be sentimental, aimless, and anemic.

Finally, the Holy Spirit dwells within us to enable us to understand the things that are freely given by God. The Spirit directs us into realms of insight that transcend merely human wisdom. Theologians refer to this as "illumination." When our search for spiritual truth leads to a sudden insight, we may exclaim: "Hey, the light just came on!" or "It just dawned on me!" Such is the quiet power of the Holy Spirit in our lives.

> Thus learn...learn the motions of your mind,
> Why you were made, for what you are designed,
> And the great moral end of humankind.
> Study thyself, what rank, or what degree
> The wise Creator has ordained for thee:
> And all the offices of that estate
> Perform, and with thy prudence guide thy fate. (Anon.)

Prayer: Dear God, thank you for that marvelous gift we call the mind and for the challenges you send our way in using it. May we never forget that when you illuminate our minds, you also set a torch to our hearts and souls. Lead us kindly with your light and may we never seek to extinguish the flame. Through the One who was the Light of this world. Amen.

3

The Grip of an Idea

N ow that we are in the third millennium C. E. (Common Era), the world seems to be changing rapidly. At least our perceptions of the world are changing. Everything, it seems, is being questioned. And what stirs these enormous changes? The answer is in a simple word: ideas.

The greatest forces in all human history have not been massive military operations or weapons of mass destruction. Not satellites and not computers. Neither jet aircraft nor rockets. The greatest force in history has been an idea whose time has come.

Two Concepts of Time

The ancient Greeks employed two words for "time" that represent two separate concepts. *Chronos*, the basis for the English word "chronological," represented a measurement of time by certain units (minutes, hours, days, etc.) at any given moment. The other Greek concept of time, *kairos*, is a moment in history which is "pregnant with expectancy." *Kairos* is a point in history when certain forces—whether historical, religious, sociological, political, economic, or other—converge in dynamic tension to create an inviting environment for a dramatic, transforming change. Paul's meaning in the Galatians text is that God had prepared just the right conditions for the arrival of his Son on planet Earth.

Philosophers sometimes speak of an Axial Period, a centuries-long period in ancient times that saw the emergence of great teachers in various cultures. An Axial Period is an era in which ancient, untenable ideas about humanity are questioned and eventually discarded and new ideas emerge that seem universally true for all humanity. Axial Period teachers included, among others, Confucius, the Buddha, Lao-Tzu, Socrates, Plato, Aristotle, the Old Testament prophets, Jesus, and finally even Muhammad. Though these great philosophers and teachers came from four distinct geographical regions, they rose above tribalism and particularities and believed in values greater than mere human existence and thus advanced principles that applied to all people. And while the specifics of their doctrines about Ultimate Reality surely varied, they all emphasized what future generations called "the Golden Rule" and they focused their teachings on what all good people should rise above—selfishness, greed, hatred, injustice, unfair discrimination, violence, and harm toward the vulnerable.

A timely idea has driven a number of significant revolutions in our past, including the American and French Revolutions of the late eighteenth century, the Bolshevik Revolution of the early twentieth century, and the final dissolution of the old Soviet Union in 1989. Powerful ideas shape our institutions and the ways we see the world and other people. The Ptolemaic way of seeing the world, with the earth at the center of everything and the sun revolving around the earth, was challenged by an idea held by Copernicus—and our world has never been the same since that point in history, despite early demurrals by those who contended Copernican theory clearly violated Scripture (as in the story of Joshua's plea to God to "make the sun stand still" in order to complete a victorious battle; see Josh. 10:13).

Perhaps the greatest idea is the existence of a Supreme Being or Higher Power. The idea of a Supreme Being has impacted history more than any other idea, whether one believes this idea was revealed to humankind through a holy book or simply through nature and intuition. The idea is so persuasive and so powerful that it is almost as though human beings have been programmed to believe in God. How comforting to know that humans are not alone, and how fascinating to consider how history has been influenced by this concept—a concept that has inspired countless millions to perform some of the most amazing, outrageous, selfless, loving, and even violent and radical acts in the name of God!

POWERFUL IDEAS CAN BE ENSLAVING OR LIBERATING

Not all powerful ideas are anchored in absolute truth and the reality of human nature. Atheism is a powerful idea, to be sure, but hardly a great and reassuring one. The idea that the strong should dominate and control the weak has been around throughout human history and certainly centuries before the writings of Niccolo Machiavelli (1469-1527), perhaps the most famous Italian political theorist, and Frederich Nietzsche (1844-1900), nineteenth century nihilist German philosopher, were published. This idea has rationalized almost any kind of injustice to human beings, beginning with enslavement of huge blocs of people. For example, Adolph Hitler, with the help of Nietzsche's sister, Elisabeth Forster-Nietzsche, claimed that the doctrine of "Aryan supremacy" and the Third Reich had roots in Nietzschean philosophy, a philosophy which ridiculed believers who appeal to a "father God" for justice and compassion.

A companion idea that has been potent throughout history is that some people, solely on the basis of race or ethnic background, are inherently smarter, superior, and more deserving of civil liberties than all other people. This idea has been the seedbed of all kinds of prejudice and discrimination against a wide range of minorities, and again illustrates the sad reality that not all *powerful* and popularly-held ideas are necessarily *great* ideas.

The greatest idea, some may contend, is the concept that human beings inherently possess unalienable rights—rights which cannot be removed or abridged except by due process of law. The concepts of liberty and freedom are vitally linked. This idea gets expressed in some marvelous documents of Anglo-American history, such as the Magna Carta (1215), the Declaration of Independence (1776) and the U. S. Constitution (in the Bill of Rights, 1791), as well as in speeches and sermons, such as Martin Luther King, Jr.'s 1963 address at the March on Washington, "I Have a Dream." We are indebted to Enlightenment philosophers such as Jean-Jacques Rousseau (1712-1778), John Locke (1632-1704), and Thomas Jefferson (1743-1826) for forwarding these great ideals on which America is founded, but, to broaden the scope of gratitude, we thank God for granting these philosophers the intelligence to reason toward those principles and the ability to articulate them. Millions have courageously risked their lives for the idea of human freedom and political equality.

Social and political history has been shaped by ideas that thoughtful and morally excellent human beings could not escape—freedom, liberty, rights, democracy, integrity, fairness, happiness, science, progress, health, education, welfare, and family. These ideas get "fleshed out" in different ways in a pluralistic society such as the United States and most European nations, yet their compelling nature in our thoughts and attitudes cannot be denied.

BETTER LIVING THROUGH GREAT IDEAS

Great ideas are linked also to invention and technology. The design of the wheel is fairly basic and simple and yet revolutionary. At one time it was not unusual for someone to live a full lifespan without ever venturing more than a few miles from one's place of birth. The wheel allowed both travel and hauling of loads as well as countless possibilities in architecture, engineering, and manufacturing. The stories of how ancient civilizations such as the Greeks, Romans, Egyptians and then, centuries later, the Maya, Aztecs, and Incas developed calendars, invented "clocks," and by remarkable civil engineering built roads, canals, reservoirs, pyramids, and temples, all seem incredibly mind-boggling even today. The invention of the cotton gin by a 27-year-old Eli Whitney in 1793 stimulated the Old South's economy at a time when the regional economy was flagging, though the negative impact of this time-saving device was the revival of African-American slavery at a time when some speculated that slavery would die out.

The idea of the written or printed word preserves and passes on humankind's knowledge to future generations. Around 1450 Johann Gutenberg invented printing with movable type, and thus, with scholars gaining access to dependable, standard-ized text, the printing press was the first form of mass media. This was the right tech-nology at a crucial time in history. The Gutenberg Bible, the first mass-produced book, came off the press in 1454. Printing press technology was soon taken from Germany to other European nations. Print technology gave people information that previously only an elite could have accessed. Books were now more numerous and cheaper. The press also gave ordinary people an impetus for literacy and an opportunity to think and decide for themselves. This revolution removed some power out of the hands of Roman clergy, the upper class, and royalty, and placed the Bible in the hands of ordi-nary people, thus fueling social reform and the Protestant Reformation.

Computer technology might also be nominated as the best idea of humankind, though there remain vast numbers of people in lesser developed nations who are untouched by computers. Still, this technology has reduced the world to a global vil-lage and continues to expand almost without limit the ways our lives can be enriched or modified. And while an entire volume could be written on the great ideas which have shaped all history, our point here is simple yet profound—God the Creator gave us our minds from whence these great ideas have been born and all truth about life in this universe is essentially God's truth.

We live in a new century that is fantastic in many ways. Imagine Rip Van Winkle awakening today after a hundred-year snooze. Think how bewildered he might be seeing people dropping coins into a machine for drinks and snacks, men and women dashing about the streets and in buildings, talking to themselves, seemingly, but with small metal devices hooked on one ear; young people sitting on the floor pushing life-like characters around on an electronic screen; older people defying death and disabil-ity with pacemakers in their chests, miniature hearing devices inside their ears, and walking quite briskly with hips and knees made of metal and plastic; many others of all ages with miniature lenses fixed on their eyeballs for better vision.

Imagine that Rip walks into a university classroom: rather than seeing students sitting in rows in auditorium arrangement with a well-dressed man lecturing behind a podium and in front of a black chalk board, he more likely will see a casually dressed woman or man walking about the classroom, flashing colorful pictures and/or text on a screen with sound and animation, some perhaps downloaded directly from a website, with students sitting at tables with lap-top computers or recorders for note-taking or diversionary distractions. One must wonder how Jesus simply sitting down on a mountainside to deliver the greatest sermon on ethics and righteousness that's ever been preached would possibly connect with today's listeners.

So we are deeply indebted to science and technology for introducing such rapid change in the way we conduct our business interaction, daily communication, and leisure-time activities. World religions and religious institution change, too, and indeed must change in order to survive. As valuable and authentic as "restoration" movements may be, any religion of the twenty-first century is not precisely the same religion of an ancient era, even if called by the same name.

Not all changes in different areas of our lives have the same impact.. Scientific technology makes major contributions to minor needs (admittedly, medical science does address important human needs). Does advancement in receiving electronic mail or the speed of air travel or the fidelity of recorded music really address the human condition? Does technology give us more meaningful answers to life's ultimate questions? On the other hand, even the smallest insights in religion and philosophy might well turn out a life-enriching or life-saving blessing for future generations.

THE LIMITATION OF HUMAN IDEAS

As humans we are limited by our individual abilities, preferences, experiences, and life situations. Consequently, we cannot rely on our own untested thinking. Both Scripture and common sense caution that we are not wise enough to direct our own steps (see Jer. 10:23). This counsel is surely a generalization, for there may be several dimensions in our lives where we have combined such extensive study with rich experience so that we have learned to act wisely. And yet, in grappling with deep and ultimate questions of a worldview, we would be wise to access wisdom from those ideas and thinkers that have stood the test of time.

How easy it is to be content with ideas that leave us feeling comfortable! And, paradoxically, it is possible to keep one's mind open to every new fact and closed to every new idea. Such mental gymnastics are necessary for maintaining an unperturbed comfort level with untenable beliefs in one's worldview. John Maynard Keynes once wrote: "The difficulty lies not so much in developing new ideas as in escaping old ones." Thomas Henry Huxley offered the opinion that "irrationally held truths may be more harmful than reasoned errors." "The whole problem with the world is that fools and fanatics are always so certain of themselves," declares philosopher Bertrand Russell, "but wiser people are full of doubts." Truly, so many seem to take great comfort in the illusion of unquestionable certainty.

Of course, one would be unwise to accept an idea from a religious leader or philosopher simply because the idea or claim is considered "great" or "significant." Defensively or impulsively rejecting an idea or claim before we have given it critical evaluation is equally foolish. One may not agree with everything that acclaimed religious thinkers and philosophers have taught about life and reality, but how can one be a good steward of the God-given mind who rejects the collective wisdom of scientists, philosophers, and theologians who have devoted their lives to studying vital issues?

Those of us who have embraced the Judeo-Christian worldview should never forget the distinction between divine wisdom and worldly wisdom. And even though a clear line between these two sources of wisdom seems elusive and difficult to draw, the insightful author of Proverbs declares a truth that remains valid even in our time: "The fear of the Lord is the beginning of wisdom and the knowledge of the Holy One is understanding" (9:10).

Devotional Reflection

"Ignorance is bliss" the old saying goes. But is blissful ignorance a serious option? Chosen or willed ignorance of great ideas in the area of spiritual life, which includes relationship both with God and others, is not a serious option. If life on earth had no terminal point, we might be able to engage in the luxury of spending a few thousand years with our ears and minds closed to new ideas. Human life is too brief and too fragile—only a momentary interim between two eternities—not to engage in serious philosophical and spiritual contemplation. Knowledge is valuable for its practical applications, but it is also valuable for its own sake. Knowledge about the present condition and mysteries of life, like virtue, is its own reward.

Our lives can be dramatically transformed by the grip of a powerful idea. Oliver Wendell Holmes once observed that "a mind stretched by a new idea never returns to its original shape." Change is the essence of life. And some change cannot be prevented, such as the cellular change in our bodies that constitutes the aging process. Transformation is more intentional and deliberate. Transformation calls for thinking about great ideas and planning the re-direction of our lives. The ability to create something valuable or wonderful with great ideas is what separates extraordinary people from ordinary people.

Our worldview is the composite and arrangement of the great ideas that focus our faith and shape our lives. The nineteenth century Danish philosopher Soren Kierkegaard entered an insightful observation in his journal: "The thing is to find a truth which is true for me, to find the idea for which I can live and die." We may respect Kierkegaard's insight that authentic living means finding an idea to which one can give the fullest measure of unceasing devotion.

All great ideas must sooner or later be "fleshed out" in some kind of observable action. The idea of divine grace or divine lovingkindness did not lie dormant as an abstraction in the mind of God. Most surely, then, the greatest and most scandalous idea in all history was the great God of the entire cosmos choosing to reveal himself in human flesh, to live and teach on this earth as a human person, to feel deep pain and anguish, and eventually to suffer an excruciatingly painful execution for our sins upon a barbaric cross. Could God have demonstrated his grace and love for us in a way that was any more sacrificial, any more meaningful, any more convincing of his sincerity?

There is an idea grip that sometimes takes hold of us and will not let us go. The doctrine of the divine incarnation is one of those powerful, compelling ideas. The sacrificial death of Jesus on the cross enables us to be totally forgiven of sins and moral transgressions that we could never make "right" by our own confessions, actions, or reparations. Perhaps it is not so much the grip of an abstract idea, but the grip of God's love and grace that makes the difference. That love reaches out and claims us, so that we may find ourselves declaring with Augustine, "Oh God, Thou hast made us for thyself, and our hearts are restless till they rest in Thee."

Prayer: Dear God, thank you for creating us with minds that can perceive reality, conceptualize new ideas, reason logically, and make sound decisions. Keep our minds open to new ideas we need to hear and willing to refute ideas that battle your will. Most of all, thank you for your abundant grace that grants us salvation from all the ways we fall short of your will, but gives us the security to grow, to learn, and even make mistakes. Through Jesus. Amen.

4

Are All Truths Created Equal?

D ecades have passed, perhaps, since the American general public became as stirred about a novel as has happened in 2003 and 2004 with author Dan Brown's *The DaVinci Code*. The blockbuster novel disturbed many Christian theologians. When the best-selling story was turned into a movie on the big screen in May 2006, the controversy reached a crescendo. Churches resorted to special classes and preachers delivered sermons on the topic and workshops, websites, DVDs, and educational materials were prepared in order to educate their members on the issues that the book raises.

And what are the issues with *The DaVinci Code*? Answer: Can a book that is listed at the top of the *New York Times* best-seller list for over a year with more than sixty million copies in print present misleading and outright non-factual material so convincingly that readers accept it uncritically as truth? Clearly, the American public enjoys reading religious material. Witness the Tim LaHaye and Jerry Jenkins' "biblical" *Left Behind* novels that by 2004 had sold 65 million copies. Are the end times presented accurately within biblical teaching in this series? And, then, in the winter of 2007, a television version of *The Jesus Family Tomb* on the Discovery Channel argued, with a mix of archaeology and speculation, that an ancient Palestinian tomb once held the bones of Jesus and his family. The show was sponsored by movie producer James Cameron (*Titanic*) and was highly promoted during the beginning of Lent. The year before, the cable TV documentary *The Lost Gospel of Judas* fueled still another bizarre, nontraditional view of Jesus. All of these stories cater to some apparent boredom with

41

the traditional story of Jesus and a fascination with a speculative version that is high-lighted with hidden truths, dangerous mysteries, and illicit sex.

The issues raised in Brown's novel and Cameron's TV documentary are far more important than those raised in the *Left Behind* series. The deeper issues included: Can people trust Christian Scripture? Was Jesus really God or just a good man and an effective teacher? Was Jesus actually resurrected in bodily form from Joseph's tomb? Was Jesus married and how did he view women?

Dan Brown narrates a romantic and marital relationship between Jesus and Mary Magdalene, a theory that has been around for centuries despite the lack of any hard evidence. *The Da Vinci Code* also claims that church leaders suppressed women's contributions to early Christianity, a conclusion accepted by several scholars and historians. The news stories on this best seller often quoted Christians who conceded their faith had been shaken by reading the book. Is truth about the lifestyle of Jesus more important than truth about eschatology ("end times")? And are most believers unable to separate fact from fiction?

"So you are a king?" Pontius Pilate asked Jesus of Nazareth, who was brought before his seat of judgment for a verdict. The brief conversation recorded between Pilate and Jesus touched directly on significant issues. Jesus asserted that the very purpose for which he came into the world and was born into humanity was to "testify to the truth" and that everyone who belongs to truth listened to his voice. And then Pilate asked a pregnant question: "What is truth?" (Jn. 18:37-38). Through the ages, both before and after the time of Pilate and Jesus, the greatest thinkers and philosophers, as well as ordinary thoughtful people such as you and me, have asked the same crucially important question.

LIFE'S GREATEST QUESTIONS

Jesus once asserted to his disciples, "You will know the truth and the truth will set you free" (Jn. 8:32). In addition to asking what truth is, a plethora of other questions about truth emerge: Does absolute truth exist? If so, what standards or criteria must be met for truth to be established? In areas of religion and ethics, how can we know what beliefs and practices are true and right? Should we accept truth claims solely on the basis of authority, such as from our parents or minister or a holy book, or must scientific methodology always be employed? Does truth ever change? If there is such a thing as truth, how can we hope to discover it?

A sobering reality: perhaps 75% of young adults today doubt the existence of absolute truth. Denying that absolute truth exists in any realm of life has become quite intellectually fashionable. The entire school of postmodernism rejects the idea that there are universal, absolute, transcultural standards (such as laws of logic or principles of inductive reasoning) for determining whether a belief is true or false, rational or irrational, good or bad. Postmoderns reject "universals" in general—nothing is the same from one moment to the next and nothing can be present at one time or place and literally be present again at another time and place.

Please don't dismiss this as heavy philosophy, because this topic crucially important. Why? The Christian religion, as well as competing worldviews and world religions, makes substantial claims about reality. These claims are either true or false.

The claims of the Christian faith have crucial consequences for both life and afterlife. We are not speaking of claims that Toyota manufactures a better automotive product than General Motors or that Lake Tahoe is better for recreation and scenery than Lake St. Clair. We are not even speaking of whether the rapture will happen before the tribulation or the tribulation before the rapture. Instead, we are making claims as to whether a Supreme Being does indeed exist, whether Jesus of Nazareth was and is the divine Son of God, and whether we are considered righteous before God on the basis of Christ's sacrifice upon the cross, and whether there exist judgment, heaven, and hell in an unending life to come.

Can you think of any questions more important than these? These are the very claims, whether we accept or deny them, on which we build our lives, focus our goals, devote our energies, rest our hopes, and build our dreams. What could possibly be more important?

If you've ever read a college-level textbook in philosophy, you may have been "blown away" by the technical terminology and complex reasoning. I may have been guilty of that already, for example when I used the term "postmodernism." Let's simply attempt some common sense about this crucially important subject of truth in the space that remains. Let's begin with that simple yet profound question that Pilate posed to Jesus: what is truth?

THREE THEORIES OF TRUTH

Philosophers have posed three tests or three theories about truth. The first is the *Correspondence Theory*, the one most commonly accepted. Truth is defined as fidelity to objective reality, the agreement between the statement of fact and actual fact. If I state that the United States is bounded on the north by the nation of Canada and on the southwest border by the nation of Mexico, then this statement corresponds with the actual geographic situation and I have told the truth.

The presence or absence of belief has no direct bearing on the issue of truth or falsity, since truth depends on the conditions of reality, conditions that have been affirmed or denied. If a judgment or perception corresponds with the facts, it is true, and if not, it is false. Of course, this theory of correspondence assumes that our sense data are clear and accurate, that they disclose the nature of the world just as it is, and that our methods of research are clearly authentic when we make assertions about events alleged to happen in history. If I state that on October 21, 2004, the St. Louis Cardinals defeated the Houston Astros to win the National League Championship and play the Boston Red Sox in the World Series, then I can consult several newspapers of record to check the accuracy of that claim. Of course, the further back into history we venture in making claims about events, the more difficult it can be to establish evidence that everyone accepts conclusively.

The *Coherence* or *Consistency Theory* of truth places trust in the consistency and coherency of all our judgments. Advocates of coherence define truth as judgment that is consistent and in harmony with all other judgments. We may reject something as false because it does not "fit in" with what we know to be true or with what has happened in our past experience.

The Coherence Theory is used when the correspondence test cannot verify reality. Suppose the Coast Guard tells a woman that the small plane her husband was flying has surely crashed in the Atlantic in the Bermuda Triangle. Officials tell this woman that, sadly, her husband is presumably dead. Some debris from the wreckage has been found, radio communication with the pilot ended abruptly in mid-flight, but no body surfaced. Days pass. No lifeless body of this woman's husband is found, yet she comes to accept as truth that he has been killed in the accident and that his body may never be recovered. And why? That conclusion coheres with all the other evidence that did surface

Sometimes new observations seem so strong that we are confronted with the need to reconsider all that we previously held to be true. That may lead to revision of previous conceptions. The Copernican worldview is an obvious example. Prior to Copernicus, almost everyone believed the earth was the center of the universe or solar system, a belief which stemmed from Ptolemy of the second century, C. E. And why did people accept this erroneous view for so long? Answer: it both made common sense and seemed to square with respected religious authority (did not the Old Testament report that "Joshua made the sun stand still"?). And why did scholars, scientists, and students embrace the new Copernican worldview? Answer: it gave a greater degree of coherence and consistency with facts already established and it explained phenomena previously unexplained. Under this coherence or consistency theory, truth must be drawn from the whole system of what is known, and by this method laws of physics are established.

The *Pragmatic Theory* for establishing truth is the test of utility, workability, or satisfactory consequences. A philosopher named Charles Sanders Peirce (1839-1914)

contended there is a question we can ask as the best test of the truth of an idea: what would be the effect of this idea in everyday conduct of our lives if this idea were true? His point: an idea is true if it works out in practice, if it leads to satisfactory results. William James (1842-1910), the well-known American philosopher and psychologist, is best known for his pragmatism. He rejected a model of truth based on pure rationality and total objectivity and emphasized the personal and contextual dimensions of truth. To James, "truth happens to an idea," especially in areas such as moral and religious belief (areas James thought vital to human happiness). An idea becomes true by the way it works in our lives.

James had a deep respect for a religion that enriches people's lives, that has "cash value." He observed that people in all cultures turn to a god (or gods) who gets things done, a active god, a god of the "strenuous mood," not a passive, ineffective god. This led James to a fascinating suggestion: if people do not believe in God, it might be because God is not doing anything in their lives. In his popularly and widely read work, *Varieties of Religious Experience*, James attempted to discover through empirical and psychological study how God works in people's lives.

A growing number of young people opt for this third operational definition of truth. Many students are suspicious of the idea that some thoughts are *just true*. They want to ask, "True for whom?" You may have heard some of your friends say, "OK, that may be true for you, but it's not true for me." It's almost as though truth can be judged as subjectively as humor. For example, two people leave a comedy club after the show, and one says to the other, "Those jokes may have been very funny to you but they were not funny at all to me." Is truth something as subjective as humor? Are moral rules and standards simply matters of personal preference? Wouldn't that be equivalent to saying (as ridiculous as this may seem), "Well, it may be true for you that the earth is round, but for me, just like for people who lived centuries ago, it is true that the earth is flat."

THE CHRISTIAN CLAIM ABOUT TRUTH

As we confront these questions, we are stepping through ground punctured with land mines. Let's continue with this proposition: Christianity claims that truth is absolute—true for everybody, at all times, at every place. Truth being absolute, Christian thinkers would reject the claim made by James and many others that "truth is what works for you." Truth corresponds with reality. When we speak of objective truth, we refer to reality that is the same regardless of anyone's attitude toward it. It can't be "true" that the earth is round for most people and flat for people of other centuries—what varies is what people have believed about the earth and not truth about the earth itself. When someone says, "Abraham Lincoln was the U. S. president during the American Civil War," that statement is either objectively true or false.

"Truth" based on feelings, preferences, wishes, or workability is dangerous. If someone says, "Jesus Christ may be your personal Savior, but I find much liberation in the teachings of the Buddha," or if another says, "You may see the Bible as God's ultimate and final revelation in written words to you, but I view the *Qu'ran* as even more authoritative and definitely the final revelation of God to humanity," then each person cannot be correct. Both may be wrong, but only one can be right.

THE LAW OF NON-CONTRADICTION

In philosophy and critical thinking, there is the *Law of Non-Contradiction*, sometimes called the *Law of Contradiction*. This is not simply a principle we may or may not observe—it is an unavoidable principle of thinking that is basic to rationality. You can read some confusingly complex definitions of this law, but let's state it as simply as possible: No statement can be both true and false at the same time and under the same conditions. Or to use symbols, as philosophers who study logic often do, *p* cannot be both *p* and *not-p* at the same time. Stated another way: the same question at the same time cannot elicit two opposite answers, both claiming to be true. Some assertions remove the middle ground. For example, this is either a religious book or not a religious book. It cannot be both a religious book and not a religious book. You might contend that this is a religious book and more, and that would not be a contradiction. The contradiction comes in mutually exclusive assertions: "This is a religious book and also it is not a religious book."

When addressing truth claims in religion, this law of non-contradiction forces a significant and imperative choice in our thinking. For example, either God as Supreme Being does exist or God does not exist. There is no middle ground. Jesus Christ was God's incarnate Son on earth or he is not the divine Son of God. Buddha's teaching is directly and divinely inspired by God or it is not. Muhammad was the last true prophet of God or he was not. The *Qu'ran* is the inspired word of God or it is not. The Bible is an authentic record of God's dealings with human beings or it is not. Now the fact that we may not agree on answers to these questions, or that a step of faith is required when we accept claims as truth, does not diminish the reality that truth is objective and absolute.

BELIEFS ARE CRUCIALLY IMPORTANT

What we believe is crucially important. Of course, there are exceptions to that generalization. One person may believe a Honda motorcycle is better than a Harley

Davidson or that ice hockey is more exciting to watch than professional basketball or that classical music is more enriching than rock music, and those convictions will not make any real difference in one's life even if you could objectively prove what is right. In grappling with life's ultimate questions, however, what we believe about God determines our worldview. And even in matters of national interest or public policy, what we believe can make all the difference in the world, at least in *our* world.

What we do depends in large part on what we believe. That is why so many conflicts in life, whether with your family or your friends or your classmates, are based on differences of belief. The strident disagreement about whether God wants Palestine to be occupied and controlled by the Jews or by the Arabs, for example, has been the cause of continual conflict. If both sides in this dispute claim certainty for their belief, and neither possesses the humility to admit the possibility of error or the need to negotiate, the disputants have foreclosed the possibility of resolving conflict peacefully through reason and compromise.

Let's be clear: there is a sense in which "truth" is difficult, if not impossible, to establish with absolute certainty. We are all subjected to so many messages in advertising, the entertainment media, political rhetoric, and, yes, even in our churches, that seem totally fictitious. The critical thinker makes distinctions between objective claims, based on verifiable facts, and subjective claims, rooted in one's values, insights, needs, and desires. If a friend of yours were to say, "Most movies today promote very few wholesome moral values," that friend would be offering a subjective claim that seems more opinion than verifiable fact.

"Truth" in certain areas of religion, philosophy, politics, and public policy is always open to debate and dialogue. Usually no one "wins" any arguments because the discussion is always entwined with personal or organizational values and also because we cannot know with absolute certainty what is right. We may urge our political candidates to "speak the truth" when they are on the stump campaigning, but when they are supposedly "telling the truth" on issues of domestic or foreign policy, how can we know with absolute certainty what future policy is right or best? Of course, what we hear or read from advocates of policy or the interpretation and application of religious teachings is all filtered through their personal values, affiliations, and partisanships.

Distinguish between what is "true" in terms of what works for you, and what is universally true. It's one thing to say, "Dr. Atkins' low-carb diet is truly the best program for weight loss" and another to simply claim, "Dr. Atkins' low-carb diet truly worked wonders for me in weight loss." Consider this statement: "150 pounds is difficult to lift." "That may be true for me," you might say, "but not for a weightlifter." Of course, we would understand what you meant by the first statement. But what truly varies between you and the weightlifter is the *difficulty of lifting* 150 pounds, not the truth that the weights total 150 pounds.

Let's return to our original question: Are all truths created equal? Truth as correspondence with reality is objective. Truth in one field cannot contradict truth in another field; truth in science cannot contradict truth in religion. Truth is consistent and universal. And truth is the point of all thinking. But, no, not all truths are equal. And, furthermore, truth and decibel level are not related.

Devotional Reflection

"Getting physical" is an expression we hear a great deal. There is a song, "Let's Get Physical," which was sung in the early 80s movie *Grease* by Olivia Newton-John. Except for the revival of this show as a Broadway musical or movie classic, of course, most in this current generation would not have heard of this show. Exercise videos sometimes use this song to set the rhythm of the calisthenics, and most of the people we see in workout videos and television ads are young and attractive.

Health clubs and recreation centers enjoy robust business. We see joggers weaving between walkers in parks; others ride bikes. Diet books are perennial best sellers. Almost everyone wants to look good. Physical fitness is in style. We count fat grams as much as we count calories. We learn about different diets, whether Dr. Atkins, Weight Watchers, Rotation or some other formula.

Most of us look in the mirror critically. We see extra flesh or other unattractive features and we ponder what to do about it—lose weight, camouflage it, or schedule cosmetic surgery? How incredibly tempting to be unhappy with our bodies! A majority of Americans would likely have trouble listing five things about their bodies that they would *not* actually change if they could.

On the other hand, what about mental fitness? Do you ever hear people say, "Let's get mental"? Mental fitness is not always a priority for the majority, or so it seems. We're not speaking here of simply getting an education, a college degree, or graduate degree. Plenty of people seem quite intelligent and possess much education who are not mentally healthy. Consider the true story of the brilliant though schizophrenic physicist Dr. John Nash in the movie *A Beautiful Mind.*

How does one become mentally fit? Back to the analogy of physical fitness. Some prefer jogging, others biking or swimming or walking or any number of other activities that provide aerobic conditioning. For the Christian, the starting point is one's study and application of the Word of God (see Psalm 119:11, 105, 127-28). How instructive to note that most appeals to first-century listeners from the earliest preachers of the gospel, beginning with Peter's keynote address on Pentecost in Jerusalem, were based on logic, reasoning, and evidence, and not on emotion. And the apostle Paul engaged in a logical dialogue about God when encountering Athenians who relished religious and philosophical discussion.

Just as the Creator designed our bodies with such great and interesting variety, he created our minds with infinite and rich variety. No two bodies are exactly alike, nor are any two minds exactly alike. This variety is how we stimulate thinking and growth in one another as we interact at deep levels. What would happen if we pursued mental health with the same degree of energy and enthusiasm that we pursue physical fitness in this culture? How would we go about it? For some it would be maintaining vigorous dialogue with intelligent people. For others, it might be taking advantage of every continuing educational opportunity available. Others may opt to enroll in university classes for credit or audit. The creative woman or man, thirsty for truth and knowledge, will find a wide range of methods and opportunities to foster mental health and grow intellectually.

Despite popular stereotypes to the contrary, mature Christians are committed to a quest for truth and to intellectual openness as a strategy for discovering truth. The problem of the closed mind has plagued the human family since the Fall, for humankind has always had something to hide. Yet it is a dangerous experience to reject light, whatever its source or however weak and flickering the flame seems. Truth is still truth no matter where one finds it. Come out of darkness and into light wherever it appears. The light illuminates reality and reality is truth. God is truth, God is the source of truth, and God's revelation is truth. To the degree that you are pursuing truth, then, to that degree you are pursuing God.

Christians are thrown in the middle of a war zone, with all manner of ideas flying around. These are not all harmless ideas, academic questions, and talking points. Major ideas have major consequences. And we are called to equip ourselves for major battle (Eph. 6:10-17). We may fight this battle of ideas with a weak body, but not with a weak mind. Given such intensive ideological conflict in the world today, especially as worldviews collide, there has never been a time in history where the search for truth and the strategy of critical thinking among citizens were more important. Pseudoreasoning may be psychologically satisfying to those who believe what they want to believe, but fallacies and insufficient evidence are poor building blocks for a better world. Conviction against all evidence is the seedbed of fanaticism.

By faith, we Christians accept Jesus' claim to be the truth. In reality, Jesus is not on trial in our court or anyone's court any more than is Socrates or Michelangelo or

Shakespeare or Mozart or Einstein. Nor are the great truths revealed in Holy Scripture on trial. What Pontius Pilate decided about Jesus revealed more about Pilate than it revealed about Jesus. And what you decide about Jesus reveals more about you than it reveals about the one whose coming did more to change history than any other event!

Prayer: Oh, God, we thank you for honoring us by gifting us with our minds. May we know that our highest form of gratitude for this gift is developing our minds, beginning with knowing your truth in our lives. May our entire lives be devoted to seeking truth and in this quest find that we have much in common with non-Christian truth-seekers and a very special intellectual and spiritual fellowship with our truth-seeking sisters and brothers in Christ. Through him whose word was truth and remains truth today. Amen.

5

We Can Prove God,
Can't We?—or Can We?

Most believers in God have heard a number of stories and jokes that ridicule the thinking and arguments of atheists. Such humor can bring a smile to believers in God because it humorously connects to a crucially important question—who or what is the source of everything that we experience in our world? Truth is, however, atheists and agnostics can produce almost as many little anecdotes and jokes that make light of Christian beliefs, practices, and arguments for God's existence as do Christians poking fun at atheists.

Does God actually exist? Is there an all-powerful, all-knowing, and all-loving personal and eternal God who created us and designed a plan for our lives? Is it reasonable to believe in such a God? Can the existence of God be proven logically without appealing to religious experience or some leap of faith? Can we be sure of our answer? No question that any worldview could answer is more significant than this one. No other issue touches our lives quite as profoundly. And how we answer this perennial question, of course, determines how we answer so many other related questions. Try as one may, the question cannot be avoided.

A REMARKABLE SCHOLAR

For centuries, mature religious people have attempted to prove the existence of God. Let's consider one of the most influential thinkers of the centuries. Thomas Aquinas was born near Naples around 1225. His father enrolled him as a boy in a

Benedictine abbey school, but as a young man he was so attracted to the scholarly ways of the Dominicans that he joined the order; he later went to both Cologne and then to the University of Paris for studies. Thomas became a true scholar. During the twenty years that he was an active teacher, Thomas wrote disputations on various theological questions, commentaries on various books of the Bible, commentaries on twelve works of Aristotle, and many miscellaneous notes, sermons, lectures, poems, and treaties. His crowning achievement was the multi-volume summary of theology known as *Summa Theologica* and *Summa Contra Gentiles.* Thomas became and remains today a giant among philosophers, theologians, and ethicists, and his influence is incalculable.

Though he lived centuries ago, Thomas' quest was one to which you and I can easily relate. Thomas knew that personal feelings are subjective states that vary with desire and personality. What is crucially important is *what is true.* Our timeless concerns are about whether God actually exists—objectively, really—and not about what we think or feel or hope is true. Thomas approached this crucial question using natural reason or intelligence.

Thomas certainly believed in God and he believed Scripture to be divine revelation to humanity, but he thought that God's existence could be demonstrated by natural reason. That is, God's existence could be proven logically even without appeal to the authenticity of Scripture, and he intended his arguments to be used by believers in defense of their faith. Thomas offered "Five Ways," all cause-effect arguments, beginning with our experience of effects and moving toward their cause, God.

The Five Ways

The Five Ways begin with the *argument from motion*. Indisputably, things are moving and motion must be given to each object by some other object that is already moving. Linear motion and "life motion" are moved by God. Thomas' *argument from necessity* is based on the idea that if nothing had ever existed, nothing would always exist; therefore, there is something whose existence is necessary (an eternal something). Thomas also offered the *argument from gradation* based on the metaphysical concept of a hierarchy of souls, sometimes called "the great chain of being." In ascending order, being progresses from inanimate objects to increasingly complex animated creatures. For example, a horse has more being than a worm, and a person more than a dog, and we can move up that chain to something greater than a human being. So these are three of the famous "Five Ways."

Enough. Let's be honest. Those arguments are difficult for to grasp because they rest on a medieval worldview and scholastic rigor that seem strange to us today. Two other arguments among the Five Ways are much more understandable. One is the *cosmological argument*, from the Greek word *kosmos*, meaning "world," "universe," or "orderly structure." Stated briefly, the cosmological argument asserts that it is impossible for any natural thing to be the complete and sufficient cause for its own existence. In order to cause itself, a thing must precede itself. For example, in order for me to be the source of my existence, I would have to exist before I existed. This is both impossible and absurd.

The cosmological argument is fairly simple. It's also a profound argument. The existence of the cosmos is an undeniable reality. Sure, the universe is a mystery which boggles the mind, but the universe is a reality. Can anyone seriously deny that reality? The story is told of a student at a major university who approached his professor with a philosophical question: "Sir, just how do you know that I exist?" The professor paused a moment, lowered his bifocals, looked the student in the eye, and asked, "And whom shall I say is asking?"

Why is there a universe at all? Why is there something rather than nothing? Where did women and men originate? And from whence came animals, mountains, oceans, rocks, hills, trees, and flowers, and on and on we could go? Is there anything in the world that can explain its own existence apart from a Creator God? No matter how many wonderful things scientists can conceive on drawing boards and invent in laboratories, can any of them come up with the soil and water which compose the substance of human and nonhuman animal life. Medical scientists can fertilize human eggs outside a woman's body (*in vitro* fertilization), they can design an incubator that simulates the womb God gave women, and they can experiment with techniques of both therapeutic and reproductive cloning—but they cannot create or invent the sperm and the egg which are vital ingredients to the human life process. And artificial intelligence is only a manufactured product of humans using an original intelligence that was bestowed by a First Cause or an Uncaused Cause.

The other argument from Thomas, who was greatly influenced by the naturalism of Aristotle, is the *teleological argument*, also known as the *argument from design*, one of the most widely known and used arguments for the existence of God. Teleological thinking is a way of understanding things in terms of their *telos* or end (from the Greek language). Thomas asserts that the entire natural world exhibits order and design. The elements in the natural universe—whether water, wind, clouds, trees, mountains, rocks, animals, and people—all behave in orderly ways. And there is a complex interconnectedness of the natural world, wherein human tampering with one dimension of the universe, such as rain forests in the Amazon basin, can impact life in other parts of the universe.

IS GOD DEAD OR ALIVE—WHAT ARE THE CHANCES?

Order, Thomas Aquinas argues, implies intelligence, planning, and purpose. Again, the argument is incredibly simple and yet profoundly effective. What is the most complex human invention that comes to your mind? Might it be an advanced, high speed computer? A sophisticated satellite communications system? A NASA space ship designed for human transportation? Maybe even a fine timepiece? How many individual parts or components do you think are fitted together in a luxury Mercedes Benz automobile? Now, could any of these products that bless our lives have simply "come together" by some explosion at a metal factory? Was there no designer for even the simplest machines we employ to do yard work or household tasks? Would that bulky phone book have come together with its thousands upon thousands of names alphabetically arranged simply from an explosion at the printing plant? Could the wind, rain, and soil erosion over many eons of time have produced the faces of four presidents on the side of Mount Rushmore?

Consider Planet Earth. Everything about our earthly habitat seems finely tuned for human habitation. Astrophysicists note that this earth is uniquely tailored in its function, position, and existence. The earth is the right distance from the sun for human existence and any variation in heat or light would mean a global disaster that Hollywood likes to portray as entertainment. Everywhere one turns there is wonder and beauty and much compelling evidence of design, purpose, complexity, and order. Perhaps reflecting on this amazing, complex cosmic system, Albert Einstein once declared, "I cannot believe that God plays dice with the cosmos."

What is the basic idea here? The whole cosmic system seems to make sense only when there is a God, a God who intelligently designs life as we know it. Remove God from the equation and there emerge a myriad of puzzling questions to answer. And yet, there are still intelligent atheists who hear the classic arguments and reject the idea of God. Einstein and subsequent generations of physicists have hoped that at the end of their labors there would be one answer—a so-called Theory of Everything—that would explain why the details of the world are the way they are and cannot be any other way: if and why there was a Big Bang, the number of dimensions of space-time, the masses of elementary particles.

Just as theists have their reasons for faith in God, atheists have their reasons for not believing in God. Does it puzzle you that atheists often seemed unmoved by the classic arguments for the existence of God? Take, for example, the argument from intelligent design (teleological argument). As for the precise nature of Planet Earth, some atheists contend that humans simply "got lucky" to be here. Rather than an earth uniquely designed for human life by an intelligent God, the earth is simply one very, very small element in a vast "cosmic landscape," a sort of meta-realm of space-times, and this solar system is zillions of times more vast than we ever imagine. Given this incomprehensible vastness, it stands to reason (the argument goes) that by pure chance some physical environment would be adaptable to human, animal, and plant life. The universe seen through telescopes, then, is just one in an endless chain of bubble universes that sprout from one another.

The "death" of God has been announced by almost every generation since the Age of Enlightenment in the eighteenth century. Back in the 1960s, a group of theologians proclaimed "the death of God," echoing what the philosopher Frederich Nietzsche had announced generations earlier. Even *Time* presented a striking cover for the lead story in its April 8, 1966, issue with a simple question in bold red letters on a black background: IS GOD DEAD? What some of these philosophers were saying, in essence, was: "I don't find God a personal reality anymore" or "modern society does not need God anymore." Currently, there are other writers from the field of science such as Richard Dawkins and Sam Harris who have been advancing logical arguments against the existence of God and some of their works have been national best-sellers (see the next chapter for some of their titles and ideas).

So did God really die? Or is God in a comatose state? Does someone need to officially write God's obituary for everyone to accept? Did people just invent the idea of God to satisfy their longings and then made that God in their own image? Or was God simply called onto the stage of life to explain all the mysterious phenomena of life—such as tragedy, disease, natural disasters that we call "acts of God"—but now the "God of the gaps" is ushered off the stage when modern science provides explanations and answers these things? Or might we sing heartily the lyrics of the late Rich Mullins, "Our God is an awesome God. He reigns from heaven above with wisdom, power, and love. Our God is an awesome God." Though our faith is never perfect, as Christians we answer life's most important question with a confident affirmation.

Devotional Reflection

God is alive and well. Let us believers proclaim that affirmation. Anyone who has experienced mighty services of praise to God, witnessed only a few of the mighty works of love and compassion given in the name of his Son, heard some of the fervent prayers offered up to the Father by countless millions of people worldwide, or seen the joy and elation on the faces of believers who know that the Father's grace has touched their souls—any witness to those experiences knows that God's vital signs are strong and healthy. God's Spirit is very much alive in the minds and hearts of those most passionately devoted to his glory and his will. He is real and the Ruler of heaven and earth, whether people believe in him or not.

You do not need to prove God's existence. After all, no one can prove God with mathematical or scientific certainty. Nor do you need to understand and explain to others the mystery of God's working in the world and in your life. The strongest arguments in the world will not convince many atheists to come to faith in God, just as the most agonizing struggles and temptations will not shake the faith of many believers. Yes, you surely need to be able to give a reason for your faith, not only for yourself but also for others who might ask, but you need not engage in non-productive and endless debate about God. Too often such debate with skeptics turns to permanent stalemate or gets bogged down in some endless "creation versus evolution" debate. God's existence does not depend on your defense or your arguments.

Our greatest need is to encounter God. You may feel there have been times in which you needed to search for God, yet many of us think of ourselves as having been found by God during moments of our deepest need. The important thing is to keep on seeking, to keep reaching out.

So how does one encounter God? How does one experience God? All of this may seem rather abstract to you. After all, we can't see, hear, or touch God the way we can experience the people or objects around us. It's truly understandable to feel that you need something more concrete, more tangible, something undeniable to our five senses, when we really need the love and help of God.

Let's enrich this encounter with God through the knowledge of the Word. No, we do not speak first and foremost of a printed page. The most reliable knowledge we have of God is through the person of Jesus Christ. Jesus was and is the ultimate Word of God (see Jn. 1:1). Then, the gospel narratives are witnesses to the Spirit-filled life of Jesus on earth. He lived a certain life, at a particular time, and did certain actions and made certain statements. Christianity is not so much faith in a set of propositions, but in a real person. All religions have stories, sometimes called myths, but the stories about Jesus happen to be true as well as inspiring. And these stories are quite revealing about God. We can encounter God by studying the written words of people who walked and talked with Jesus or learned about him through first-hand witnesses.

Then we can encounter God in the world he created for us. We can see something of the divine in every good thing in our lives. We can see God in the beauty of nature. No, we're not transforming theism into pantheism, but simply recognizing that God sends powerful messages about his majesty and glory through the world he made for us. And we can see God in our relationships. Holy Ground is never a private real estate investment—it is always communal property. So we can encounter God in the face of that baby child, in the love of a father or mother or son or daughter, and in the constant support and hugs of a loyal friend.

And, finally, we may encounter God by deepening our kinship with our older brother, Jesus. In a world with so much evil and brokenness in human relationships, we are called to be "little Christs" to the distressed and hurting people we meet. Taped to my computer monitor is a quote, not even a complete sentence, that was passed on to me by my sister Nan, and it reminds me daily of my calling: "To be Christ in whatever way I am able to be, with whatever gladness I have, and in whatever place, and among whatever brothers and sisters I am called to."

Prayer: Dear God, give us a mind totally open to all the evidence and logical arguments for your existence, but, far more that that, give us a passionate heart for you that people can see through acts of deep love and humble service for others. Through Jesus. Amen.

6

Smart People Don't Need God—Or Do They?

Sharon entered my Nashville State classroom in ethics and sat on the front row. She was typically the first student to arrive and always ready to converse on almost any topic. She had an engaging personality and warm smile. What most caught my attention about Sharon were the slogans and statements on the strip stickers plastered to her notebook. In big letters were messages that surely did not endear her to the devout Christians in our class. One message: "Atheist and Proud of It." Another asserted: "The Bible Is Myth-Understanding." Still another message proclaimed: "Atheists Are the Reason There is Reason."

Sharon was a very bright student. I informed her that the brief messages intrigued me and rather than, as a theist and believer, taking offense at her declarations that I would use them as springboard for dialogue. One day, when my Introduction to Philosophy class was studying Aquinas and the question of God's existence, I invited Sharon to visit my class and explain the reasons for her atheism and respond to comments and questions from class members. As intelligent and articulate as I knew Sharon to be, I knew she could hold her own against any challenges to her position and I certainly did not want to ridicule or embarrass her in any way. I asked about her willingness to engage in "friendly debate" with me in the class on this topic. Sharon enthusiastically accepted the invitation.

After opening the class, I asked her to speak first. Her major arguments were three-fold: (1) She did not see anything supernatural occurring in the world today, and there was no good reason for any supernatural event in previous history; (2) the Bible is filled with folklore and myths and cannot be trusted for any authoritative word on the existence of God; and (3) over the centuries, some of history's greatest moral evil and atrocities have been committed against other people by believers in God.

In almost all my classes on this campus a few atheists have been enrolled. Most remain modest and quiet about their beliefs. And many of them are like Ryan, who proudly announced in class, "I don't believe in God." When I countered, "Well, since you threw that out there for all of us, Ryan, do you want to say why you don't believe in God or is that question too personal?" "My dad's a scientist and he's a pretty smart man," Ryan replied, "and he says he does not need God to have a better life, and I trust my dad's opinion."

Atheists and agnostics live all about us. In a recent semester at a Christian university, much to my surprise one student announced he was an atheist and two other students, one male and one female, announced they were agnostic. Most of them, as did Sharon, can give a more logical and persuasive explanation as for why they do not fit a personal God into their worldview than did Ryan, but the idea that highly intelligent people do not need God is a premise that many accept uncritically. You may have wondered at times if belief in God is only for those who are emotionally and intellectually weak and struggling through life with their fears and insecurities. Or, your faith in God may be so strong that you can hardly imagine why anyone seriously questions God's existence.

Worldviews rest on foundations. Whether one believes or does not believe in God is, undoubtedly, the most important element in the formulation of one's worldview.

In the past three centuries, Christian claims about God and the Christian faith have hunkered in a defensive posture. The assaults on God have come from various directions. Often a cluster of anti-God and anti-Christianity views are linked together and an effective refutation of one is not considered an answer to the other objections to Christian faith. The German philosopher Frederick Nietzsche declared, "God is dead." Assuming we want to face challenges to our faith with our eyes wide open, then why have people declared the death of God? Smart people don't really need God—or do they?

THE MARCH OF REASON THROUGH HISTORY

Intelligent atheists may begin their rejection of God by exalting the human reasoning process. As far back as the ancient philosophers of Greece, humanists have contended that ultimate truth about our world, others, ourselves, and God (if indeed there is a God) can be learned through human reasoning without any divine revelation. This system is called *Rationalism*, which is not quite the same as "reason." All of us must reason by critical thinking with claims and evidence, and, truth is, many of us do not reason as effectively as we are capable. Reason is theologically neutral. It poses no threat to our faith. But when reason is proposed as the ultimate and exclusive source of truth about God, our destiny, and ourselves it then becomes Rationalism.

Many historical developments contributed to the elevation of reason as the ultimate source of truth. During the eighteenth and nineteenth centuries, there was an intellectual revolt against the established church and its historic doctrine. A variety of philosophers and scientists sought truth about our world and human nature apart from divine revelation.

Sigmund Freud (1856-1939) built a theory of personality on the basis that the subconscious dimension explained one's behavior. Karl Marx (1818-1883) contended that some have used religion to protect their privileges and that among the industrial workers whose wages were inequitable religion functioned only as an "opium for the masses," thus alleviating their social misery. Charles Darwin (1809-1882) clearly pushed the origin of life well past the 4004 B.C.E. point of origin determined by a well-intentioned Archbishop Ussher (an indefensible date based on an overly literal reading of the book of Genesis). From his research, Darwin launched a revolution in thinking that everything evolved by natural processes apart from a Grand Designer. Though Darwin himself was a believer, Darwinian thought eventually rejected a Creator God. By the late nineteenth century, the methods of science were all that were necessary for some to reach truth and understand their world. Darwin had been influenced by an early nineteenth century thinker named Ludwig Feuerbach, who argued that "God" is nothing more than a projection of human ideals and desires onto an imaginary plane—that is we "project" our desire for eternal life, meaning, and love and call the imaginary result "God."

Other philosophers offered more "down to earth" arguments that questioned God. To the utilitarians, such as John Stuart Mill (1806-1873), religious faith was a tool that served some people well and did not benefit others. By 1869, Thomas Huxley, eminent scientist, humanist, and grandfather of biologist Julian and writer Aldous, coined the word "agnostic," now meaning someone who does not know or cannot know whether there is a God. And the eminent twentieth-century philosopher Bertrand Russell (1872-1970) wrote a popular volume entitled *Why I Am Not a Christian*, which, among other arguments, cites cruelties done to humanity in the name of religion.

In the first decade of the twenty-first century, there seemed to be renewed debate about the existence of God among scholars in theology and science. Some hoped science could replace religion as a worldview. Richard Dawkins wrote *The God Delusion* with a position so clear that the book needed no subtitle. The book attacks Christian faith historically and philosophically as well as scientifically. Neuroscientist Sam Harris is the author of *New York Times* best sellers *The End of Faith* and *Letter to a Christian*

Nation. Both Harris and Dawkins insist that they are atheists, in part, because there is insufficient evidence for the existence of God. Even more recently, journalist and professor Christopher Hitchens, making his rounds on numerous U.S. network news and talk shows as a kind of celebrity atheist, offered caustic comments about God and religious people. Hitchens' book, *God Is Not Great: How Religion Poisons Everything* (the God of the Bible is spelled with a lower case "g" throughout the book) offers a familiar case against God and the Bible, reminiscent of the attacks on Scripture by Robert Ingersoll in the late nineteenth century.

Most Americans want to reconcile the Christian worldview with the scientific worldview, believing the two approaches to truth fully complement rather than contradict each other. Foremost among scientists and Christians arguing for common ground has been Francis Collins, whose *The Language of God: A Scientist Presents Evidence for Belief*, offers intellectually reasonable and persuasive arguments for the existence of a personal, creator God.

All these skeptics we have referenced reached the conclusion that nature is a closed system and nothing has ever entered the natural order from the "outside." Science is inherently and unavoidably naturalistic—atheistic, in one sense. Thus, there is no place for biblical miracles. And there is no sense in praying for divine intervention in our lives. Prayer is an exercise for weak, helpless, and at times desperate people offered to a God who likely is not even present anyway. Atheism offers as the ultimate evidence only those experiences which are tangible—what humans can see, hear, touch, taste, and smell—and nothing else exists. In interviews Sam Harris has pointed out that all people today are atheists with respect to Zeus and thousands of other deities of past cultures whom nobody worships today. Ultimate reality corresponds to what people observe and how most people live on a day-to-day basis. Surely, smart people do not need God—or do they?

The "Practical" Argument Against God

Many intelligent people do not feel a need for God in their lives. They argue that they can be just as good in their moral lives, if not better, as those who are believers in God. Occasionally on a university campus one hears comments such as, "Well, Christianity can't be of any real value. My roommate is a Christian and I can't tell that her religion has done any good for her." Another might state: "I can tell you that the most regular church member I ever knew was one of the most racist and sexist persons I have ever met in my life." The unstated premise of these statements is that a religion or philosophy is not to be judged on the basis of its ideas, but on the basis of its effects (or lack thereof) on selected individuals or institutions.

Pragmatism virtually deifies "what works." For the pragmatist, standards of morality are all subjective and relative to the circumstances in which you find yourself. And pragmatism is yet another way to say that all truth is relative. Both secular humanists and pragmatists believe the answers to some of life's most difficult personal problems lie within their own intelligence and moral character and not within the pages of some divine revelation. And it is science, not the Bible, that gives us a better world! Secular-minded people may question a person's Christian faith and commitment, but they seldom if ever question the intelligence of either the humanist or the pragmatist.

Many intelligent people look at the evil, pain, and suffering in the world and find all of it incompatible with a God who is both all-loving and compassionate, yet also all-powerful. Would not an omnipotent and compassionate Supreme Being step in to prevent intense human suffering? (This objection is so important and persuasive to many and it surely must not be discounted; thus, we will deal with this issue separately in chapter 15.)

THE MEANING OF APOLOGETICS

You've probably been exposed already to the kind of argumentation from unbelievers and skeptics. This line of reasoning, persuasive as it is, long ago gave rise to the study of apologetics. "Apologetics," in this usage, answers important questions and offers a defense for important truth that is under attack. Apologetics does not create faith—it creates a fertile and intellectual climate in which seeds of faith can be planted and grow. While apologetics seeks to persuade thinking people that God is real and Christianity is true, such truth is no guarantee of one's acceptance of this truth and placing trust in God and living the lifestyle of his Son.

THE PRACTICAL ARGUMENT FOR GOD

Some argue for the existence of God and the validity of the Christian religion not so much because their convictions are logically persuasive but because they are workable. Yes, quite obviously both believers and unbelievers deploy this pragmatic argument. The noted American philosopher and psychologist William James (1842-1910) spoke of the "validity" of a religion on the basis of how faith works in a person's life. Two well known preachers of the mid- and late-twentieth century, Norman Vincent Peale (major theme: positive thinking) and Robert Schuller (major theme: possibility thinking) rose to national popularity on the thesis that simple Christianity serves as the best self-help and self-esteem building formula available to everyone. Some evangelicals have cited research completed in hospitals of how prayer "works" for ailing patients. Televangelists often unashamedly preach a "health and wealth" gospel wherein the God of Scripture is just waiting to bestow material riches and other physical blessings upon those who trust and obey. Our culture is clearly oriented toward pragmatism. We look for a product or service that is useful and discard what no longer works for us. And yet, something seems not quite right here—is pragmatism the strongest case that can be made for a compassionate God and the Christian faith?

Practicality seems such a subjective and slippery standard for judging the authenticity of any worldview. Yes, we want our Christian faith and discipleship to make a real difference in our lives, but Christ does not call us to a new life by promising "Hey, this really works!" as though he were speaking of some new detergent that removes tough stains or some deodorant that protects us from odor or moisture for up to twenty-four hours. And yet, our hearts and minds must be open to truth from whatever source it comes. Most surely, truth comes to us from many directions. There are "truths" learned in the disciplines of natural science, of physics and biology, and then in the social sciences of psychology, sociology, and anthropology; then, of course, truth is conveyed in the arts and humanities such as religion, philosophy, art, and literature. There is no reason for scholars in science and intellectuals in religion to wage battle against each other as though their worldviews were irreconcilable. And, finally, there is the truth that we learn existentially—from real life personal experiences. And do these "truths" contradict each other at any point along the way? Not really. Absolute truth is non-contradictory. Only our views and interpretations of reality can be contradictory.

Yes, we are all indebted to intellectuals and to bright people in general. We find them in our schools and universities. We find them in our places of business and in the professional world. We find them in hospitals and laboratories. And we find a good many in our churches, government, Christian schools, and civic organizations. Are these bright people, whether believers or unbelievers, capable of living responsibly and honestly and of demonstrating a commitment to great justice and compassion in our world? Our answer: absolutely yes! And do these bright women and men need God? Well, they certainly do *not* need archaic concepts, old prejudices, non-critical thinking, useless traditions, sterile institutions, non-authentic relationships, and narrow-minded people—but they *do* need God!

The Judeo-Christian worldview is credible because it provides the durable foundation and vast framework in which a coherent, consistent view of the world with all the many "truths" garnered from all the disciplines can be placed. And this worldview is valid because it gives that vast body of truth from all the academic disciplines an overarching meaning and significance. As C. S. Lewis, perhaps the greatest Christian apologist of the twentieth century, aptly stated: "Christian theology can fit in science, art, morality, and the sub-Christian religions. The scientific point of view cannot fit in any of these things, not even science itself. I believe in Christianity as I believe that the sun has risen not only because I see it but because by it I see everything else." The functioning of a Christian worldview could not have been more eloquently stated.

------·-·------

Devotional Reflection

Do smart people really need God? Perhaps it is better to ask, Can smart people actually afford the "luxury" of living without God? Can reason alone give you the wisdom and insights you need in order to live with meaningful relationships, serve higher purposes, hope when all ordinary strengths and joys fade, and die with confidence that you will live on in another realm of existence? Smart people, who in their "intelligence" have reviewed, dismantled, and dismissed the idea of God, will follow this worldview to its logical and eventual conclusion: a determined universe where every man or woman is simply a cog in the wheel that turns in endless cycle and goes nowhere of ultimate importance. Life becomes one purposeless chain of cause and effect, morality develops only by some evolution of noble human thought, and good and evil have no ultimate meaning. And all of us live in what is, on balance, a wonderful world that happened by complete accident.

Be firm in your rejection of such pessimism even if you need increased understanding of God and his purposes. Be joyous in acceptance of the God of your fathers and mothers even when your personal faith cannot answer all questions. Your intelligence is a gift to be used in the service of your faith. Throughout the centuries, some of the most brilliant and creative men and women who made their mark on history were devout believers in God and fervent worshipers of God. To people such as Augustine, Thomas Aquinas, Isaac Newton, Francis Bacon, Martin Luther, John Calvin, John Wesley, Charles Wesley, Dietrich Bonhoeffer, Mother Teresa, Martin Luther King, Jr., Billy Graham, and a host of others who are not so well known, God was not simply an idea, a construction of the human mind—God was and is a reality to be encountered and experienced!

This God is outside of nature and also outside of space and time, and God's thoughts and ways are far beyond our human understanding. God is the one who ultimately engages us, calling us beyond the narrow limits of the human mind. God has reached out to us through his Son Jesus and invited us to become his children, heirs in his kingdom.

Prayer: Great God of heaven and earth, may our minds never become so filled with knowledge that we crowd out every thought of your existence nor our hearts so consumed with worldly values that we crowd out our passion for you. Through Jesus who revealed you to the world. Amen.

7

Some Certainty
About Doubt

I was raised in a family of preachers. Unless I was seriously ill, I was taken to Sunday school and worship assemblies twice on Sunday and on Wednesday nights as well. I was taught all the exciting narratives of Scripture, and there seemed to be more drama in the Old Testament than in the New. I knew the stories of the Garden of Eden, Noah and the Ark, Daniel and the Lions' Den, Abraham offering Isaac, and Moses and the Ten Commandments, just to name a few, far better than I knew the stories of the Pilgrims coming to America, George Washington and the cherry tree, the American Revolutionary War, and even the Civil War. These stories were not only true in every detail, but they were to be taken literally.

The stirring of first doubts happened in my freshman Bible class at a Christian college, so nagging that I felt the need to make an appointment with my respected Bible teacher and ask such questions as, "If Moses died on the mountain, how could he have written about his death and then delivered it to the Israelites at base camp?" In my sophomore year, I began more intensive study of later Hebrew history. I confronted the stories of stark barbarism and cruelty, not to mention some fairly amazing claims of the miraculous working of the Almighty. Though I thrilled to the basic message of the later prophets calling Israel to righteousness and social justice, I began to wonder about the basic point of some supernatural events narrated before those prophetic messages.

Several years of graduate school re-shaped the contours of my intellectual life and presented new concepts and ideas to ponder. A common thread ran throughout all my doubts—my guilt over harboring doubts in the first place. These stories had been passed to me by highly trustworthy and, in some cases, notably intelligent men and women. I wondered: How could they be wrong, even in the slightest way? What exactly is wrong with my faith? How could I not be inadequate or unfaithful in some way to God by allowing such nagging doubts to linger in the corners of my mind?

DOUBTERS ARE IN GOOD COMPANY

Years ago, thankfully, I came to inner peace about the struggle and hereby offer some lines of analysis that might be helpful. If as a thinking Christian you are dealing with your first doubts, it surely helps to know that all mature Christians have struggled with doubts. As Philip Yancey eloquently states it in *Reaching for the Invisible God*, "Everyone dangles on a pendulum that swings from belief to unbelief, back to belief, and ends—where? Some never find faith....Others have faith, then lose it....Doubt is the skeleton in the closet of faith."

Your doubting places you in the company of some outstanding saints of the biblical era—Adam, Sarah, Jacob, Job, Jeremiah, Jonah, Martha, and Peter are among better-known stalwarts who doubted God or his purposes. For centuries, the Apostle Thomas has been dubbed "doubting Thomas" though a better name might well be "cautious Thomas." The annals of church history are filled with the names of great church leaders who, like Jacob, wrestled with God. Martin Luther—whose bold act of posting 95 theses on a church door at Wittenberg, Germany, sparked the Protestant Reformation—constantly waged war against unyielding doubt and depression. In more recent times, the private correspondence of Mother Teresa, awarded the Nobel Peace Prize for founding the Missionaries of Charity as a global beacon of care for the sick and dying, reveals that this widely acclaimed "saint of the gutters" in Calcutta agonized over her doubts about the reality of Christ in her life. "Jesus has a special love for you," she wrote a clergyman friend. "[But] as for me—The silence and the emptiness is so great—that I look and do not see, Listen and do not hear."

ALL DOUBTS ARE NOT CREATED EQUAL

Consider that not all doubts are equal. First, we may have doubts that emerge from the system of interpretation of Scripture that we were taught. There are several ways to read and date the Creation narrative, for example, and when any one interpretation among several plausible ones is taught as absolute truth then seeds of doubt are sown easily. As we attribute absolute truth to Holy Scripture, we must be on guard against attributing absolute truth to our personal system of interpretation of Scripture (one's hermeneutic, if you will).

Second, there can be doubts about the ethical values that we were taught or that we assimilated from the culture at large. As a boy I thought little or nothing about the practice of polygamy among Old Testament characters; it did not matter at all how many wives these ancient saints had married. (Of course, had the American president taken on several wives, then I would surely have deemed that strangely inappropriate and morally wrong.) Nor did it particularly matter how many Canaanites were slain by Joshua in conquest of the land God was giving his people or how barbaric some of monarchs of Israel acted in dealing with their enemies. I was comfortable enough with those stories so that I did not need to place them in some historical or cultural context or allow them to raise questions about biblical ethics.

As a boy I was taught a subtle, but insidious, form of racism. White people enjoyed their schools and churches and blacks had their schools and churches, and this "separate but equal" doctrine was reinforced by the Bible college I attended—a college to which I could not have been admitted had my skin been black! My first graduate school years at a large urban university brought a gradual awakening, an awakening which started with doubting some traditional moral values and cultural standards.. The process is continual (at least I hope).

Third, there can be doubts about some of the crucial, central tenets of our faith. Clearly, tenets of faith define us. We believe there is an eternal, transcendent, beneficent and gracious God who created us and called us to become like his Son. We believe that God revealed himself in many ways, and the Bible contains the record of his revelation, but that Jesus is the fullest incarnation of his divine nature. And we believe that Jesus died for our sins, experienced a bodily resurrection, ascended to the Father, and continues to provide true life for us in his Father's kingdom. And finally, we believe there is an eternal life beyond this relatively brief span of time on planet Earth. The essence of these convictions has already been stated centuries ago in the Apostles Creed. Yes, these convictions are far more important than our beliefs about whether Samson's strength lay in avoiding buzz haircuts or whether Peter discovered a coin in the mouth of the first fish he caught one day that could be used to pay taxes. When we question these central beliefs from which we draw answers to life's ultimate questions, the foundation of our lives seems to be crumbling beneath us.

Seeds of doubt vary. For many university students, doubt arises from the challenges propounded by professors, textbooks and other readings, and even classmates. One's confidence in biblical authenticity might be shaken by an encounter with science or with the claims of another world religion. For believers of all ages, doubt may arise from intense pain and suffering. And most of us are truly shaken when we are betrayed by church leaders or disillusioned by individual Christians. For others it might be a keen awareness of the immense evil and injustice in the world.

SOME GOOD WORDS ABOUT DOUBT

Some people make a distinction between doubt and skepticism. If you are a doubter—and what thinking Christian is not?—the good news is that doubt only comes to a person who believes in something substantial to begin with, whether the belief is in God or Allah or Krishna or the Buddha. "Who knows nothing doubts nothing," declares an old French proverb.

Doubt is not to be confused with the skepticism, it is argued, held by a person who has not yet come to faith. Doubting might be, for some at least, a lazy option to avoid careful study and reflection for those who want to make quick sense of their world. For most others, doubting is not taking the low road but the high road. Doubt could be a prelude to faith. To doubt is to hold reservations. To make judgments tentative. To raise serious questions. To delve into more study. To disdain dogmatism and exercise a searching and inquiring mind. To look at all the evidence. To honestly doubt is to maintain genuine humility about who we are and what we know.

Doubt can most certainly be a sign of growth. Consider how you came to faith. You may have simply accepted without question the faith bequeathed to you by your parents and grandparents. Hopefully, you have moved beyond what they taught you. You may have refined your faith through your own study of Scripture and the reading of books, commentaries, and lessons about Holy Scripture. From these you have drawn presuppositional truths or conclusions about what is true and right and how they apply to your life. You accept these truths or conclusions because they are logical, real, and relevant. This then is called *faith*—certitude in the basic principles that emerge from the sources of your knowledge and your critical thinking. No one else has written out a "laundry list" of religious non-negotiables and required you to mindlessly sign off on it—this faith is your own!

Your growth never stops, however, as you continually place the tenets of your faith within a matrix of the love and grace of God in Jesus and your own experiences. You learn new things that alter your perception of self, other people, or the world at large. Life may throw such a devastating challenge at you that your worldview is greatly tested or damaged: a classmate is killed in a tragic accident; a sibling dies; a friend loses a son or daughter; a niece is physically and sexually abused; the minister you respect confesses to having an adulterous affair; a church leader is arrested for business fraud. Suddenly and startlingly, all the pieces do not fit so easily into the worldview or the matrix that your parents and earliest Bible teachers constructed.

Doubts Putting Us at a Fork in the Road

Doubt is unavoidable. "Doubt isn't the opposite of faith," the late theologian Paul Tillich once declared; "it is an element of faith." Although we cannot control doubt that surprises us suddenly like an uninvited guest or nags at us incessantly like a siege of mosquitoes, the new doubt born of personal tragedy plunks us squarely at a fork in the road. Now, a thoughtful person cannot simply sit down for long at that fork in the road—movement in one of two directions is demanded.

First, as we all know, deep doubt can lead to despair and an eventual decision to abandon faith and hope. This choice does not happen overnight, but is a painful downhill spiritual process similar to a degenerative physical disease. And there is another road, perhaps the one less traveled. This road is for those who hang on to their commitment while watching others abandon the faith. Many believers have been blessed with the gift of deep, resilient faith. The bottom-line answer for other believers, such as Yancey, is a practical, if something less than honorable, response: the lack of viable alternatives. Peter's plaintiff cry, "Lord, to whom else shall we go?" speaks powerfully for why many of us remain in the fold.

The healthy direction in which we can move, of course, promotes spiritual growth within a more realistic matrix of faith. Armed with what passes for rational, clear-cut truth, tempered and tested by real life experience, we adopt the principles upon which we will stake our lives and our reputations. Doubts are not trivial, but they are important—even necessary! Frederick Buechner, in *The Alphabet of Grace*, confessed: "Without somehow destroying me in the process, how could God reveal Himself in a way that would leave no room for doubt? If there were no room for doubt, there would be no room for me."

Uncertainty in faith? Isn't this oxymoronic? In practical terms, how are they reconciled? Here are two suggestions: First, doubt should be disassociated from the simple reality of not knowing all the truth we want to know. Wouldn't it be reassuring if we could truly fathom the mystery of the Incarnation, how God could visit Earth and live simultaneously as fully God and fully human? How can there be the union of two incommensurate natures in one person? Can anyone harmonize the doctrines of predestination with free will? And who is going to be lost and who will be saved? For me, it would be reassuring to convincingly resolve the notions of God's justice and of divine compassion in the Canaan conquest stories of the Old Testament. You probably have your own religious conundrums. While there should be no retreat from pursuit of truth and knowledge, the reality is that mystery will always be part and parcel of the Christian faith. In our quest for certitude, could it be that we try to understand too much? Even if all mysteries could be fathomed, the apostle Paul counseled, the Christian virtue of love is more foundational to the actual practice of our faith (1 Cor. 13:2).

Devotional Reflection

Why not doubt your doubts? Yes, the advice may seem much too simple, but consider its practicality for worldviews. The same principles of critical thinking that are applied to our beliefs must also be applied to our doubts. Kathleen Norris, gifted writer and author of *Amazing Grace*, has written: "Perhaps my most important breakthrough with regard to belief came when I learned to be as consciously skeptical and questioning of my disbelief and my doubts as I was of my burgeoning faith."

If you imagine a faith that will be perfect, or near perfect, at the end of a long Christian life of commitment, then abandon that fantasy immediately! Salvation comes by God's grace, his unmerited favor toward us. God's grace is always fulsomely perfect—our faith always falteringly imperfect! Surely, one of the most honest utterances to Jesus was an exclamation by an anonymous father of a diseased child, "Lord, I do believe; help me overcome my unbelief!" (Mk. 9:24). That plaintive cry may well describe the faith-condition of your heart and mind, too. And that father's faith was enough for Jesus to bestow lovingkindness and compassion. Jesus never commended someone by saying, "You have perfect faith." Likewise, Jesus never condemned any individual seeking him by saying, "Sorry, I'd love to accept you as my disciple, but you have too many doubts."

Consider faith to be a gift and be a good steward of that gift and the other gifts the Spirit has given you at this point in your life. Don't be afraid to ask any question—any question! No stalwart Christian will faint nor any solid church collapse upon hearing your honest doubts or inquiries. After 2,000 years as a mighty faith, no question you can ask publicly or privately is going to bring Christianity crashing down. Study with an open mind and open heart all the spiritual and moral concerns that God has laid on your heart, but do not despair over inability to arrive at clear conclusions. And remember that secret mysteries belong to God (Deut. 32:32).

Faith is trusting God. Faith is not absolute certainty that tolerates no reservations. There may be times when we feel that God is totally absent from our lives. Yet we must live by the Word of God, exemplified in the teaching and example of Jesus, and not by how we feel. Faith is more like a blank check than a laundry list of favors we want God to grant us. Faith is tough at times, to be sure, but so is life sometimes. And faith is the only way to survive.

Prayer: Dear God, you are the both the object and the subject of our faith. And yet, while some have found faith in your existence and providential care to be as natural as inhaling and exhaling, others of us feel at times as if we are dangling by a brittle thread over the chasm of what we do not understand or what we cannot possibly solve. Our doubts persist. Surely your grace and love are greater than our biggest doubts. Thank you that our faith does not need to be perfect simply because your grace is perfect. May our doubts provoke study and spiritual growth as we open our minds and hearts to the ways you strengthen us in our weak places. Through Jesus. Amen.

8

Ultimate Mystery/
Ultimate Reality

Driving along a well-traveled highway to my home one day, I noticed a message on one of those ubiquitous billboards. The message read succinctly, "We Need to Talk—God." Over time a number of other clever messages began to appear: "I love you and you and you—God." "Come on over and bring the kids"—God. "My way IS the highway—God." "Tell the kids I love them"—God. Apparently God has a way of cleverly making his point, as in "What part of THOU SHALT NOT do you not understand"—God." God can use rhetorical questions, as in "Do you have any idea where you are going?—God." and "Need directions?—God. Still another: "Have you read my #1 best-seller? There will be a test—God." Apparently, God has a sense of humor: "Big Bang? You've got to be kidding!—God." Or, "Loved the wedding. Invite me to the marriage"—God. And then there were threatening messages: "Keep using my name in vain and I'll make rush hour longer—God." "Don't make me come down there—God."

These billboard messages, which have appeared both on Internet and church marquees, stir mixed reactions. On the one hand, the billboard messages may be effective in reminding people who might never enter a house of worship of the reality of God. Perhaps we should rejoice any time the name of God is lifted up in public places. On the other hand, these messages project a message that the great God of heaven and earth can be easily grasped by the human mind and that God's message can be reduced to clever, casual sayings that are brief enough to be placed on billboards and marquees. So we have a folksy God who seems to have read the latest pop psychology books and engages in a little humor, a little affirmation, and a little chiding for his way-ward children. And overall, this God is a rather affable deity whose ways are common sensible and who would not object to being portrayed most casually in a laid back, folksy manner by Morgan Freeman in *Evan Almighty* and *Bruce Almighty* and George Burns in *Oh God!*

Various worldviews offer a wide range of insights and interpretations on the existence and nature of God. Little wonder. God is the ultimate reality with whom all of us deal—and the ultimate mystery of our lives. We do well to understand, at least in brief form, the major conceptions of deity in the dominant worldviews. A popular cultural tendency today minimizes the differences in various religions in the push for tolerance. Yet, all religions are not alike in doctrinal tenets, however similar they may be in ethics. The diversity of religious worldviews is nowhere more evident than in their teachings and depictions of ultimate reality and supernatural power. Many different words and expressions have been used to name and describe this ultimate reality. We will begin in the ancient world, painting this historical picture with a broad stroke.

Concepts of God in Various Worldviews

Animism is a view common among the world's native religions and has been revived in current pagan and neo-pagan practices. Animists believe that all elements in nature are imbued with spirits. Thus the tree has a soul, the mountain has a soul, and the deer has a soul. These nature spirits may indeed be relatives of the living and must be considered and honored, especially during times of seasonal change, life cycles, or potential adversity. Many animists have believed that among the many spirits, there is one great superior spirit that is more powerful than all other spirits. Any line between animism and polytheism is vague. Some polytheists, for example in the ancient Greek and Roman tradition, believe that many gods administer the world in a disorganized, unpredictable fashion. Other polytheists, such as those in the Hindu tradition, conceive the role of deities in maintaining balance and order in the universe. Some polytheists give special honor to a creator god and others give special honor to one god who rules over a hierarchy of gods. Ancient peoples often paid homage to a chief deity, but were more concerned with deities believed to be actively engaged in affecting their survival.

The native peoples of the Americas thought of the absolute in terms of gods and goddesses that possessed human characteristics. In that sense, Native Americans were no different in worldview from ancient Sumerians, Norse cultures, or South Asian Aryans, just to name a few cultures. The major elements of nature—sun, moon, stars, earth, water, weather, and seasons—were perceived as deities who were characters in a ceaseless drama. In ancient Egypt the sun, sky, earth, and river were considered sources of life, and thus were deified and symbolized as humans, animals, and combined human-animal forms. In ancient Europe as well as in Northern Africa and the Americas, many of the major cities and city-states adopted a patron deity, and symbols and rituals were attached to that deity; the Athenians' adoption of the goddess Athena provides a well-known example. Deities of hunting and gathering peoples were sometimes integrated with deities of agriculture and bounty. The gods of the ancient Greeks and Romans were also "bigger than life" characters who possessed very human-like emotions such as anger, love, jealousy, and envy. Ancient Mesopotamians worshiped the gods of nature, but their best-known and most loved deity was Ishtar, the goddess of fertility, whose popularity earned her worship under other names in other cultures.

Deity in Religions Originating in India

Hinduism is perhaps the oldest of the major world religions still in existence and it has encouraged a wide variety of beliefs and practices over the centuries. There are almost innumerable deities within Hinduism. Hindus start with the guidance of the *Vedas*, the earliest collection of Scriptures of knowledge and wisdom (recorded around 1200 B. C. E.), and from that scriptural basis move into manifold expressions of faith and action. They consider ultimate reality, Brahman, as being an impersonal oneness that is beyond all distinctions, including moral and personal distinctions. Hindus may choose to believe there is only one true God or they may embrace the concept of 3,000 deities or even 300 million deities.

Some Hindus may choose one god or image above all others. Hindu families may adopt their own personal deity; after all, much Hindu devotion is expressed in the home. Since the Middle Ages, three gods have been important in the worship and artistic life of most Hindus: Brahma, Vishnu, and Shiva (who form the *Trimurti*, meaning "triple form"). Brahma represents the creative power and artistic genius that made the universe; he is often depicted as a four-faced, thoughtful king sitting on a throne and looking in all directions and seeing everything. Shiva's creative energies permeate this world, but this god has a wrathful side and is linked with punishment and destruction. Some devotees of Shiva consider their deity to be the most powerful force in maintaining a cycle of world creation, fertility, and destruction; in contrast with western religions, the Hindu notion of destruction is both necessary for new forms of cosmic life and is simply another dimension of divine energy in the world. Vishnu represents the cosmic force of preservation, the deity who underlies all reality; his presence bestows light and warmth that destroy darkness. Vishnu also bestows lovingkindness and can appear on earth at different times.

Vishnu's incarnations, called *avataras,* are usually in heroic figures; the best-known avatar is Krishna, revered for his sweet disposition and wise counsel as a guru. Gurus are teachers of Hindu scriptures, thinkers whose insights and reasoning lead seekers to believe they have been illumined by the gods. Hinduism expresses a strong sense of the feminine in their understanding of divinity. Hindu goddesses (*devis*) are born of the earth and from the earliest era of this religion each village or community had its own *devi* who protected it. The Great Mother, also called Devi, is portrayed in different forms but is worshipped throughout all India. Colorful, detailed stories are connected with all the major Hindu deities. For example, Krishna becomes a friend to milkmaids who tend herds of cows, plays the flute, and develops a romantic relationship with Radha, his closest milkmaid companion. Though many varieties of Hinduism have developed over the centuries, what gives this broad tradition a measure of unity is the deeply-held conviction that something supernatural underlies the material world experienced by our senses.

Radha Babu, a life-time Hindu born in India and a personal friend, expressed a more contemporary view of God. "God is like strong electricity that brings light to all kinds of seekers," she has told me more than once. "The wide variety of legitimate religions enlightens a wide variety of people in different cultures. There are big light bulbs and small ones. There are incandescent bulbs and fluorescent bulbs. Though the amount of light may vary, all are powered by the same electricity."

Hindu deities have been depicted graphically in design and color. The well-known figure of Nataraja, or Shiva, as lord of the dance, has four arms and hands extending from his shoulders. The upper hands with drum and flame symbolize creation and destruction. Ganesh, a popular deity and son of Shiva who offers aid during distress as well as worldly prosperity, appears with an elephant head with a pot-bellied human form. The many body parts of human-animal combination are meant to express a deity's capacity to fulfill many functions. In contrast to Jews, iconoclasts within the Christian tradition, and Muslims, Hindus have not considered image worship to be competing with their deities. Most Hindus believe that they are in their true selves (*atman*) extended from Brahman and one with Brahman, their conception of Ultimate Reality. In contrast with the polytheism of ancient Egypt and ancient Greece, Hindu doctrine holds that beyond all the deities there is an Ultimate Reality. The philosophical Hindu would explain the separate deities as ways to approach this one true reality.

Buddhism is typically considered to be a philosophy toward life rather than a religion, if we consider religion primarily concerned with knowing and honoring a deity. Because Buddha did not worship a god, many people have concluded that he was an atheist. In his reported conversations with his monks, clearly Buddha did not have an experience with any god that he found worthy of describing. He also questioned whether the Brahmins who taught so much about gods and sacrifices knew from experience what they were teaching. He seemed to question whether these Brahmins were only repeating hearsay, tradition, or doctrine instilled in them. Could not the same question be posed to all traditions?

Buddha did not consider the matter of God's existence to be significant, for this concern did not pertain to the issue of how to escape suffering. And is there an unchanging Divine Reality called Brahman in the Buddhist philosophy? Early Buddhism expressed skepticism on that question, too, for Buddha considered that everything was in constant change and he never experienced anything that was not changing. The Buddha might best be described as a nontheist. He opposed the concentration of religious power and authority, dogmatism in religious teaching, and blind devotion to gurus or other religious teachers. He believed that reason could be used to answer questions about the existence of deity and his followers over the centuries have followed his advice to experience reality for themselves and to trust their own reasoned judgment.

Most Buddhists today will insist that the Buddha was not a god, but a mere mortal. Westerners who visit a Theravadin Buddhist temple, if not oriented to the ritual, would surely conclude that the devotees are worshiping the Buddha. Buddhists generally believe, as do most Hindus, that a spiritual reality embraces all meaningful experiences. Mahayanist Buddhists opened the door for all kinds of spiritual beings. They teach that there are many *bodhisattvas* or saints qualified for *nirvana* who remain in contact with the world to help suffering. Devotees can pray to them and offer adoration. For most Buddhists, the closest entities to gods are deified ancestors and other persons who personify aspects of the Absolute.

Deity in Religions of the Far East

Early Shinto, the religious life that flourished in Japan before Buddhism arrived in their country in the sixth century after Jesus, focused its worship on the goddess of the sun, Amaterasu-Omikami. The Japanese saw this goddess not as a universal deity, but as a deity especially partial to the Japanese. Nature *kami* (deities) are worshiped and emperors can be revered or worshiped at shrines because they are viewed as descendents of the goddess of the sun. There are many *kami* and they are procreated by other gods. The *kami*, which can be either helpful or hurtful, dwell in both material objects and the natural world and may commune with those who are ritually pure and wait for their presence.

Two other traditions of the ancient Orient merit attention. Confucius' philosophy about life formed a belief-system with values that have been cherished by billions of

Asian people as well many non-Asians over the centuries. Before the time of Confucius, God was spoken of as a personal Being and was called *Ti* or *Shang-ti*. Confucius, on the other hand, spoke of ultimate reality as *Tien*, which had the less personal meaning of "heaven;" the mandate from "heaven" was to advance the moral order of things within nature. There are hints within the *Analects*, the collection of Confucian sayings, that the great Chinese philosopher considered the ultimate reality to possess personal attributes. Yet Confucius focused on practical lessons for daily living and wise government. *Jen* is the goal of an ideal humanity that is symbolized in the *Analects* by the terms "superior man," "gentry intellectual, and "a person of *jen*." Such a person has reached an ideal in which one's full potential in moral goodness has been reached.

The beginnings of Daoism remain more obscure than its later developments, but its earliest teachers drew contrasts with the teachings of Confucius and his disciples. The Daoists were more speculative than Confucians about universal truth. The sage, the wise person in Eastern tradition, realizes that in the final analysis humans cannot conquer nature. Although no one can completely comprehend the *Dao* as the mysterious cosmic power of the universe, the *Dao* does manifest itself to those who patiently observe, carefully reflect, and seek to live in harmony with it. This *Dao*, the impersonal and invisible way that the universe follows, is the Ultimate Reality for Daoists who discover the harmony of tensions between opposites. Humans who died became ancestors that were worshiped as gods. Illustrious emperors and rulers were worshiped as folk heroes, much in the manner of Buddhists worshiping their ancestors.

In attempting a picture of Ultimate Reality as conceived over the centuries and in various environments, you might conclude that the notion of deity is "all over the map." Both animism and polytheism, perhaps a combination of the two, seem to have been natural for peoples attempting simply to survive and understand threatening forces of nature they could not control. We could scarcely begin to make a definitive list of the names of all the gods and goddesses and forces that have been worshiped by men and women over the many centuries of human history. And could any artist capture on canvas all the ways that deity has been imagined in the human mind?

Among the cultures of the ancient world, none developed an enduring concept of only one god, a monotheism, though there were attempts to conceive a unified cosmic system. Egypt was clearly and pervasively polytheistic except for the efforts of Akhnaton (1367-1350 B.C.E.), a young and inexperienced Pharaoh who wanted to revise national religion to worship a single sun god, Aton; the ruling priests vehemently opposed the idea and it was not to be heard of again until the emergence of Judaism centuries later. The Zoroastrianism of ancient Iran, rooted in the experiences of Zarathrustra and the *Avesta* (Zoroastrian scriptures), provides a possible example of acceptance of monotheistic doctrine independent of Judaism. Zoroastrians of the sixth and seventh centuries B.C.E. taught that a high god, Ahura Mazda, expressed himself through good spirits whose names are virtues. Whether the good spirits are independent beings or character traits of Ahura Mazda is not clear, but this religion also teaches about an evil force that opposes God named Angra Mainyu.

THE JUDEO-CHRISTIAN-MUSLIM CONCEPT OF DEITY

Our human need is to visualize God in some way. How easy and seemingly necessary for scholars and theologians to speak of God with abstractions! Given the deep mystery about God, little wonder theologians and scholars employ terms such as "ground of all being," "universal spirit," or "ultimate being" to describe this Ultimate Reality. For the Christian, the biblical worldview and biblical doctrine about God constitute the most authoritative sources on the nature of Ultimate Reality. These sources begin first with a biblical portrait and then also include centuries of experiences, doctrine, and teaching in church history.

The Judeo-Christian-Muslim worldview advances a faith in one God. There is evidence that early in their history the Jews practiced henotheism. As alluded to in Hindu practice, henotheism refers to beliefs and practices that, while recognizing the presence of numerous gods, accepts and worships the ascendancy of only one God above all others. Some have interpreted the first commandment in the Decalogue forbidding "no other gods" before the Lord as evidence of belief in the existence of inferior deities. The ancient Israelites often wavered in their loyalty to Yahweh, and the enticement to adopt and worship the gods of nations and tribes around them seemed a persistent temptation.

God's covenant people were clearly taught the reality of monotheism. God has no legitimate rivals in some other world religion, and idolatry is strictly forbidden for true believers. A beginning point is the *Shema* in ancient Judaism, a brief declaration: "Hear, O Israel! The Lord is our God, the Lord is one" (Deut. 6:4-5; see also Isa. 45:5-7). This is a statement of doctrine: *there is but one true God*. The second part of this ancient creed is an ethical command: "Love the Lord your God with all your heart and with all your soul and with all your strength" (6:5; Jews continue by reciting daily the command to place this instruction "on your hearts" and "impress them on your children," vss. 6-9).

While Judaism offers contributions in morals and ethical behavior, this concept of monotheism is arguably its abiding contribution to the religious world. As other religions were steeped in either animism or polytheism, the Judaism that began with the call of Abraham out of paganism offered to the religious world the compelling concept of the oneness and unity of God. The one Almighty God is granted absolutely unique authority, shared with no other being. The theistic doctrine first revealed to

Abraham became the foundation for three great world religions, two of which constitute the world's most populous religions. Islam especially declares condemnation against all polytheists and any flirtation with "other gods" is a drastic, condemnable transgression called "shirk," the associating of any person or thing as though placed on God's level. And the source of such a doctrine of one true God? Answer: Most surely in the divine, self-revelation of the Father-God to his chosen people and the chosen people's fulfilling the commission to take the message to the world.

Does God Have a Name?

Insights from Islamic and Jewish Traditions

How unimaginable to think of ourselves or any of our friends without possessing a name! But does God have a name? Is "God" God's name? The word "God" is only the English name for God, the word we use to translate "theos" from the Greek New Testament, and it came to English from the German name for God, which is "Gott."

Muslims say that God's name is "Allah," which is an Arabic word meaning "the God." From the *Qur'an*, Muslims teach that in addition to the name Allah, God has ninety-nine other names. Some of these ninety-nine names for Allah are: the First, the Real, the Far Away, the Real Close, the Light, the Maker of Everything Else, the Good, the Merciful, the Compassionate, the Loving, the One, the Wise, the Great, the Judge, the Forgiver, and the Rewarder. These expressions are like nicknames for God. One meaningful name is *al Salam*, "the place from whom peace comes." The Islamic idea is that God is always more goodness than we can imagine. We can think up even more good and wonderful names and expressions for God and there will always be more because God is always more than we can know and more than we can express in human language.

Islamic theology simply followed Judaism. During the Old Testament times, God was called by richly descriptive personal names and titles. This was an era in which names described the being, character, personality, reputation, and authority of individuals. In order to know God it is important to understand the names he used to communicate himself and his purposes to humankind. In the Old Testament, we encounter these and other names: *El* (God, Gen. 17:1); *El-Elyon* (Most High God, Gen. 14:18-20); *Elohim* (literally "gods;" Gen. 1:2); *Adonai* (Lord, Josh. 3:1); *El-Shaddai* (God Almighty or, literally "God of the Mountains," Gen. 17:1); *El-Olam* (God-Everlasting, Gen. 21:33); *Jehovah-Jireh* (the Lord our Provider, Gen. 22:13-14); *El-Berith* (God of the Covenant, Judg. 9:16); *Jehovah-Shalom* (the Lord is Peace, Judg. 6:24); and *Jehovah-Sabaoth*; 1 Sam. 17:45). Faithful Jews teach us that the real name of God (YHWH from the Hebrew Scriptures) cannot be pronounced, and they simply substitute another name, *Adonai,* meaning "my Lord." For Jews, God's real name must remain both sacred and ineffable.

The Judeo-Christian-Muslim worldview believes that God is a personal God, not a remote sky god like Zeus, but a God with moral attributes who intervenes in human affairs. How tempting to speak and sing of "our God," yet no one and no party "owns" God. Let us also concede a paradox about this Almighty God: God's complete essence is beyond human comprehension and God cannot be made to fit into our limited human categories, and yet God has chosen to give the human family a compelling picture of the divine nature.

KNOWING GOD

How much can we know about our God? What is God like? What does God think and what does God feel? What is God's will for America? And what is God's will for me? In what ways am I accountable to this God? How does God want me to live? What can I do for the God who created me? How will God bring human history to a climax? More crucially important questions could not be asked.

At this point, let's acknowledge our human finitude and limitations. Have you ever listened to hymns or sermons and drawn the impression that certain preachers and hymnists seem to know all about God? They may give you the impression they know infallibly what God is willing to do and what he is not willing to do, what emotions God must be feeling, how God is active in the world, the church that God wants all Christians to attend, the career God wants someone to pursue, the income someone should earn, the position that all "good" people should take on moral issues, or the candidate for which true Christians should vote. Such attitudes are heretical at worst and spiritually perilous at best. Let's recall one apostle's caveat that concluded his burst of doxology: "Oh, the depth of the riches of the wisdom and knowledge of God! How unsearchable his judgments, and his paths beyond tracing out! Who has known the mind of the Lord? Or who has been his counselor?" (Rom. 11:33-34).

The mystery and awesomeness of God can scarcely be fathomed by the human mind. How absurd to think that anyone could ever fully define or describe the great God of heaven and earth, or penetrate the mysteries of divinity, eternity, and the unseen world? It would be analogous to expecting a lowly insect to understand the intricacies of life as a human being. God is someone of whom we catch glimpses, someone of whom we have moments of insight, someone we see only through a dark glass (I Cor. 13:12).

When we turn to Holy Scripture, we find these ancient authors encountered the same challenge of describing God. Though God is Spirit, the Bible depictions of deity use the analogy of a person. While Greek philosophers preferred to conceive of God as an unchanging force and remote from the created order (*cosmos*), the Bible is a record of God's personal traits, his mighty acts on behalf of his human creation, his words to people through his spokespersons.

Holy Scripture gives us several figures and analogies toward knowing God. The figure of a loving shepherd who cares for his aimless sheep is grounded in the everyday world of the Middle East. There are figures that speak to almost any culture in our contemporary world: God is the faithful husband who grieves over the unfaithfulness of his wife, but still loves her passionately and seeks her return to him. God is the loving mother who in no way would consider abandoning her own child (Isa. 49:15; see also 42:14; 46:3; 66:13). Most of all, God is the loving father who unfailingly seeks what is best for his children, grants them their rightful freedom, grieves when they become wayward and rebellious, and longs for their return to his home. He hears the cries of those who are enslaved and seeks to deliver them. He is on the side of the weak and oppressed. He is compassionate to the fatherless, the barren woman, the poor and indigent, and even the foreigners and prisoners. He is ever-ready to hear the voice of those who cry out to him.

These clear depictions of God within biblical Scripture point to the one authentic portrait of God in Jesus Christ. In Jesus, God is embodied as a human being. Jesus expressed his basic organic unity with the Father. Any image or depiction of God's character or behavior which we cannot square with what we know for certain about Jesus must be rejected as inadequate or erroneous. God not only reached out to draw us to himself by sending his Son, but he dramatically demonstrated how to live through the actions and teachings of this Son.

God takes the initiative and *actively seeks us* for the purpose of establishing relationship. We were created for the purpose of relationship with our Father, and, yet, of course, we can waive this privilege of divine relationship just as we can pass up opportunities for specific human relationships or refuse an honor that some person or organization wants to present.

And how do we know that the biblical worldview gives us, however incomplete, an accurate picture of ultimate reality? How can we know that this Jesus of Nazareth was truly God in the flesh walking, talking, working, teaching, and socializing like you and me? Isn't the entire doctrine of Incarnation illogical and impossible?

Finding answers to such important questions would mean a march deep into the field of Christian apologetics, and a plethora of books on the subject are easily accessible in libraries and bookstores. Suffice it to say here, the doctrine that Jesus on earth was truly the Christ and Lord of history was not some bizarre conclusion reached by some lonely, eccentric, emotionally-disturbed philosopher—it was the considered conviction of the entire Christian community of the first century as these early disciples responded to unmistakable evidence they knew first hand or trusted in witness accounts of the life, the cruel execution, and glorious resurrection of Jesus Christ. These were convictions for which the early Christians were willing, if necessary, to sacrifice their lives as martyrs even by barbaric forms of execution.

The testimony of the centuries holds no other viable explanation for the devotion of millions and the presence of both magnificent cathedrals and humble meeting-houses of worship and service in the name of Jesus. If Jesus Christ is indeed not who he claimed to be, all of Christendom and much of history rest on bold deception.

Devotional Reflection

Could it be that the great "Hound of Heaven," an expression of the poet Francis Thompson, is seeking you or me for some mighty calling or purpose? Perhaps you can sing with assurance in praise to God "How Great Thou Art" but have you felt the closeness expressed in the lyrics of "My God and I"? Is God a friend with whom you can, figuratively speaking, "walk and talk and clasp hands together," or does this over-sentimentalize the great God who created the entire world?

And do we truly know God? Can we, like Jesus, call him "Abba Father"? We may know theological teachings and philosophical concepts *about* Ultimate Reality, but that does not mean that we truly *know* God. Any theology that precludes the possibility of our truly knowing God, not simply knowing facts in sacred history, must be discarded as sub-Christian and dishonest.

And do we seek God's movement in our midst, the dance of divine grace in and out of our lives? Just as we need to think outside the box in forming our worldview, we must not de-mystify God and place him in a box of our own ideological limitations and comfort level. We may never effectively determine the will of God in our lives so long as we have already determined the boundaries within which he can operate.

Prayer: Dear God, we seek to know the totality of you that you have revealed in the past through holy men and women moved by your Spirit as well as to know you through the way you move in our lives today. Thank you for reaching out to us even in times when we were not reaching out to you, for always being more willing to listen than we are seeking to talk to you. May we never limit your work in the world or in our lives by our own ignorance, prejudice, or selfishness. Through the One who blessed our world with the most concrete embodiment of Ultimate Reality, even Jesus our Lord and Savior. Amen.

9

Blessings, Curses, and Free Will

The tee shirt reads: "ANY TEAM CAN HAVE A BAD CENTURY." The satirical shirt was worn around Chicago at the end of the 2003 baseball season. For decades the windy city's lovable Cubs have come so close to earning their way to the World Series, only to find chances foiled time and time again. Is there a special curse on the Cubs? In the 2003 National League Playoff series, the Cubs were three runs ahead and five outs away from bringing a pennant to their famished fans. A fan named Steve Bartman interfered with a high foul ball that the Cubs outfielder likely would have caught for an out. The Florida Marlins went on to score eight runs to win that game and returned to beat the Cubs in the seventh game; thus, alas, Cub fans were thwarted once again from seeing their favorite team reach the World Series.

The day following the disastrous 2003 game a reporter visited a Chicago public school and asked students how many blamed themselves in some way for the collapse of their beloved team in that fateful game. Had they worn something different? Eaten a different snack in front of the TV? Sat on the couch instead of the chair? Nearly three-quarters of them raised their hands. Most of us would not doubt the overall sanity of people who lapse into some superstition during stressful moments. Have you ever dressed in a "lucky tee shirt" when competing for victory? Or have you ever stopped watching your favorite team on television, thinking the team must fare better when you are outside the room?

Think of the many interesting events that have occurred in your own life, some joyous and happy, others sad or even tragic. Who is responsible for these events occurring in your life? Were all of them "bound" to happen no matter what you thought or wanted?

Do you control what happens in your life? These questions are important. A variety of worldviews provide a variety of answers.

Freedom

Few words have such diverse meaning as freedom. The word might mean physical freedom, as in the freedom to move our bodies as we want. There may be civil freedom, political freedom, and psychological freedom. To a philosopher the meaning is a little different—the capacity to choose freely. Being free seems to involve an alternative. You and I can make choices. Well, we certainly *feel* as though we make decisions—whether to trade for a new car or repair the one we own; whether to attend church services on a Sunday or use the morning for sleep or recreation; whether to take a special class or spend the evening with the family; what to order from the menu in a restaurant; what clothes to purchase in a department store; what topics to use for our term project, and so on, *ad infinitum.*

So how did God create us? Are we truly free? Some say "no," that our deliberations and decisions are merely the expressions of unconscious drives and desires. We do not blame people for the color of their eyes or skin or for their height and should not blame them for their socially significant activities and behavior. We should not, then, blame them for their choices. Or is every act caused and pre-determined? Do we have real choice or do we entertain only the illusion of real choice?

Probably no other issue in metaphysics is any more controversial, is more significant, or has a larger impact on other concerns in our lives. For example, if everything is rigidly controlled, what is the point of making future plans in an attempt to guide future events? And what about moral responsibility? Could anyone really be punished in a court of law for some crime when the defendant had no choice but to commit the crime? If a person could not have acted differently, how can we hold him or her responsible? And how could God label any behavior as sin or punish behavior as sin if the "sinner" has no choice?

Free Will and Determinism

This perennial issue in philosophy is the age-old conflict between free will and determinism. "Will" refers to the ability to choose. We assume we can choose who we date, whether we will marry, and who we marry. We can decide what our religious expression and affiliation will be—we could be Roman Catholic, Southern Baptist, or we could become Muslim or Buddhist. Or could we?

Given all the factors that influence us—our parents and other relatives, early teachers, our peers, our political and religious leaders—is there real choice or only the illusion of choice? Is there any imaginable way that poor factory worker in Beijing,

China, someone who never heard of Jesus, could become a Christian? And is there any realistic way a young person in Nashville, Tennessee, raised in a conservative Christian church and educated in a Christian school, could become a Hindu? Sure, the person in Nashville, who has worshiped and studied in a Christian church all her life, has heard of Hinduism, may have studied Hinduism in a college-level class in world religions, and may have even visited a Hindu temple as part of a field trip—but does she really have the freedom to become a Hindu?

The world of science moves with different assumptions. In the scientific world it is assumed that everything is determined by natural laws and there is an orderly causal sequence. Effects follow causes with regularity. *Determinism* is the theory that everything in the universe, including human beings, is entirely governed by causal laws. The assumption in determinism is that whatever happens is governed by something that has happened right before it. This relates to sunrise, pollination, orbiting of planets, or any other process in nature. Yet in sociology, psychology, and biology we discover that humans, too, are ruled by cause and effect. A person's life is ruled by glands, unconscious drives, training and teaching, hereditary and environmental facts, DNA, *et cetera*, that are beyond that person's control. According to determinists, everything has a cause regardless of whether it is recognized.

Predestination is the doctrine that God has decreed that every event that is to take place or that each person's destiny is fixed by divine decree. In salvation, some people are chosen for eternal bliss and others are arbitrarily rejected. Therefore, everything is determined by the sovereign will of God. (Sometime you may want to study such passages as 1 Peter 2:9 and Ephesians 1:4-5, 11, as well as three challenging New Testament chapters: Romans 9, 10, and 11.) In extreme predestination, everything is determined. In more moderate form, predestination means God is seeking people before they are aware of divine calling.

The doctrine of predestination is represented in all three major monotheistic religions, although, of course, scriptural passages are open to varying interpretation. From Paul to Augustine to John Calvin, the doctrine of election seems clearly stated. Historic Calvinism has contributed a rich tradition to church history in past centuries. God is sovereign and human beings are responsible and both assumptions are simultaneously true. This is an antimony or paradox, to be sure, that cannot be fully resolved in the human mind. For Reformed Christians, the Bible teaches both points of doctrine and faith demands that Christians accept both—but understanding is beyond any of us. Christians are chosen of God, yet they have chosen freely to come to Christ. The apparent answer lies in a regeneration that changes hearts and gives sincere students the ability to hear the gospel and be responsive to his call. Thus, when we come to God, we come willingly, not kicking and screaming, and we enter his kingdom.

Fatalism is the belief that some, perhaps all, events are irrevocably fixed and human effort cannot alter them. All events are predetermined from the beginning of time. Certain events will happen at the appointed time, such as a person's death or other tragedy. The question of causes remains an inscrutable mystery. In the ancient Greek and Roman worldview, the concept of fate was prominent. To the ancient Greeks, the will of Zeus was all controlling and there was nothing that could be done to alter the future. A fatalist is pessimistic about the future and about life in general.

And what about luck? Is there a role for luck? Suppose you buy a new coat at Dillard's and upon arriving home you discover a $100 bill in the pocket. Could this have been God's answer to your prayer for some needed cash? Was it pure luck? Could it be that some absent-minded shopper stuck the bill in the coat as it was being checked for size and simply forgot to return it to a billfold or purse? Does any good thing happen to us solely on basis of luck? If so, is it ever appropriate to give thanks to God for "good luck"?

Most of us think we experience more bad luck than good luck. You buy a used car that you've wanted and the transmission goes out in three months. The important flight connection you needed to get home on time gets canceled and you are stranded in another city. Your new laptop computer gets stolen almost right under your nose. You waited until the night before the exam to do intensive study, and then realize you have misplaced your full set of class notes needed for preparation. We all have heard the old saying, "If it were not for bad luck, I wouldn't have any luck at all." Truth is, of course, that when many of us complain about our "bad luck," we have been guilty of focusing on atypical negative experiences and overlooking the many good experiences and the wonderful realities that bless our lives.

There are times that we all make the wrong choices. Not all wrong choices, of course, are sinful choices. You may have purchased the wrong textbook for the new course in which you enrolled. You may have chosen the wrong route to reach your vacation spot. You may have selected the wrong garment to wear to the party or purchased the wrong tool to complete the repair. When we willfully make wrong choices about moral behavior, behavior that has a serious negative consequence on others or self, we have sinned and become morally accountable.

BIBLICAL NARRATIVES OF FREE WILL

Many Christians are repelled by the doctrine of determinism and believe it is inconsistent with biblical doctrine, but also incompatible with freedom and moral responsibility. The first narrative in Scripture tells of God creating both male and female and then giving to them the precious gift of freedom, along with some directives in using that freedom. The fact that Adam and Eve eventually chose to abuse their freedom and rebel against a clear command of God is prototypical of all human moral nature.

The Bible is filled with stories about men and women who made important choices. Noah chose to obey God's command to build an ark. Joseph chose to resist the temptation to indulge in sexual relations with Mrs. Potiphar. Moses chose to identify with his own people in ancient Egypt, though they were enslaved, than to pursue a rising political career in Pharaoh's dynasty. Israel's King David made many good choices, obviously, but he also chose to seduce a married woman named Bathsheba, resulting in an unplanned pregnancy, and the death of her husband Uriah through his attempted cover-up scheme. Though Saul of Tarsus obstinately resisted all the signs that might point him to Jesus as God's Son, the Damascus Highway experience convinced him that he had been rebelling against the will of God. A paradox regarding free will worked in Saul's life—he felt compelled with no other logical choice but to follow Jesus, and yet he still consciously made the decision to preach Jesus and give his life for this new Savior and new faith.

The best biblical example of freedom exercised in a challenging crisis is, of course, that of God's own Son. Jesus had the choice of two roads before him. One was to suffer unspeakable physical and emotional agony by scourging and execution by public crucifixion, The other was to become a non-participant in God's plan to redeem sinful humanity by returning to heaven at any time before the awful sacrifice was offered. Though Jesus prayed for his ability to submit to the Father's will, agonized at length, and surely contemplated a fail-safe rescue by a host of ten thousand angels, he still consciously chose the path of self-sacrifice.

The ultimate question is whether God is involved in our lives and, if so, just how involved is God? Certainly, God knows all things and his knowledge is eternal. He knows what we are going to choose before we ever choose it, yet we are still free to choose between other paths and alternatives. There is not just one path that leads from the past into the future. Of course, only one of those paths can be ultimately chosen.

A MIDDLE GROUND BETWEEN DETERMINISM AND FREEDOM?

As thinking adults, we want the world to be "open" rather than "closed." We value novelty, creativity, openness, and spontaneity. The American philosopher and psychologist William James became an outstanding proponent of the open and free position and he called this doctrine "indeterminism." James contended there is a lot of "loose play" in the universe of events that are not causally related (an insight that sounds like "luck" to some people). James did not shun the word "chance." Though freedom is a postulate (*i.e.,* unproved rule or basic assumption from which people reason), so also are causality and uniformity. James asked how we can either feel good for taking the right way in life or bad for taking the wrong way if we really had no choice—we have no basis for self-judgment.

So, how do we resolve this issue? Most philosophers contend that no matter how persuasively one argues and reasons, neither position can be proven absolutely. Be careful to avoid extreme claims and unreasonable conclusions. Fatalists will relish the line from the player in *As You Like It*: "All the world's a stage and all the men and women merely players." Others refuse to accept the assumption in that famous stage line and declare that determinism is false.

Is there a middle position possible, one that links determinism and freedom? Surely a man or woman is a creature of one's environment, genes, age, and all those predetermined factors, but might one also be both critic and a creator of one's personal environment? Yes, surely some decisions are dependent on antecedent causal factors, but we also reject rigid, hard-line determinism that negates human freedom and, as a logical concomitant, also negates personal moral responsibility.

Self-determinism might be the name for this position, where the self does act in creative ways and can make responsible decisions. Yes, there are some limits or boundaries, but within these boundaries of time and place a person possesses the capacity for personal initiative and response. And why do we believe that, within certain boundaries, we humans can creatively reshape ourselves and even influence others within our social environment? We cannot go to a science laboratory to find definitive answers to these important questions, but we can offer a list of sound reasons:

1. People possess an immediate consciousness of freedom. We believe we can choose alternative courses of action.

2. There is a sense of personal responsibility that expresses itself in feelings of obligation, especially when we use words such as "ought" and "should." Sometimes we have a keen feeling of blame and guilt—are these ill-founded concepts or do they actually make sense?

3. We render moral judgments on human conduct and character. We hold both ourselves and others responsible for certain choices and actions. For example, just examine your language. How often do you use words such as right and wrong, good and bad, praise and blame, approval and disapproval, reward and punishment—words that all assume the reality of freedom? How could you use those words if you did not feel people were free to make choices?

Consider the fact of deliberation. Reflective thinking is another dimension of human experience. Sometimes we stop to deliberate before we make a big decision.

Why should we take the time for deliberation if such pondering and reflective thinking do not influence us?

So, yes, there is a cause for everything and yet I, myself, am one of the causes, just as you are one of the causes of your behavior and its consequences. A degree of freedom and some kind of determinism may be combined. All animals can seemingly be conscious, that is, aware of their physical environment. Yet only human beings are self-conscious, which includes the additional awareness of the thoughts and motives of one's own mind or self. Self-consciousness makes reflective thinking and the sense of right and wrong possible. It enables a person to consider oneself as a subject and as an object of action, a prerequisite of freedom of choice.

THREE CATEGORIES OF CONTROL OR NON-CONTROL

As serious-minded Christians we are then summoned to make important distinctions between three categories: (1) events or circumstances over which one has no control; (2) decisions over which one has what seems to be complete control; (3) events or circumstances that one can influence.

Consider first the things over which you have no control: the identity of your parents, their DNA or genetic endowment to you, which includes your physical features such as color of skin, height, color and texture of hair, physique, metabolism, and predisposition to certain diseases and conditions. Nor did you choose the relatives in your family of origin. You certainly did not choose the time and place of your birth nor the birth order of you and your siblings.

Thankfully, by contrast, there are important matters we can control. We can choose our values. We can choose our commitments, either personal or organizational. We are free to develop our own faith and worldview. Though we do not choose our relatives, we are free, thank God, to choose our friends and associates. While many of us may feel we do not have enough time to do all the things we need and want to do, each person is given a gift of twenty-four hours each day and each has the choice of priorities in spending that block of time. And, of course, we have choices in managing our financial resources. What an irony that many of us expend a great deal of anxiety and effort to manipulate those components of life we cannot control (height, hair or lack thereof; the effects of aging on our bodies) while almost ignoring those areas we can control!

Finally, there are those areas wherein we do not have ultimate control, but that we may influence significantly. For example, if you are a university student, you cannot control your final grades in classes, though you do have considerable influence over them. The same effort in a chemistry class at Abilene Christian University that is awarded an "A" under Professor Jones might be awarded a "B" under Professor Smith atthe University of Texas. Professors vary in terms of course standards, expectations, and, quite frankly, concepts of fairness. Their personalities and values influence the grading process. Our point: you are foolish when you simply resign yourself to fate and exercise no effort on your own behalf. You did not choose all the features that would make you physically attractive or unattractive, but through exercise, proper diet, and good grooming and dressing habits you can influence how you present yourself to others and how others perceive you.

The Stoics of ancient Greece would say that ultimately the results of our efforts remain beyond our control. We see so many illustrations of this principle. Jim Fixx was a running enthusiast whose diet and exercise regimen were challenging in discipline, but sensible, and yet he died in his 40s with a cardiac condition. By contrast, all of us know at least a few characters who eat what they want at any time and become easily placed in the category of obesity, totally disregard exercise and other healthy habits, smoke tobacco like the proverbial industrial furnace, and wind up living into their 60s or even 70s. No one needs an excuse for self-indulgence. We do not control our destinies, but we do influence them just enough so that we should do our best to make wise moral and lifestyle choices.

Most importantly, you cannot totally control your reputation. Yes, you have considerable vital input and influence into how others perceive you and talk about you with others, but how they see and think of you are their choices. You do control your personal moral character. And God is the only one whose approval or disapproval ultimately matters. Recall the old saying: Your reputation is what people *think* that you are and your character is what God *knows* you are.

Blessings may come in unexpected and even undesired providential occurrences that most Christians would label "providential" and others would label as "luck" or "coincidence." (You may have heard the saying, "Coincidence is God's way of remaining anonymous in your life.") Christopher Reeve portrayed on screen the comic superhero "Superman," but a freakish catapult to the ground while horseback-riding left him totally immobilized from his neck down. And yet Reeve became an even greater "Superman" as a moral hero whose marvelous attitude toward the gift of life and his gutsy determination to walk again and champion spinal research granted him far more influence for good in real life than did his relatively brief career on the silver screen. With his tragic death in October, 2004, Americans mourned the loss of a courageous moral hero who had blessed the world more in 52 years than had he lived a normal and otherwise highly predictable lifespan. (Sadly, Reeve's widow Dana lost her battle with lung cancer less than two years after his death.)

The bottom line is one's confidence in God's providence. If you are a university student, you know there are some required courses that are a real "pain," but you surely trust they fit into your curriculum for a meaningful purpose. The individual parts of a ship when tossed into the ocean would sink, but tightly fitted together the well-crafted ship will sail safely above the ocean depths. These are simple analogies for grasping divine providence. If we belong to God and are called according to his purpose through Jesus in our lives, then truly all experiences in our lives—the excellent, the routine, the mediocre, the unfortunate, even the tragic—will work together for the good of our spiritual character (see Rom. 8:28).

Devotional Reflection

If you are puzzled by events that have happened in history or by narratives you have read in Scripture, remember that God is sovereign. That point of doctrine likely will not answer all our questions, but it does remind us that God is unlimited in his freedom and can do anything he chooses to do within his perfect will—regardless of whether we understand it. We humans, too, possess freedom. While God has the power, right, and authority to do whatever he pleases, we only have the freedom and power to do whatever we want within our bounds of time and place. Thus, our freedom is always limited by the higher freedom of God.

Reject fate with its entire pessimistic outlook. Embrace freedom realistically if not absolutely. After all, there is never the absolute human freedom to live a life without needing God. God is not a cosmic entertainer, having placed us on earth as puppets with him pulling all our strings. Neither is God a cosmic hypnotist, making us do his bidding when we think we are acting on our own.

God created us, grants us freedom within the sphere of our time and place on earth, invites us into relationship with him through his Son, and yet never coerces us to submit to his will. We are free to reject God and to rebel against him. The wise person embraces the God who created all humans and seeks to draw them into relationship with himself, and then lives life courageously and responsibly, willingly accepting everything that happens as a process that can mold one more completely into the image of Christ.

Prayer: Dear God, we as finite humans cannot resolve all the intellectual challenges and complexities of human existence. We simply know that you created us, you gave us freedom, and you seek to bring us into close relationship with you as our eternal Father. Let us seize our freedom boldly to make wise choices, find security in your grace for our poorest choices, and trust in you totally that you will cause all the puzzling events in our lives to fit together in a harmonious whole that honors you. We acknowledge you as the One with complete control of the entire universe and that your ultimate will shall surely be done. May we be instruments of your will and your peace. Through the One who chose to go to the cross and die for the very worst of our moral choices. Amen.

10

When Socrates Stands Beside Jesus

T ake time to confront one of the most widely known, inspiring, powerful, intriguing, challenging, and, at times, annoying teachers of the western world. He was also one of the most widely misunderstood figures in the history of ideas. Other great teachers have claimed him as their chief inspiration and model. The influence of this person is incalculable. Centuries later, this great teacher and role model is still relevant to us today with the same compelling immediacy that he addressed his friends, followers, and critics. He belongs to the ages.

Surely we are speaking of Jesus. Or could we possibly be speaking of Socrates? Actually, we could be speaking of either person. We know the influence of Jesus on the world. Socrates, too, has achieved a kind of immortality in the world of ideas. He is one of the few great philosophers to whom people of many eras, cultures, interests, and abilities have turned for wisdom. Socrates' power to awaken and provoke intellectual thought and growth lives on from ancient to contemporary times.

When Socrates stands beside Jesus, what do we see? It may surprise you to learn how much these two teachers of antiquity were alike. Just as Jesus' way of life was inseparable from his teaching about the kingdom of God, Socrates' entire personality and lifestyle were also inseparable from his philosophy. Both Jesus and Socrates are such titanic figures in history that some philosophers and theologians call them *archetypes* or *paradigmatic* people, individuals who serve as an uplifting model for all humanity. Whether people study either Socrates or Jesus, no one is left untouched by the unusual character of either man.

An Unusual Life in a Golden Age

What do we know about Socrates? Nothing, actually, from his own handwriting or dictation. Yes, surely he wrote some messages, and Aristophanes, the writer of comedies in Athens, refers to Socrates in one of his plays; but nothing Socrates wrote has survived. His main form of communication was the lively conversation or dialogue. Later, Socrates' method of teaching was called the "dialectic method" or the "Socratic method," which uses lively, probing questions in a disciplined, "give and take" manner to facilitate learners' discovery of truth about complex issues for themselves. Over the centuries, the influence of Socrates has been channeled through the "Dialogues," written by his best-known student and disciple, Plato.

We do know that Socrates lived in Athens from 470 to 399 B. C. E. He was married to Xantippe and fathered children. In fifth century Greece, political life was volatile with arguments between democrats and aristocrats. Socrates was one of several teachers of philosophy, science, and rhetoric in Athens during a "golden age" of learning and artistic achievement. While philosophers before Socrates typically studied the workings of nature (physics), Socrates was the first major philosopher to focus deep inquiry about the nature of human beings and wisdom about human life.

Socrates conducted his classes in public and typically in the *agora*, or open marketplace, where crowds would gather for political rhetoric and discussion; this style was customary prior to the formalization of classes, schools, and academy life. He had great influence among young men, many of whom came from the homes of noblemen and might be expected to exert political influence in the future. This teacher masterfully employed irony, a rhetorical statement that has at least two conflicting levels of meaning—a literal or obvious level and a hidden or real level. His irony served to expose the ignorance and foolishness in his dialogue partners, laying the groundwork for understanding the complexity of an issue and a humble approach to knowledge. Socrates often engaged politicians and sophists (liberal arts teachers who could be hired for good salary to teach young men) under the pretext of an "aw, shucks" kind of ignorance to induce the other person into revealing his own ignorance or prejudice on the subject. His admirers loved this "questioning of authority." And many may have missed the genuine humility of Socrates in pursuit of truth. He did not accept anything as reality until it had been investigated, tested, and discussed in the light of reason.

A Clear Stand for Values

Socrates held the conviction that the improvement of the soul constitutes the central project for philosophical thought and the chief project for each person. He stood clearly for some values and clearly against other values. His uncompromising respect for justice, courage, integrity, humility, temperance, decency, balance, and beauty was particularly appealing in countering a cultural climate that endorsed crass materialism, cutthroat competition, and sensual excesses. Socrates was resourceful enough to incorporate philosophy into any random event or conversation, even joking among friends. His simple, yet profound, guiding motto of "Know thyself" has been challenging to people all over the world throughout the centuries as an antidote for drowsy sleepwalking through life.

Indeed, as with all great philosophers, Socrates struggled with several of the great problems of every age: Who am I? How can I discover my true identity? What are the great virtues? How shall I live? What should my life be all about? To him, the pursuit of wisdom begins with a march to one's interior. "The unexamined life is not worth living," he asserted boldly. This dictum suggests that every person has a responsibility to craft a rich, meaningful life guided by an enlightened personal philosophy.

Against the norms of his time, Socrates taught rejection of materialism and simplicity of lifestyle. He resisted any temptation to meander through life, predictable in all one's habits, submerged in mundane routine, and uncritical of the prevailing cultural values of the time. He believed beauty should be determined by function and usefulness and not by mere appearance. His entire teaching mission was rooted in his conviction that we are our souls; that is, the "real person" is not the body, but the psyche. Happiness is a matter of inner qualities and not external advantages.

Socrates was a walking embodiment of this teaching. He taught and practiced self-control of the physical appetites. This disciplined sense of values and self-control left him indifferent to fear. He was universally acknowledged to be "extraordinarily ugly," a condition to which he made humorous references. Obviously, he was "comfortable in his own skin." Nor was he worried about image, perfectly content to walk about Athens in a tattered garment and barefoot, even in extremely cold weather. His enemies accused him of being "unwashed," perhaps not without justification.

Socrates' appeal comes from possessing many of the same desires as all of us, but being able to keep his appetites and passions under strict control. He was wise enough to know that the best *things* in life are not things. His intellectual quest for both truth and justice was life-long. His passion for life and truth was not based on some naïve "goody-goody" view of human nature. As married man, father, and citizen, he understood the struggles of being human. He loved life to the fullest, wrestled with its deepest issues, and challenged other sincere seekers to join his "enduring quest."

The Death of Socrates

Such a "gadfly," a figure by which Socrates thought of himself, can threaten the mainstream of conventional society. Eventually, Socrates' enemies took action. They resorted to what appears to be a standard charge: that Socrates was "offending the gods and corrupting the young." Socrates was tried and declared himself not only innocent, but even deserving of a retirement paid by the city of Athens. The jury's verdict was to render their fellow citizen guilty. The sentence was death by poison. Socrates could have simply left the city and taken refuge in one of many places within the Greek realm that stretched into Italy as well as the Middle East. His friends had urged him to depart before the trial, but this courageous and wise man argued that by leaving he would be admitting guilt. When Crito suggested that Socrates ought to escape because he had been convicted by unjust laws, Socrates replied that two wrongs do not make a right. And the laws of Athens had supported him throughout his life; even though unjust, he argued, they are still the laws of Athens.

Thus, the great philosopher had chosen death for a rational principle over life because of compromise. The final scene in the life of Socrates is tender and poignant. As described by Plato in *Phaedo*, Socrates' friends and students are gathered to say goodbye. Though they are on the verge of tears, Socrates does his best to boost their spirits. Even the jailor apologizes for the role he must play and hopes Socrates will not hold it against him. Socrates assures him that he will not and swallows the poison, an extract of hemlock. He then lies down. Such a "lethal injection" was humane by ancient standards of justice. The end approaches quickly. His last words are uttered to friends to make certain they pay back a rooster he owes Asclepius, and they promise to do so, perhaps wondering if there is a double meaning to this final request.

The effect of Socrates' death upon Plato was profound. Plato had watched his respected mentor, a teacher whose life and teachings were in total harmony, be indicted, convicted, and executed as a traitorous blasphemer. Socrates was transformed from a truth-seeker and wandering teacher into a sage who became the very archetype of a wise man. On his death bed, once eyes were set, Crito closed his eyes and mouth, and Plato concludes his narrative: "Such was the end...of our friend; concerning whom I may truly say that of all men of his time whom I have known, he was the wisest and justest and best."

Remarkable Parallels with the Life of Jesus

Jesus entered the stage of history during a time of political unrest in first century Palestine. Though Jerusalem was never known as the great cultural center for which

Athens was reputed, it was still a major city known for heritage, religious festivals, and observances. Socrates did not travel far from Athens, nor did Jesus travel far from Jerusalem. Both teacher/philosophers (yes, it may be a little stretch to think of Jesus as a philosopher) taught exclusively in their own nation, but wielded an influence that would be universal and timeless.

Jesus' teaching, like that of Socrates, challenged conventional wisdom and conventional morality. Both relied on the power of questions to penetrate the minds and hearts of seekers. Each called into question the cherished traditions of the majority. Each was subjected to ridicule and efforts to discredit his teachings. Jesus hearkened the religious establishment to the true meaning of the Torah and summoned followers to a lifestyle befitting heirs within the Kingdom of Heaven. Jesus, too, seemed totally oblivious to material values. Though both master teachers were willing to receive gifts and hospitality from friends, neither possessed many material goods. Their chief mode of transportation was walking. Their typical venue for teaching was outdoors wherever a throng of people would gather or wherever one or two eager minds were inquiring and seeking truth.

Socrates and Jesus each instructed their learners that mere appearances were not enough to attain moral goodness, and that true happiness comes through wholehearted devotion to justice, integrity, humility, and courage. And just as Socrates could infuse his philosophy into the simplest occasion or turn of events, Jesus could take the simplest stories to teach lessons about the Kingdom of God and turn the barbed questions of his enemies into opportunities for sharing profound truth about his Father or spiritual life.

SOME IMPORTANT DIFFERENCES

When Socrates stands beside Jesus, some differences seem trivial and others crucially important. Besides birth in different centuries and in different nations, Socrates was both husband and father wherein Jesus was neither. Socrates lived to age 70 and Jesus' life was ended at age 33, though there is something patently absurd about their deaths by execution—in the former case, putting to death a defenseless old man due to allegations he had "corrupted the youth" of Athens and that he did not "believe in the gods whom the state believes in, but in other divinities," and, in the latter case, putting to death one relatively young man who was absolutely no threat to the political state and had come to bless his own people and the entire world. Socrates was obviously much more interested in politics than was Jesus, whose all-consuming passion was his Father's Kingdom.

Socrates was known for his pursuit of truth and wisdom, and he was truly humble in that pursuit. Jesus was known for his deep love for humanity. The Lord did not simply pursue truth—he *was* and *is* the Truth. Jesus was the truth of God's will revealed to humanity. He did not ask his followers to accept logical propositions and a cogent reasoning process to determine reality. He asked people to recognize him as God's Son and accept the Father's abundant grace and, in gratitude, to live the Kingdom lifestyle. And while both were truly humble, Jesus' humility was exhibited not in some academic pursuit of truth but in a servant role that directed his steps all the way to the cross.

Like other great philosophical and religious teachers of antiquity, both Jesus and Socrates attracted a dedicated group of followers who loved and followed their Master and thrilled to stirring discussions about the nature of truth and life. Both Socrates and Jesus believed that learners had a choice about the kind of life they wanted to live and that true knowledge (wisdom) produces behavioral change. Each believed that a blessed and fulfilling life must be based on rock-solid principles and virtues rather than on the shifting sand of sensuality and materialism. Socrates would surely have appreciated Jesus' appeals to logic and common sense and his use of irony and rhetorical question. Had Socrates been on the mountain when Jesus delivered his greatest sermon and heard those simple words, "the wise man builds his house upon the rock and the foolish man builds his house upon the sand," one might imagine his being the first to shout "Amen!"

One great difference emerges from Christian doctrine about Jesus and all other great teachers. The Founder of the Christian faith promises to live in the hearts and lives of his followers. Socrates, Plato, Aristotle, the Buddha, Confucius or any other great teacher makes no similar claim. All these great teachers changed history, for sure, but none lives on in a special indwelling among his disciples.

To non-Christians, the claim is preposterously absurd. Nor can Christians explain this mystical and mysterious union with their Savior. Yet we believe the mind-boggling promise that Jesus gave his closest disciples prior to his death, that he would send the Comforter or Holy Spirit to guide and empower them when he was physically absent (Jn. 14:16-18). Little wonder that Paul exclaimed, "Christ in you, the hope of glory" (Col. 1:27) and "anyone who does not have the Spirit of Christ does not belong to him" (Rom. 8:9). The key to being a Christian is not simply revering superlative teaching about life, as in other great philosophies and religions, but receiving God's free gift of salvation and welcoming in the indwelling Christ.

The most intriguing parallels between the lives of Socrates and Jesus emerge from their indictment on charges of blasphemy and constituting a threat to political society, their unfair trials with stunning convictions against an innocent man, their acceptance of their sentence of execution at the hands of the state, and their serenity in their closing moments of life. Jesus called for the forgiveness of his tormentors, and Socrates seems to have possessed the same attitude toward those who called for his execution. At the time of their deaths, each one was unselfishly thinking about others. How fitting that the life of each is judged in light of his death, for in the face of adversity, in the ultimate "situation beyond control," each martyr for truth remained in full control of himself. The point of this martyrdom: some things are more important than human existence itself, such as being true to one's principles and true to one's calling no matter how others may feel or act.

Devotional Reflection

Our Christian worldview compels us to consider the most crucial distinction of all between Socrates and Jesus. When Socrates stands beside Jesus, the portrait is that of a sinner standing beside a Savior. What an intriguing dialogue might have taken place if Socrates and Jesus had lived in the same time and same culture and sat down together for a visit!

Beyond any doubt, the world has been blessed by the life and the quest for truth of Socrates. And Socrates was wise enough to believe in the "Universal Spirit" that we call God. Likewise, the narrative of Socrates' death is one of the most stirring and inspirational stories ever told. Only the death of Jesus, however, was offered to satisfy the justice demands of God. "Yes, if the life and death of Socrates are those of a philosopher," declares philosopher and romanticist Jean-Jacques Rousseau (1712-1778), a famous French philosopher, "the life and death of Jesus Christ are those of a God."

Yes, all of us would be far wiser, more knowledgeable, and more fulfilled if we imitated the life of Socrates. But we are made righteous before God only through Jesus—accepting his Father's grace through that agonizing sacrifice of blood and then in gratitude living a lifestyle that molds us into the likeness of his Son!

Prayer: Dear God, we thank you for the lives of great teachers such as Socrates, who blessed the western world immensely with his pursuit of truth, wisdom, and justice. Thank you that the life and death of Socrates have inspired countless students throughout the centuries. The words "thank you" seem so inadequate in response to what you have done for us through Jesus who has brought us not only your blessing and modeled an ideal life, but also brought your salvation. May our every thought, every attitude, and every action reflect in some sense our deepest gratitude for your greatest gift. Through Jesus. Amen.

11

When Buddha Stands Beside Jesus

Prepare to confront one of the most widely known, inspiring, powerful, and challenging teachers in the entire world. This teacher, who was also a preacher, has been revered and respected on all continents and throughout many centuries. Though raised in one spiritual tradition, he is highly regarded as the founder of one of the world's oldest and most significant religions. His life is greatly interwoven with great events which defined him and, rather than detailed biographies which chronicle every year of his life, sacred tradition offers a realistic portrait of what all good disciples should strive to become. The man's life was so intricately connected with his teachings. The influence of this leader is incalculable. He belongs to the ages.

Surely we speak of Jesus. Or could we possibly be speaking of the Buddha? Actually, we could be speaking of either man. Buddha has achieved a kind of immortality in the world of spiritual ideas and spiritual disciplines. Buddhism has spread through almost all of Asia, influencing diverse cultures, and now gaining new followers in western nations. Like Socrates, the Buddha's power to awaken and provoke thought and growth in character lives on from ancient to contemporary times.

When Buddha stands beside Jesus, what do we see? Just as Jesus' way of life was inseparable from his teaching about the kingdom of God, Buddha's lifestyle was inseparable from his philosophy. Despite the intriguing parallels between the lives of these two religious leaders, we will surely discover that the differences in purpose and doctrine are greater than similarities between the two men.

EARLY LIFE

About the time that some of the Hindu *Upanishads* were being written, around 560 B.C.E., a young prince was born in northern India. Legend says that a virtuous woman named Maya had demonstrated purity and excellence during previous existences in 100,000 ages of the world and that one night she dreamed that a white elephant, bearing in his trunk a white lotus flower, entered her womb—the moment of conception of the future Buddha who was born miraculously from her side. The earth trembled and the birth event was witnessed by supernatural beings.

These honored parents, King Suddhodanna and Queen Maya, named their new son Siddhartha ("he who has reached his goal") Gautama (a name derived from a famous Hindu teacher). Siddhartha's father was the prince of the Shakya tribe in what today is Nepal and, wanting his son to succeed him, sought to shield his son from exposure to the harshness of the world and the reality of suffering. Hence, the young Siddhartha grew up in a large, walled palace compound. He lived a life of luxury, married at an early age to a young woman his family had chosen, and fathered his own son, who was named Rahula. He was educated in the arts and sciences and trained as a warrior. He later conceded that he was spoiled by the easy lifestyle.

The king's plan ran smoothly for a considerable period. When Siddhartha made brief excursions outside his palace he was confronted with what are called Four Passing Sights. He first came across an old man, toothless and crooked in stature; then he encountered a sick man, wasted by disease; next a corpse being taken for cremation; and finally, a wandering holy man who had renounced all possessions but seemed to be at peace. At age 29, he realized his life had been spent in a pleasant prison and that he was just now learning some of life's deepest lessons: all human beings must grow old; sickness and suffering are part of human existence; death is an experience common to all human beings; and release from any attachment to material possessions offers the only way to deal with life's harshest realities. The seeds for Siddhartha's future identity were planted.

THE GREAT RENUNCIATION AND ENLIGHTENMENT

Having learned of suffering that was part and parcel of the human condition, Siddhartha could find no comfort in the palace. He knew then his life had been a pampered prison, a life he did not want to continue into old age. He then made the radical decision to escape life as he knew it. Legend tells of how he took his last look at his sleeping family, rode to the boundary of the palace ground, gave his horse to a servant, removed his jewels, shaved off his long black hair, donned simple clothing of a wandering ascetic, and then ventured into the world with nothing but life's greatest questions.

Siddhartha first honored the tradition of Indian spirituality by turning to teachers for dialogues on philosophy, but he was ultimately unsatisfied in the quest. He also strove for knowledge in the traditional Hindu way by constant yoga exercises intended to unite his self *(atman)* with the origin and meaning of the world *(brahman)*. Again, even under the guidance of gurus, this path failed to satisfy him or lead to true knowledge. He became emaciated from six years of fasting. As long as a man is enjoying the pleasures of the flesh, this earnest seeker reasoned, he could neither find the light of truth nor escape the endless cycle of rebirth. His diet was sickening. His shell of a body became so thin that his ribs projected and he could feel his spine by pressing on his abdomen. The ascetics who were his friends expected him to die from such self-mortification. When he realized he had followed the path of asceticism to his absolute limit, he received food from Sujata and gained strength to return to life. Surely there was another path to enlightenment.

In the despair of his futile search for release from rebirth, Siddhartha remembered how he had succeeded in his first meditation at home under an apple tree. He then abandoned the rigid disciplines that were so ineffectual and turned to a form of meditation that did not cause such bodily pain. He immersed himself in rigorous thought and mystic concentration along the lines of Hinduism's *raja* yoga. Sensing a breakthrough, he sat down under a fig tree, eventually called "the tree of enlightenment" or *bodhi*-tree (usually shortened to Bo tree), where at last he finally reached the highest knowledge. Now the enlightened one, he became the Buddha. Buddhist tradition describes several steps in the enlightenment process. The bottom line: Siddhartha realized that destroying desire would eliminate suffering, leaving him awake, free, and enlightened. He had achieved a profound understanding, called his Awakening or Enlightenment *(bodhi)*.

First Sermon and Four Noble Truths

From the sight of his enlightenment, the Buddha traveled west. The enlightenment had changed his outward appearance so much that five reluctant ascetics accepted him again. In the Deer Park of Sarnath, outside Banares, the "enlightened one" delivered his first sermon. The Buddha expounded the Middle Path between the two extremes of self-mortification and self-indulgence. Buddha himself had doubts about whether humankind was ready for this message, but his early sermons captured the attention and interest of a group of followers—early disciples impressed more by Buddha's calm serenity and reassuring authority of his manner as by the content of his teaching. His preaching and the allegiance of these early disciples constituted the beginning of the Buddhist religion. He began a religious order called the *Sangha*, which included people of all walks and stations in life. Clearly, Buddha had discarded the Hindu caste system. All became *arhats*, ones instructed in the *dharma* (teachings) and who attained enlightenment.

After his enlightenment, Buddha traveled about India for some forty-five years, living and teaching as a beggar-monk. He and his followers would sometimes stay in parks in the towns. The doctrinal core of Buddha's preaching is summed up in the Four Noble Truths. The first noble truth recognizes the reality of misery and suffering. The universal human experience of suffering is mental and emotional as well as physical—having a body means that we can be tired and sick and having a mind means that we can be discouraged and troubled. The second noble truth affirms that the source of all suffering is desire and ignorance. The word for desire might best be translated as "thirst" or "craving," suggesting an addiction and fear of loss. The third truth deals with destroying desire and suffering. Suffering must be totally extinguished, thus granting the individual eternal release from suffering and the endless cycle of rebirth (*samsura*) and permitting entrance into the blessed state of *nirvana*. The fourth noble truth is that a release from suffering is possible and can be attained by following the Noble Eightfold Path. The ultimate goal of Buddhism, then, is *nirvana*: the end of suffering, inner peace, and liberation from the limitations of worldly existence.

The Way to Inner Peace: The Noble Eightfold Path

The foundations of Buddha's ethical teaching are found in the Eightfold Path. The eight "steps" constituted a program that Buddha taught would lead his disciples toward liberation from suffering. Though sometimes called "steps," they were not to be practiced sequentially, but concurrently. Keep in mind the word translated "right" might better be translated "correct" or "complete." We will state these the way a loyal Buddhist might affirm them:

1. Right knowledge or understanding. I understand the brevity and impermanence of life, the dynamics of desire, and the real cause of suffering.

2. Right attitude or intention. My thoughts and motives are pure, not tainted by ugly emotions or selfish desires; I have good will toward others and keep myself from all sensual desire, hate, and malice.

3. Right speech. I will not lie, slander, or use abusive or idle talk. I speak kindly and in positive ways, avoiding exaggeration and harshness.

4. Right action. My behavior must never hurt another being that can feel hurt. This means I must abstain from taking life, from stealing, and from sexual conduct that would bring hurt.

5. Right work. My livelihood does no harm to anyone. I will work to prevent evil in myself and any others and will awaken to good potentials.

6. Right effort. Living in moderation, I constantly seek to improve. I will develop noble thoughts and deeds.

7. Right mindfulness. I use the disciplines of meditation and focused awareness to contemplate the nature of reality more deeply. Through meditation I continue to overcome the craving so easily a part of thought, speech, action, and emotion.

8. Right concentration/contemplation/composure. By staying aloof from sensuous appetites and evil desires, I cultivate states of blissful inner peace.

Essentially, the Eightfold Path is a middle way of ethical living that avoids the extremes of strictness and severity. This middle way cannot be called a compromise—it offers a challenging lifestyle that is both practical and balanced. Belief in the self is rejected. "I" and "my" are concepts which bear no relationship to truth.

Like Hinduism, Buddhism has a vast collection of sacred writings. Buddhists have been meticulous in collecting, preserving, and interpreting everything about the Buddha, the *dharma*, and the *sangha*. The earliest stories about Buddha were passed through the generations orally. In the early centuries of Buddhism, several schools claimed to follow most closely the original, unchanged teachings of the Buddha. The Theravada (meaning "the way," *vada*) school takes its name from the goal of passing on the Buddha's teaching unchanged; the heart of this school is the community of monks. The second great branch of Buddhism is Mahayana, a word typically translated as "big vehicle." This school proclaims that *nirvana* is possible for everyone and not just monks and that enlightenment is a call to compassion; the ideal in Mahayana Buddhism is the *bodhisattva*, the person of deep compassion.

When he was 80, legend says, the Buddha ate a meal offered by a well-meaning blacksmith named Chunda, but the food was spoiled and the Buddha became deathly ill. Sensing his death was imminent, he called his disciples to his bedside. To those who were weeping, he reminded them that everything must die and that the Buddha was no exception. He gave them final instructions to trust their own insights and use self-control to reach perfection and inner peace. His final words have echoed through history: "All compounds grow old. Work out your own salvation with diligence." Colorful legends describe his ecstatic entry into *nirvana*, and a powerful earthquake reportedly shook the land when his body was cremated.

Buddha and Jesus So Much Alike

When the lives of Buddha and Jesus are placed side-by-side, we see so many similarities. First, the circumstances of their birth, beginning with conception, are reported to be miraculous. As Buddhists point to the initiative of a sacred elephant that entered the side of Queen Maya, Christians point to the initiative of the Holy Spirit which brought about conception in a teenaged virgin named Mary. Clearly, both of these men were considered to have experienced a special origin that pointed to a special role in history.

There is a deeper comparison regarding origin. Siddhartha, Gautama's given name, was the handsome son of a king. He lived the boyhood years in the sheltered comfort and luxury of a palace. As a teenager, he married a pretty princess who bore for him a son. Siddhartha seemed to have everything that any young man could possibly imagine: wealth, social standing, appearance, a model wife, a son, and a throne he would eventually inherit. What good fortune! Despite all this, a passion and restlessness lay deeply in his heart that all this good fortune could not satisfy.

And so for Jesus, too, there remained a throne and all the riches of heaven and fellowship with the Father. The Father, however, designed a will and a mission on earth for the Son. All the blessings of heaven could be relinquished for a segment of time in order to assume a mission in the poverty, the dirt, the suffering, and the pain of sinful humanity. Or, as the apostle Paul stated it, it was through the Lord's grace for all of us that, "though he was rich, yet for your sake he became poor, so that you through his poverty might be rich" (2 Cor. 8:9). Just as Jesus left the glory and comfort of heaven to dwell among humans, so Siddhartha Gautama five centuries earlier left the glory and comfort of a palace to seek truth and enlightenment.

Both Jesus and Gautama encountered the most desperate men and women as they trod the roads and streets of the ancient world. Jesus' encounters with the beggars, blind, deaf, diseased, and grieving people remind us the Gautama's Four Passing Sights, the major difference being that Son of God possessed the power to do more for these suffering people than feel empathy. Both Jesus and Gautama were so easily moved to compassion. With their outreach to those troubled people on the margins of society, both seemed to exclude nobody from their radius of deep concern. During these young adult years, Gautama completed a mission for personal learning and enlightenment, while Jesus fulfilled a mission of ministering to the deepest spiritual, emotional, and physical needs of all who would receive him.

Both Gautama and Jesus as young men experienced a defining moment. For Gautama, after such a long period of outdoing his Hindu teachers in asceticism and self-denial, rigorous concentration led him one evening to the Bo Tree as a setting for a breakthrough in his long search. The first event of the night under the Bo tree was a series of temptations from Mara, the Evil One, reminiscent of Jesus in the desert wilderness. Gautama resisted Mara's challenges and the earth thundered, "I bear you witness." Under the Bo tree, he finally realized his goal of enlightenment. The defining moment for Jesus, separating his private life from his public ministry, was his baptism by John in the Jordan River. Emerging from the water of baptism, the Spirit of the Lord descended upon him and declared, "This is my beloved Son in whom I am well pleased."

Both Jesus and Gautama were raised in the religions of their homeland. They rejected some of the popular and traditional interpretations of those religions. Jesus was born a Jew and lived his life as a Jew. And yet, his public teaching was persistently at odds with the dominant legalistic interpretation of the Law of Moses. The apostle Paul interprets Jesus' death as nullifying the legalistic covenant code of the law of God revealed through Moses.

Gautama, who became the Buddha, was born a Hindu and had studied under two great Brahman teachers, but the teachings of his native religion brought him no lasting peace. Just as Jesus struggled against the notion of righteousness before God as embraced by the tradition-bound religious leaders in Judaism, Gautama struggled with the question of how to be freed from the misery of endless re-births. Little wonder some historians see Buddhism and Christianity as reform movements. Scholars and students hotly debate whether either man intended to found a new religion, but just as clearly as Buddhism emerged from the life and teachings of Siddhartha Gautama, so Christianity emerged from the life and teachings of Jesus. How fascinating, also, that for literally billions of people over the centuries, the title that each man came to wear, Buddha for Gautama and Christ for Jesus, has served as a personal name for his followers and the world!

There is similarity in the ethical teaching of Buddha and Jesus, and thus also in the teaching of Buddhism and Christianity. Both religious teachers emphasized the doctrine of non-harm for all living creatures and pursuing peace in interpersonal relations. For Buddhism, the doctrine of *ahimsa* (non-harm) is fundamental. This teaching holds that to cause harm and suffering to any being is unnecessary and cruel, and the weakest members of the human family deserve the greatest protection.

The number "eight" is a superficial and coincidental matter, really, when noting Buddha's Eightfold Path or the eight beatitudes offered by Jesus in the Sermon on the Mount. What is striking is that both Buddha and Jesus taught that our lives are impoverished from wanting what we cannot have and from never being satisfied with what we do have. Some of our desires are understandable—such as for food, clothing, shelter, security—as all humans have basic physiological needs, but we must be continually trusting of their provision rather than obsessing over them. And some of our desires are "wants" that are cultivated by our society and can only be acquired honorably through personal wealth. Both teachers warned against such desire. For Buddha, this desire spawns all kinds of suffering; he could have certainly identified with Jesus' warnings to those who put their trust in material prosperity. For Jesus, obsessive desire constitutes covetousness, which spawns all kinds of evil, an alienation from God, and apathy about the material needs of others.

Buddha and Jesus both began their ministries as fervent preachers and teachers. Both rejected all the trappings of material prosperity and comfort and walked and taught in large measure depending on the generosity and good will of supporters. Each gathered about him a small band of followers who began to preach his message. And each saw an immediate favorable response to his message, especially among ordinary men and women who were simply seeking hope and a better way of life. Each religion has emphasized the vital role of believers coming together in a special community, the church *(ekklesia)* for Christians and the *sangha* for Buddhists, to encourage one another within the community and keep faith alive. The earliest disciples of each became, in effect, a missionary order and each group had a universal mission that their founders shared that had no parallel in Hinduism or Judaism.

JESUS AND BUDDHA SO MUCH UNALIKE

Despite such intriguing and significant ways that Buddha and Jesus were alike, a few differences in these two religious leaders emerge as crucially important. No difference is greater than the quest of their followers. Siddhartha Gautama sought enlightenment about the cause of suffering and the meaning of life. Once the experience of enlightenment had been achieved, he became the Buddha, the Enlightened One. And Buddha offered no conception of a Supreme Being who was above himself. He did not consider his meditation to be prayer to an Almighty God. For both Buddha and his followers there is no God to whom they can go with their petitions, deepest needs, or deepest longings. And the goal of Buddhists is to cease the mad, debilitating cycle of re-birth and enter *nirvana*: inner peace, end of suffering, and liberation from the limitations of the world.

The quest of Jesus was all about his Father, the Almighty God and Supreme Being of the universe, and bringing honor and glory to the Father by submitting fully to his will. Being filled with the Spirit of God, Jesus did not need enlightenment. Nor did Jesus ever teach that all desire was either evil or harmful. The mission of Jesus was about salvation, not enlightenment. His passion was the very Kingdom of Heaven. In his teaching and life, he taught and demonstrated how his disciples could find meaning and life in the Kingdom of God. More than simply another moral teacher, Jesus taught a demanding kingdom ethic that placed total, uncompromising love of God as the first great commandment. He encountered the barriers that divide the powerful from the weak, the rich from the poor, the female from the male, and the slave from the free person. He also taught clearly the difference between a false, hypocritical "righteousness" and a genuine, humble righteousness before his Father. And Jesus willingly faced his death as a means of satisfying God's sense of justice against all humans because they are sinners.

The goal of Jesus' followers throughout the centuries has been reconciliation with God and a destiny much greater than a *nirvana* which seems to be defined in terms of "negatives" or "absences" (no earth, water, air, space, sun, moon, foundation, or anything bringing joy other than the end of suffering). The destiny is eternal salvation that culminates in a heaven filled with God's glory and praise and God's people.

Buddha's teaching about the absence of the self cuts a swath through all other major beliefs. He had turned from Hinduism because it claimed there was an essential self that Hindus call the *atman*. Buddha's claim was that once followers realize there is no personhood, then all suffering ceases. Jesus, on the other hand, accepted the self or the person. He did call for self-denial, not in obliteration of personhood, but in acknowledgment that God be placed at the highest place and others must be considered at least as equals. He reminded his followers that at the heart of the Mosaic Law were the commands to love the Lord God with all one's heart, soul, and strength and to love one's neighbor as oneself. Jesus clearly did not deny the reality of suffering and personal identity—he invited troubled and burdened souls to lay their burdens on him and follow his way!

Buddhism Today

When Buddha stands beside Jesus we see two remarkable religious leaders after whom two great world religions have been named. The photojournalism depicting Buddhist monks seated with candles and praying for victims of the December 2004 Tsunami, while Christian volunteer workers were unloading supplies of food and medicine for the survivors, provides evidence enough that their influence continues mightily in today's world. Nearly one-third of the world's population is Christian. The number of Buddhists today is around 380,000,000 worldwide, ranking them fourth, after Muslims and Hindus, in total population (if we include the 405 million under the wide umbrella of traditional Chinese religion, then Buddhism becomes the world's fifth largest faith). There are an estimated 700,000 ordained Buddhist monks and nuns worldwide. Globally, there are as about as many Buddhists as there are Protestant Christians.

Buddhism is gaining Western followers based on its ideals, especially among university students and young adults. The theme running through all the varieties of Buddhism is that suffering does exist and that all individuals seek a way out of suffering that is part and parcel of the human condition. To the Buddhist, escape from human suffering is more important than any other quest in life or death and happiness in life has less to do with circumstances in life than with how a person perceives them.

Christianity also accepts the reality of pain and suffering. In addition to the suffering through sickness and death, the followers of Jesus also experienced and acknowledged the reality of suffering from political and religious persecution. Rather than attempting to escape all suffering, an unrealistic goal, the early Christians were challenged to see a redemptive purpose in their suffering. Suffering could serve as refining fire, enhancing one's spiritual growth and moral character and preparing the believer for the glory of an eternity where pain and suffering were obliterated. The Buddhist is challenged to look within oneself for enlightenment on life's most basic truths and the cessation of suffering; the Christian is challenged to look beyond oneself for divine wisdom and guidance and for the strength to endure the pain and suffering of ordinary existence and any persecution from hostile unbelievers.

An interest in the contemporary relevance of the lessons about the impermanence of life and the connection between our attachments and disappointments is triggering a renaissance of Buddhism in the United States. While roughly three-quarters of American Buddhists are Asian, the religion is growing in the mainstream of the United States—there are approximately three million practicing Buddhists and millions more believe that Buddhist teachings have served an important influence in their spiritual lives. A number of young Western adults have converted from Christianity to Buddhism, believing that most Christians have abandoned Jesus' simple teaching on non-violence and non-attachment to material possessions.

Devotional Reflection

Buddha did not seek the worship of his followers. Nor did he claim the ability to do miraculous deeds. He was a practical man who made no great claims of deity and sought only great truths. His concepts were not based on faith, as demanded in other religions, but on empirical observations of ordinary life experiences.

Christians accept the claims of Jesus. He is the light of the world. His words are the bread of life. His words are truth. For our worst sins as well as our ordinary ones, he is the Lamb of God sacrificed for our total forgiveness. He is the Good Shepherd, leading us in the right paths. While on earth, Jesus was the very incarnation of God. He came to give us a life of fullness, not detachment. Thus, the truth of Buddha's teaching on enlightenment and human suffering does not depend on its relationship to the historical Siddhartha Gautama in the same manner as the Christian gospel of salvation is integrally connected to the historical person of Jesus of Nazareth.

The fatal flaw in historic Buddhism, at least from a Christian worldview, is not simply that it rejects the unique claims of Jesus. The fatal flaw is that it is a well-developed philosophy that is bereft of God. Buddhism demands no real faith of its followers, but only requires a sense of realism. This is a philosophy of how one can end suffering and be good without God, lifting oneself by one's own strength and discipline. There is no higher authority than self. Buddhism is the religion for those who want to be totally in control and so fully insulated from the world of care that it declares that the self is an illusion. For Jesus, the challenge for all of us is not obliteration of self through enlightenment, but the abundant life in its fullness which begins with a new birth.

The death of each is crucially significant. The peaceful death of a calm, reposed, and tranquil Buddha might soothe and reassure his followers, but cannot atone for sins. By contrast, the suffering Christ who experienced rejection, agony, and torture while being nailed and hung on a cross is the price is the Savior who made the ultimate sacrifice for our sins. To many Buddhists, and Gentiles in general, the cross as the locus of God's scheme of redemption may seem foolishness. To others, the cross can be a stumblingblock in their consideration of the Christian faith. (Incidentally, the apostle Paul drew the same conclusion about the message of the cross in his mission experiences of the first century.) For Christians, however, the cross is central to our identity and how we live!

Prayer: Thank you, Lord God, for giving our world the interesting life of Siddhartha Gautama, the man in relentless quest for great truth about life that he became the great Buddha. Thank you for the positive way he has influenced so many millions. Thank you also for the compassion and service of so many of his followers over the centuries. Their pursuit of world peace and compassion for suffering people should put many of us as followers of Jesus to shame.

And even more, dear God, thank you for sending your Son to teach us how to live and how to endure suffering, especially the suffering one does not deserve. Thank you that your Son came to die for wise and dedicated men and women such as Buddha as well as for the poor and lowly that so many of his followers have served. And when life gets tough and pains are intense, thank you for being one to whom we can turn. May we always be confident in declaring with your apostle Paul, "I know whom I have believed, and am convinced that he is able to guard what I have entrusted to him for that day." Through the One we trust with all that He has blessed us and called us to be. Amen.

12

When Gandhi Stands Beside Jesus

How ironic to think that some non-Christians seem more convincingly and effectively to embody the teaching and ethics of Jesus than do many Christians! Is it possible that some Hindu could be more "Christian" than most Christians? Could we possibly learn more about Christianity by studying the lives of certain spiritual leaders who chose not to embrace Christianity than by reading about the lives of acclaimed Christian religious leaders? Can the life and example of someone who rejected the Christian faith serve to convince others of the truth of the Judeo-Christian faith? Could someone find "the way, the truth, and the life" about Jesus without being convinced of all the claims declared about Jesus in Christian scripture?

If these questions set the wheels of your mind in motion, they have served their purpose. Different people answer them in various ways. Many university professors, reform activists, and students have pointed to Mohandas Gandhi, the great spiritual leader, reformer, social activist, and politician, as an ideal role model for today's generation. How ironic for Americans living in a culture that puts so much emphasis on material prosperity, physical conditioning, athletic competition, and youthful sex appeal. With such an unimpressive appearance and a frail body (weighing less than 120 pounds and possessing an oversized nose, flared ears, and the arms and legs of a malnourished teenage boy), there's no way Gandhi could compete in a contemporary political campaign for almost any elective office or pass a screening test in a casting call for a romantic lead in a movie or television drama.

And, yet, even in his time, Gandhi became known as "Mahatma," meaning "Great Soul." Even today, he represents the termination of a long era of global history under colonialism, and he emerged one of the greatest world figures of the twentieth century. What about Gandhi's life and devotion commend him to us today? When Gandhi stands beside Jesus, which man stands taller? Might we consider them near equals? How were Jesus and Gandhi alike and how were they different?

Years of Preparation for a Remarkable Life

Mohandas Karamchand Gandhi was born in 1869 in the seaside town of Porbandor in western India, north of Bombay, into a traditional Hindu family. The India of Gandhi's birth was controlled by Great Britain and many Indians urged violence as a response to British domination. As a young man, Gandhi learned the ideals of nonviolence from Hinduism and Jainism. Like many others of his religious faith, Gandhi was a vegetarian, though he suspected, as did other Hindus, that the British were strong because they ate meat (a theory he tested for a year until he had a bad dream of a goat crying in his stomach). His marriage at the tender age of 13, arranged by his family, was to a girl named Kasturbai, also 13. As a bright young man, Gandhi was encouraged to study law in London, although his pious Hindu mother, fearing the negative influences to which he would be exposed in England, urged him to take a vow that he would not eat meat, drink wine, or teach a woman while away from home. A Jain monk administered this vow and a young Mohandas departed for London at the age of 19.

Gandhi studied law in London from 1888 to 1891 with the intention of returning to India to work as a lawyer, but the years of study in London were pivotal to his intellectual growth and political activism. Feeling rebellious, he adopted British ways. He wore English clothes, enjoyed western manners and entertainment, and even took dancing lessons. In London, he became familiar with the Bible and was particularly moved by Jesus' summons to forgiveness and nonviolence, which he found in the Sermon on the Mount. He also read books by European intellectuals such as Tolstoy and Ruskin and the American Thoreau. And, ironically, it was in England that he first read the *Bhagavad Gita* and discovered outside his native land the wisdom in Hindu literature. He took to heart its ideal of the active but selfless human being who is, in Gandhi's words, "without egotism...who is ever forgiving, who is always contented, whose resolutions are firm, who had dedicated mind and soul to God, who causes no dread, who is not afraid of others."

Gandhi did return to India to work as a lawyer, but two years later decided to accept an offer to practice law in South Africa, then a British colony with a large Indian minority. There he witnessed first hand the inequities of *apartheid*, the official system of racial segregation that endorses legal restrictions against non-European people, including Indians. These were years of ferment for the young attorney. He read Thoreau's famous essay, "On Civil Disobedience," and Tolstoy's book, *The Kingdom of God Is Within You*, which advocated simplicity and nonviolence. The Johannesburg experience was turned into a laboratory which tested the strategies of nonviolent political action.

Gandhi's purpose in life was steeled. Toward the beginning of World War I, he returned to the land of his birth with the conviction that his country was equipped for *swaraj* (self-rule). He devoted his life to the overall liberation of the Indian people, a movement he led for more than thirty years. He organized social movements, led marches, founded religious communities, provided grass-roots education to develop the self-reliance and well-being of villagers, served as a mediator between Indians and the British government, and protested social injustices against India's lower classes. Accepting the basic Hindu doctrine that all life is one, Gandhi viewed the quest for reform and independence to be a spiritual and religious duty of universal dimensions.

THE FORCE OF TRUTH

When Gandhi stands beside Jesus we see a man who embodies so much of what the Master taught and modeled centuries earlier. Perhaps foremost is the emphasis that both Jesus and Gandhi placed on the force of truth. In John's gospel narrative, Jesus speaks of the human ability to know truth and the power of truth to set people free (8:32). Gandhi believed the realization of truth was the only force that could bring reform. The term *satyagraha* was coined by Gandhi to identify his teachings. It means literally "holding on to Truth" and has been translated as "truth-force" or "soul-force." As Gandhi explained it, "Truth (*Satya*) implies love, and firmness (*Agraha*) engenders and therefore serves as a synonym for force." Thus, *satyagraha* was "the Force which is born of Truth and Love or non-violence." It is an ethical and spiritual principle that translates into political and social action as a means of liberating not only the oppressed, but also the oppressor.

Gandhi implemented this great "reality force" of Truth whenever he felt it would be effective. He made use of every nonviolent strategy that he thought would be effective: marches, hunger strikes, demonstrations, speeches, and all other forms of publicity. He contended that violence only breeds violence and brutalizes those who use it, no matter how just their cause. Nonviolence begets admiration, spiritual greatness, and eventual freedom for those oppressed. In an age where terrorism strikes without warning and national security issues move to the top of the national agenda, such a doctrine seems impractical, even dangerously careless.

One famous example of his nonviolent strategies was the Salt March of 1930. In those days, the British not only taxed all salt eaten in India, but also made it illegal to possess salt not bought from a government supplier. Gandhi led a trudging, slow 250-mile march to the ocean, picking up new demonstrators along the way, and collected natural salt left by waves on the beach. In seaside communities around the continent, people began doing the same in violation of British law. Gandhi, like many times earlier in his career, was once again put in prison along with many of his followers. The civil disobedience was too massive for British occupying forces, already weakened by expenditures during World War II. British forces agreed to leave the great subcontinent of India in 1947. Then, Gandhi began to be called "Great Spirit" or "Great Soul," the moral leader of the second most populous nation in the world, thus helping to establish the largest democracy in world civilization.

THE POWER OF TOUCH

Gandhi and Jesus both demonstrated the power of touch in their lives. Defying social conventions of his culture, Jesus reached out to touch those who were powerless and even dispossessed by society. Jesus touched and embraced children, so precious and so innocent and so powerless. Spurning rabbinic tradition which strictly separated genders, Jesus touched women and allowed them to touch him. And Jesus touched those who were sick, even the dreaded lepers along his path. The centuries-old Indian tradition of a rigid caste system was defied by Gandhi, who believed the doctrine of *ahimsa* (non-harm) applied to every person and every creature. This great soul reached out and literally touched those outcasts in society known as "the untouchables," whose miserable and wretched physical and social conditions were accepted as their punishment for misdeeds in a previous life, thus defying a tradition about ritual purity that had been entrenched for millennia. Indeed, both Jesus and Gandhi taught the masses more by the persuasion of moral example than by the persuasion of the spoken word.

Both Gandhi and Jesus could be compared in other ways. Both were born in relatively unknown villages. Both were trained in traditions of their people. Both lived under a yoke of political domination by a foreign political power—an oppression at times that seemed innocuous and at other times seemed cruel. Both demonstrated a spirit of sacrifice and forbearance and not of violence. And both could stir the ire of political and/or religious authorities; both were hauled into court and threatened with the maximum sentence. And though they taught loving tolerance even of one's enemies, extremists within their own religion and nationality executed both Jesus and Gandhi. (Gandhi was assassinated early in 1948 by one of the Hindu militants who wanted revenge for what they perceived as wrongs done by Muslims to Hindus in the new Pakistan; his last words were *Ram, Ram* ["God, God"].)

Gandhi's career exemplified the paradox announced by Jesus that greatness is found in humility and that by becoming weak we may become strong. Throughout his life, Gandhi insisted that nonviolence was not a "weapon of the weak" nor a last resort for cowardice and impotence and that one must be willing to die (or learn "the art of dying") in order to become courageous and overcome fear. The moral philosophy and legacies of Jesus and Gandhi were not lost on a young Martin Luther King, Jr., who implemented the same strategies for justice and equality against adamant resistance in the American civil rights movement during the 50s and 60s. Peace activists today are likely to invoke the quotations of Gandhi on nonviolence and peace more than quotations from Christian preachers and teachers. In fact, Gandhi sometimes noted the irony that all serious religious people of the world interpret Christ's command to love one's enemies in a literal, nonviolent sense with only one major exception: modern Christians.

Despite his greatness on the world scene and the great respect held for him by so many of today's university students, we must resist any proposal of making Gandhi into a deity. His eccentricities notwithstanding, Gandhi was a "great soul" whose influence has rippled through modern world history, to be sure. He risked his life for his own people. He spent many days in jail as an unjustly accused man. He relinquished nearly all of life's material blessings and lived and dressed simply to identify with his people—few behaviors are more Christ-like. And yet his decisions, his thoughts, and his actions were not perfect. Gandhi was a sinner. He had his share of moral failures. And though Gandhi died for his own people, Jesus died for Gandhi. And for everyone else. Gandhi's life work was crowned in 1947, when at long last India gained independence from Great Britain; Jesus' mission on earth was culminated by his death on the cross and was validated by his resurrection from the dead.

Political boundaries, national independence, and self-rule were important to Gandhi, and truth was a force to make those values a reality for Indians. Jesus cared little or anything about political ideologies and national boundaries, and the truth he extolled was the truth about God and the truth about our spiritual reality before God. Both Jesus and Gandhi were driven by a passion for the poor, the disenfranchised, and the downtrodden. And both valued humble service even in the most menial and despised tasks—just as Jesus washed the feet of his disciples, Gandhi cleaned the latrines of the untouchables. Gandhi valued fasting as a strike against a domineering political power. Jesus valued fasting as a strike against our self-centeredness and self-righteousness before God. Yes, what remarkable similarity when we place Gandhi beside Jesus!

Devotional Reflection

Interestingly, Gandhi considered his life and teaching to be compatible with the ideals of Christianity. He was once quoted as claiming to be both Hindu and Christian. Both religions teach a strong ethical doctrine about strong relationships and right living. While the broad and tolerant nature of Hinduism could well embrace Christianity (indeed, the term "Hinduism" is used to indicate the amalgam of spiritual traditions originating in South Asia and it never stood for any single way of being religious), the Christian claims about God and his Son necessarily exclude Hindu concepts of deity and after-life.

And yet, this short, frail-looking human being may well have projected an image which was more reflective of Christian lifestyle in first century Judea than did American Christians of the latter twentieth century. Gandhi was able to see the major obstacles to successful Christian missions in his native land. Once he was asked by Christian missionary Howard Thurman, "What is the greatest enemy Jesus Christ has in India? Gandhi simply replied, "Christianity."

Whatever inspired and drove Mohandas Gandhi must surely be a "cut below" the resources that inspire and impel a Christian. There is no superficial sense of sin in authentic Christianity. However poorly Christianity may have been practiced around the globe, any respectful study of Jesus' teaching must concede a challenging call to meaningful discipleship like no other the world has ever known. In Gandhi's own land, the next generation produced a remarkable woman who was driven by the sacrifice and teaching of Jesus and her commitment to follow him—Mother Teresa, who saw the face of Jesus in disguise among the poor and weak in the filth and squalor of Calcutta streets.

Any major religion with roots as deep in history as Hinduism, and one that has gained the adherence of billions of people over its long centuries of practice, merits our appreciation and attention. Yet, whatever the strength and inspiration that can be drawn from devoted Hindus such as Gandhi, there is no cross in Hinduism. To lift up the cross of Jesus, with all its meaning and mystery, is to dramatically proclaim a message of enduring relevance to every citizen in the world.

Prayer: Father God, we thank you for the lives of great men and women in the world whose stories of sacrifice, integrity, and courage touch us all. We thank you specifically for the life of Mohandas Gandhi and for the ways he called us to great truth about ourselves and our world. And while we admire and appreciate great people in our history, may we more deeply adore and praise the one who leads us to the source of all truth. Through Jesus. Amen.

13

The Rejection of Jesus—Jews Are Not the Only Ones!

"And tell me what you think of Jesus?" I thought this was an appropriate question to pose for Lynn Fleischer, librarian at the Jewish Federation of Nashville and Middle Tennessee. We had just spent an hour or so discussing the strength of Judaism in our geographic area. I was fulfilling an assignment to lecture at a local church on the topic of contemporary Judaism and, in preparation, was consulting local rabbis and professionals for additional perspective, though I truly felt it far more appropriate for the church to invite a Jew to address this topic. Lynn's reply was both friendly and terse: "I think he was a very good rabbi of his day."

Actually, I was not expecting any other answer.

A worldview about God and his nature is a complex, interwoven tapestry of history, heritage, ideology, and personal and collective choices. The historic Jewish rejection of the divinity of Jesus is not simply a matter of willful ignorance or stubborn rebellion. If we seek to understand Judaism and maintain dialogue with Jewish people, we need to get inside their worldview. Unfortunately, too many Christians have discussed Judaism with an excess of judgment, too little insight, and too much mindless stereotyping and insensitivity.

A Jewish "Take" on the New Testament

Why do the Jews reject Jesus both as the Messiah and the divine Son of God? The question would at first seem problematic to Jewish thinkers, though they grant this is a common way of asking the question. After all, Muslims reject Jesus as Messiah and divine and, in fact, the only people who accept and proclaim Jesus in these terms are Christians. In understanding Judaism, however, the question remains important.

Let's begin with the New Testament narratives. In the earthly ministry of Jesus, there were essentially two types of Jews—those who followed Jesus and those who stood in opposition to him. Undoubtedly, there must have been many other Jews who admired his ethical teaching, but did not see him as divine. And many were fickle, embracing and celebrating Jesus' triumphal entry into Jerusalem and soon thereafter calling for his execution. The Jewish rejection was likely more complicated than commonly understood by Christians. One factor was the perception of Jesus as a false prophet by his claim of religious authority ("you have heard it said....., but I say unto you") and having broken with the law of Moses. For Jewish scholars today, the high priest's accusation of blasphemy against Jesus was a trumped-up charge, and the deeper reason for rejection was Jewish conviction that no messianic age had arrived.

Some thoughtful Jewish people contend that the New Testament writers painted a negative attitude toward Jews and Judaism because they were addressing a growing, receptive Gentile audience. There were first-century Jewish congregations that were vibrant and active in service and ministry, but as the decades passed the vast majority within the Jewish community did not embrace Jesus as their long-awaited Messiah. And while the rabbis in the Talmud (a compilation in writing of the oral traditions of the rabbis and juristic tradition completed by 465 C. E.) did not disclaim the miracles of Jesus, they attributed them to sorcery and magic. Other Jews, noting other Jewish miracle workers in various generations of Judaism as well as in the earlier Scriptures, contended miracles alone do not prove Messiahship.

The Messiah was the subject of some of the most comforting and hopeful prophecy in the Hebrew Scriptures. So, then, why was Jesus not embraced as Messiah? The prophecies heralded the dawn of world peace and political harmony, a time when swords would be converted to plowshares and spears into pruning hooks, a time when people lived in peace and security and would "study war no more." Jesus came into a society that was loosely governed as a province by totalitarian Rome and experiencing at least some religious division at home by Jewish sectarianism. He was executed by the Romans for being a threat to the delicate political balance in the land. And shortly after his death, there was certainly no dawning of peace and prosperity for the Jews. In fact, just the opposite occurred. The ranks of Jews were further decimated by the Romans, their temple was destroyed, and exile and persecution became predominant themes in their collective history. Nor has there been any change in modern times— witness the turmoil and bloodshed in the nation of Israel since its inception in 1948.

Many Christians do not seem to appreciate the Jewish roots of their faith. Jesus was born a Jew. At age 12 in the temple he may have been a participant in a religious ritual, perhaps becoming Bar Mitzvah, though we have no evidence of such ceremonies at this time. He lived his brief life in Judea. His closest disciples were Jews. His message was intended for Jews. He dressed like a Jew, talked like a Jew, prayed like a Jew. Jesus expounded the Law of Moses. All that he taught was based on the Hebrew Scriptures. His prophetic teachings on social justice and compassion were drawn directly from the sermons and writings of Israel's most courageous prophets—Amos, Hosea, Micah, and Isaiah. The spiritual meaning of his "last supper" has been argued by scholars, but the shared meal was essentially a Jewish celebration with his closest disciples. He declared that he had not come to destroy the Law but to fulfill it (Mt. 5:17). Clearly Jesus upheld the Law and expected his followers to do likewise.

Jesus could have been an Essene, a small, often monastic sect within Judaism, with his baptism an initiation into this party (consider that all Jews engaged in ritual immersion). Thus, Jesus did not come to establish a new world religion to compete with Judaism or Hinduism or Buddhism or any other religious system. He never took the scrolls of the Hebrew Scriptures and said, "You can put these on the shelf and never use them again, unless for historical insight, because very soon some new replacement Scriptures will be in place for all humanity." According to one rabbi friend of mine, Jesus was the first reform Jew—his mission was to proclaim the true meaning and spirit of the Torah.

Modern Jews do not believe that the birth, life, and teaching of Jesus heralded the birth of Christianity. To them, the birth of a new religion eventually to be called Christianity was not inevitable. Christianity did not emerge until after the death of Jesus, and the first Christians were Jewish and thought of themselves as Jews. Judaism, though it has evolved over the centuries like any other dynamic faith, is considered complete within itself. The Christian doctrine that Judaism was legalistic and inadequate and therefore superceded by a new system, and that the church superceded the synagogue, is considered sadly misguided and inimical to Jewish-Christian dialogue.

If Jesus did not found Christianity, who was the founder? Jews do not typically make pronouncements about Christian origins, though some answer clearly and emphatically: the apostle Paul, a Jew who as a "renegade Pharisee" converted to the small "cult of Jesus" and accepted a calling to spread his own interpretation of the life and teaching of Jesus into the Graeco-Roman world. The narratives of Jesus in the New Testament were written long after his death, and these stories adopted and adapted mythic themes that were associated with the birth and life of special figures. Paul and other writers of New Testament documents simply adduced the story of the crucifixion of Jesus and transformed it into a glorious drama of offering divine grace and satisfying God's demands of justice through sacrifice of his son.

As for the doctrinal tenets of first- and second-generation followers of Jesus, Christianity largely defined itself in opposition to Judaism. In time, the Christian message was spread beyond the borders of Israel, and the grand story of God's grace and Jesus' atoning death constituted a message that the polytheistic and sometimes decadent Gentile world embraced so readily. The Gentile world of the first century must not be stereotyped as totally evil and depraved, for there were many who practiced devoted family life and good moral character; additionally, there was much political, artistic, and scientific achievement within Graeco-Roman culture. In this cultural context, this new religion, a new faith with such a powerful narrative appeal and its summons to follow a risen Lord and practice a disciplined moral life, enjoyed widespread appeal. And when Emperor Constantine was converted and announced Christianity as a legal religion within the vast Roman Empire (and later was named as the official religion of the Empire), this relatively new religion spread like proverbial wildfire.

Do Christians Have Moral Standing to Confront Jews?

And finally, there is a practical explanation for why Jews reject Jesus and Christianity: Christians are perceived by many Jews as possessing no moral standing from which to convert Jewish people to Christianity. Anti-Semitism is among the most ancient and most persistent of the many enduring prejudices to afflict the human race. If one moves past Egyptian bondage, a time before Israel was called into covenant relationship with Yahweh, then the book of Esther tells of Haman's seeking to wipe out all Jews of Persia because Mordecai, a Jew, refused to bow down to him. And that was only the beginning.

Since the time of Haman (sixth century B. C. E), Jews have been despised and persecuted in a manner no other nation has experienced. Sometimes, there have been laws that sanctioned discrimination against the Jews in blatant violation of their civil rights and liberties. In medieval Europe, Christians were considered to be loyal citizens, whereas Jews were treated as suspicious and even traitorous characters. In the Crusades, an effort by European Christendom intended to rescue the Holy Land from heathen, the crusaders conquered defenseless ghettoes (secluded communities originally established to keep Jews apart from "good Christians"), which they plundered and looted while slaughtering thousands of Jews in the name of their Savior and his church.

To read any detailed history of Europe during the Middle Ages and into modern times will bring readers face-to-face with atrocities, discrimination, extortion, stereotyping, and utter hatred of Jews. At times Jews were given the option of converting to Christianity or leaving the country. Jews were constantly accused of deicide (the killing of deity) and this became justification for pogroms and deprivation of civil rights and liberties for this despised people known as "the children of the devil" (a phrase from John 8)—a people many Christians believed God had rejected because of their role in the execution of Jesus, the Son of God. Jewish people were often scapegoated for many of the problems that beset nations. During the time of the bubonic plague (also known as the Black Death, 1347-1351, and sporadically afterwards), they were sometimes blamed for massive deaths. From such oppressive nations they fled, scattered, and sought refuge elsewhere; at best, Jews were tolerated as a minority in some nations.

The Worst Atrocity in Jewish History

Anti-Semitism reached its most evil, most horrifying depth with the Nazi Holocaust that began in the 1930s. This *Shoah*, the term preferred by most Jews, was the one event in world history that ushered in a postmodern realization of unspeakable evil and mass death. Millions of Jews were trapped in Europe when Poland, Hungary, and Czechoslovakia fell into Hitler's control, then later felt trapped in such nations as Greece, Spain, France, Croatia, and Russia. Hitler's genocidal intent was senseless by any standard. The Jews of Germany in the 1920s, 30s, and 40s were not the enemies of the nation in which they dwelled, but were citizens. They posed no threat to German national security, nor were they military combatants. The Nazi military regime gained absolutely no military or territorial advantage by systematically eliminating the Jewish population. Jews were marked for systematic extermination simply because they existed.

Hitler's intent to eradicate an entire people by systematically and "efficiently" killing them was rooted in antecedents of past centuries, as we have noted, as well as more recent developments in their German homeland. The Holocaust was preceded by all the Christian sermons which condemned Jews for rejecting Jesus (some even from well-known Christian reformers), the general hostility which such sermons stirred, the stripping of all legal rights from Jews, the requirement that Jews wear a special badge that distinguished them from other people, the burning of Jewish books and Jewish synagogues, and the ordering of Jews to abandon homes and businesses and be enclosed in ghettoes. What a dreadful irony—the very land in which Martin Luther launched a Protestant Reformation was the locus of the evil machinations of the Holocaust!

When anyone—Jewish, Christian, or adherent to any faith—considers the Holocaust, two responses, seemingly paradoxical, are in order. One is silence. How can one even dare to speak a definitive word about such massive evil and such an unspeakable tragedy? We run the risk of our words being so trivial or so inadequate. Six million Jewish men, women, and children were shot and/or gassed to death, approximately one-third of the world Jewish population and a majority of European Jewry at the time. Two million of these victims were children. Among Jewish adult victims there were rabbis, doctors, lawyers, teachers, artists, writers, nurses and other professional and well-educated people who still had much to offer the world.

On the other hand, to remain silent in the shadow of such unspeakable horror is to run a greater risk—that the Holocaust is forgotten or denied, its lessons lost on future generations, its evil repeated. All Jewish people today consider themselves survivors of the Holocaust, for, after all, Hitler's plan was genocidal. So the second response is to speak out. This terrible story must be told and retold and never forgotten, and its lessons continually sought and reflected on.

Jewish philosophers and commentators reach no consensus on what the Holocaust and the recent past really mean. "Holocaust" means "burnt sacrifice." Richard Rubenstein, an author who now has removed himself from the Jewish community, declared that God died at Auschwitz and that Jews can continue their rituals and stories without God. After all, how can Jews after the Holocaust continue believing in God's promises of guidance and protection when they have been subjected to seeming abandonment and unspeakable cruelty? Other Jews such as Emil Fackenheim and Elie Wiesel argue that God is still present in history and that the Jew has every right to be angry with God and argue with God about his purposes in history; these Jews believe in a new command to remain Jewish lest they permit Judaism to die, thus giving Hitler and his henchmen a posthumous victory.

Yet Judaism does not exist only for cosmic spite or for the mere sake of survival, for this would suggest this grand religion has no compelling philosophy and teaching on its own. Would the majority of Jews remain Jewish primarily so that Hitler would not have been granted the final victory? This defines the mission of Judaism negatively, at best.

Thoughtful Jewish men and women concur that the world's leaders must not deny, ignore, or explain away the evil of the Holocaust. For Jewish and non-Jewish people alike, two awesome questions emerge from the Holocaust. The first: Where was God? Was God silent for a reason? Why did he not respond to the pleas of his special people? Was God powerless in the face of massive human suffering? Or was he uncaring? How can they ever again have a trusting faith in a loving, just, and compassionate God? Can Jews still believe in the inherent goodness of humanity? Can they still believe in covenant, "chosenness," and divine destiny? What did the mission to be the light of the world mean in such circumstances? And how can Jews listen to conservative Christians almost boast about how God answered their prayers to find just the right car, the right chandelier for the dining room, the right parking place near the mall during Christmas shopping rush season, and then reflect on how God seemingly turned his ear away from the anguished cry of his special people during the Holocaust?

The second question is even more pointed: Where was man? Did man lose his sense of elementary humaneness and decency? After all, the Holocaust was not inevitable; it was not a given. Men chose to follow Hitler's orders. Men shot Jews at point blank range. Men designed gas chambers to exterminate Jews in large numbers and men herded these groups into these death cells and turned on the gas valves. Men stripped Jewish bodies of jewelry, gold fillings, and even of clothing, glasses, and shoes. Men conducted ghastly experiments on both living and dead Jews. And most of these men were not only "loving" family men with wives and children at home, but also baptized members of some Christian denomination within "enlightened" Germany. We might assume that these men were connected to mothers, wives, and sisters who supported and comforted the men in their lives who committed such pernicious deeds. Indeed, such mystery in the nature of evil!

A Worldview Hammered out on the Anvil of History

What a twist of irony that adherents of such an ancient religion that found its promise and security tied to a homeland have spent the bulk of their history in dispersion and exile and thus far removed from a homeland! And how fascinating that Judaism was the parent to both Christianity and Islam, and that the latter two religions claim approximately three billion adherents while Judaism today claims less than fifteen million followers! And while a nascent Christianity rose quickly to popular acceptance in the Roman world, Judaism emerged slowly on the world scene and suffered unrelenting persecution. A young Christianity was soon at home in the Roman Empire and later throughout all of Europe, while Jews have lived for much of their history in exile. And finally, how almost cruelly ironic that the Jews offered the world the concept of a scapegoat, wherein guilt for wrongdoing is symbolically transferred to an animal to carry that burden so that the sinner may realize his or her complicity in sin, and yet over the centuries Jews have been victimized as literal scapegoats for social and economic ills of their own political society!

While Judaism's history and heritage are filled with paradoxes and ironies, so it is no different from other worldviews. Jews seeking dialogue with Christians and adherents to other world religions ask that they not be viewed in terms of stereotypes and inadequate information. Modern Judaism is not simply the Old Testament Judaism that has leapt over the many centuries basically unchanged. It has been a living, growing, dynamic, and ever-changing faith. Not all Jews truly long to go to a "homeland" in Palestine; most find their homes and first loyalty in their own country of origin. Nor do practicing Jews find dismay in their small numbers since Jews neither evangelize nor believe one needs to be a Jew to be in right relationship with God.

Is it possible to present Jesus of Nazareth with objectivity to people within the mainstream of Judaism? Many Jewish people, perhaps even the majority, have become secular in their outlook, having turned their backs on religious faith and observance. Little wonder in light of historical circumstances. And while a very small number have embraced Jesus as Savior but held onto their Jewish traditions, the mainstream of Judaism suspiciously sees Messianic Jews as among the worst of heretics. The modest growth of Messianic Jews has warmed the heart of Christian evangelicals, but has offended traditional Jews, who contend that for Jews to accept Jesus as Messiah constitutes a detestable repudiation of authentic Judaism.

So most Jews have chosen not to accept claims of the divinity of Jesus. If their minds could ever be turned toward Jesus as more than some first-century reform rabbi, such a turn could only be based on open and honest dialogue. Friendly discussion with a view toward mutual enlightenment is a commendable beginning. The exposure of false stereotypes as the basis of information is necessary for interfaith discussion. Then, depth dialogue proceeds by Christians owning and appreciating the vast indebtedness of their theology and moral values to ancient Jewish roots. Conversation must be based on looking at historical evidence for the claims made about Jesus, especially the evidence for the resurrection.

Dialogue must also be based on contemporary Christians disowning the heinous sins of Christians past and renouncing them in no uncertain terms. It also means stating clearly that the validity of one religion's ideals is not repudiated by the failures of adherents to live up to those ideals. And honest dialogue might mean reminding others that while "Christians" were guilty of planning the Holocaust, there were unheralded Christians, specifically motivated by their Christian faith, who valiantly attempted to save as many Jews from certain death as possible and others who died in fighting the Hitler war machine. Unlike Oskar Schindler, though not a particularly religious or moral man, yet one who valiantly and ingenuously rescuing Jews from a certain death, Corrie Ten Boom's family courageously hid Jews during the Holocaust and this family's actions were directly motivated by trust in Jesus. And a German Christian named Dietrich Bonhoeffer, though not considered by Jews as friend, was executed one Easter Sunday for having joined an assassination plot against Adolph Hitler.

There is no way we contemporary Christians can fully empathize with the Jewish experience. We might reflect on the subtle ways that Christians have dissociated Jesus from Judaism. This move happens with statements such as "The Jews of ancient times offered only legalistic compliance [or name some other spiritual or character short-coming], but Jesus, on the other hand...." Or "Unlike the Jews, Jesus actually...." No wonder many Christians believe Jesus distanced himself from the faith of his heritage and that authentic Judaism came to an end with the death of Jesus and the closing of the New Testament canon. A respected friend, Dr. Amy-Jill Levine, professor of New Testament at Vanderbilt University, told me, "You or your students can walk into a synagogue and visit a service and never hear a word about Jesus or about Christianity, and certainly not in some negative sense. However, Jewish visitors in a Christian church might very likely hear a discussion of Jews and Judaism during the biblical era and the judgment on Jews and their religious practice is almost certainly to be condemning and serving as a negative example. Jews are clearly depicted as enemies of Jesus and the church."

Let us attempt to be eminently fair and balanced in our judgment of sincere adherents to any faith. Let us visit each other's house of worship and learn from one another. Let us focus on what principles of our heritage that we hold in common. Let us exercise the right to evangelize; let others exercise the right to say "No, thank you." Let us advance the point made by the ten Boom family during the Holocaust as narrated in *The Hiding Place*—devout Christians can be true friends of the Jewish community, for they are God's people and they are always welcome in our lives, in our homes, and in our churches. Let us make the effort. The issue is of utmost importance!

Devotional Reflection

When we consider the theme of the rejection of Jesus, we Christians must first look at ourselves. Clearly, mainstream Jews are not the only people to reject Jesus. Is it not possible that "Christians" reject Jesus? When we allow legalism to tighten its grip around the throat of the bride of Christ, aren't we joining forces with the kind of Phariseeism Jesus denounced? When we resist the Holy Spirit's life-giving oxygen, or the sin-cleansing blood of Christ, aren't we rejecting the very nourishment through which Jesus would provide us new hearts? When we despise or oppress our neighbors, then attend Sunday assembly worship and enthusiastically sing "O, how I love Jesus," are we not rejecting Jesus and his ways? As he did with church members at Laodicea, Jesus still stands on the outside of many hearts and lives, gently knocking on the door, seeking entrance to enjoy genuine communion with those who wear his name.

Prayer: Dear God, we Christians are so indebted to the Jewish heritage for so much of our own insight about you as our Father, our moral values, and our spiritual roots. May our minds and hearts always be open to what we can learn about you and about life from our Jewish brothers and sisters. May we enter meaningful and sensitive dialogue with Jewish people that will lead to understanding and hope.

Most of all, O Lord God, as Christians we too often are blinded to the reality that we can reject Jesus, too—not by denying his divinity, of course, but by not taking with the utmost seriousness his words about legalism, peace, materialism, interpersonal relationships, and the meaning of discipleship. We can thrill to narratives of Jesus' birth and sing with fervor the Christmas carols that announce his birth, all the while leaving Jesus in the crib by not taking the words of the adult Jesus seriously. Until we take a careful inventory of our own commitments and performance, may we never judge others. Thank you for never giving up on any of us. Thank you for giving us Jesus. In His name. Amen.

14

When Muhammad Stands Beside Jesus

A founder of a new world religion that now attracts over one billion adherents. A man of God who called for the destruction of all idols. A man who claimed that there is only one true God and that all people are commanded to seek and obey his will. A child who was born many centuries ago to an impoverished family in the Middle East. A man whose teachings met wide acceptance but also some strong resistance even though most of his message was non-threatening. He was a teacher who promoted the need for honesty, kindness, support of the poor and protection of the weak. A man who was ministered to by women as well as by men. A man undaunted in preaching his message despite opposition all about him. And a man who, upon his death, inspired his followers to unify in one faith and promote their new religion throughout their immediate empire and even around the world. And that religion was positioned to make a mighty contribution to the history and civilization of the world.

Of course, we speak of Jesus Christ! Or do we? Actually, at least a billion people in the world might zealously contend we are speaking of Muhammad. Many people who are neither Christian nor Muslim likely think of Jesus and Muhammad as counterparts and equals in the world's religious scene, each beginning his own faith and each attracting his own followers.

And so how are Christians to think of Muhammad? Do we think of him as a counterpart to Jesus? Do we accord him respect as a great religious leader? Or was he a crazed fanatic, perhaps self-deluded, who has inspired his followers to unsheathe the sword and deploy it freely against all those who reject or seem to threaten Islamic doctrine and practices? Or could he have been an authentic prophet of God whose life must be respected and words heeded by the entire world? When Muhammad stands beside Jesus, which religious leader stands taller?

Islam Originally and Today

The majority of Americans, most likely, knew almost nothing about Muhammad and Islam prior to September 11, 2001, except to make some vague connection between the man and the faith. For a long time, many Christians misleadingly called this religion "Muhammadanism," which is misleading and unfair. Muslims are never summoned to a personal, saving relationship with Muhammad nor are they asked to worship him. Now, our peace of mind about the world and its cultural and political tensions surely demand that we become better informed about this dynamic, rapidly growing religion.

Islam belongs to the Abrahamic family of great monotheistic faiths, though its lineage is through Hagar and Ishmael rather than through Sarah and Isaac. Originally, Jews, Christians, and Muslims were "natural allies" because all three great faiths were "peoples of the Book." The word "Islam" means surrender and a Muslim is "one who surrenders" to the will of God, known as Allah to Muslims.

Just as with Christianity, there are so many faces of Islam today. Islam, and all major religions for that matter, is influenced not simply by a reading of its sacred texts, but also by the cultural, historical, political, and socio-economic conditions of a specific geographic environment. As with Christianity, Islam has developed within an expanding diversity of cultures, peoples, values, and traditions. The largest Islamic nation in the world is not in the Middle East, but in Indonesia, and the Islamic practice there is certainly different from the Islam practiced in Saudi Arabia or Iran. Accepting the challenge to think critically and fairly about such a controversial religion, we must not simply seek evidence that reinforces popular stereotypes. There is a mainstream Islam which adheres to *Qu'ranic* teaching about coercion ("There is no compulsion in religion" 2:256) and there is a radical, extremist minority of Muslims, such as Osama bin Laden and *al-Qaeda* adherents, which has hijacked the historic faith for its own political warfare against western culture and western nations.

Many Muslims will claim that Islam is the true universal faith and that Islam did not really begin with Muhammad. Islam, in their view, is not a new religion, but the "original" faith of divine origin and can be traced to the doctrine revealed to Abraham and also to Ishmael, Isaac, Jacob, the tribes of Israel, Moses, the prophets, and Jesus. Muhammad, then, becomes more of a "restorationist" than a founder, and he is the last in a line of true prophets after Abraham, Moses, and Jesus. He was a mere conduit, an intermediary, who received God's pure message and proclaimed it for the balance of his life. Even still, Muslims adore

Muhammad and they look to his example in all dimensions of their piety. Little wonder that the name Muhammad is by far the most common name for Muslim males.

Today, Islam is the second largest religion in the world and it is also the second largest religion in Germany, France, Belgium, Holland, and Canada. And Islam is the fastest growing religion in the USA and Great Britain. Hundreds of mosques and Islamic cultural centers have been established in Europe and the USA in recent years. Journalist and author Bruce Feilor in his book *Abraham* points to a fascinating irony "that in the seventh century after Christ another religion would arise out of the Middle East, use the same basic narratives as Judaism and Christianity, then quickly supplant them in terms of political and religious power." No longer considered "natural allies," Christians and Muslims today are often victimized by negative stereotypes—Muslims often seeing Christians as infidels (unbelievers) and Christians often seeing Muslims as *jihadist* terrorists.

Muhammad's Early Life

Muhammad, Messenger of God to Muslims, appeared on the world scene several centuries after Jesus' earthly life, in Arabia of the seventh century. By that time the Hebrew Bible and the Babylonian Talmud had been assembled. The New Testament canon of Scripture had long been complete and Christianity was the official religion of the Roman Empire. Constantinople thrived as the center of the Byzantine Empire. And Muhammad's sermons and recitations of God's word to him set in motion both political and religious zeal that threatened and even toppled Christian and Jewish strongholds around the Mediterranean.

Muhammad was born in 570 C.E. in Mecca, in what today is known as Saudi Arabia, and much of our knowledge of him comes from his sermons and revelations in the Muslim sacred book, the *Qur'an* ("recitation") and from *hadiths* ("recollections" or "narratives"), the remembrances of his early followers. He was born into a cultural environment of the Arabian Peninsula that might be characterized as a confusing diversity of Judaism, Christianity, Zoroastrianism, and traditional tribal religions. The local polytheistic practices included the worship of tree spirits, mountain spirits, tribal gods and *jinni* (capricious spirits thought to inhabit the desert and even to enter people).

Even before Muhammad's rise to fame as a prophet, Mecca was a center of religious pilgrimage. The city was the site of a black meteorite that had fallen to earth and was long venerated as having come from heaven; a squarish shrine had been constructed to contain it called the *Kabah* ("cube"). By the time Muhammad arrived on the scene, several hundred images of tribal gods and goddesses had been placed within the *Kabah* or around the central square of the city. Mecca was a kind of Arabian Athens of the Middle East in the seventh century, C. E.

Not much is known about Muhammad's early life. His father died not long before he was born and his mother seems to have died when he was just a child. He was raised by his grandfather and an uncle. As an adult he worked as a caravan driver for a prosperous widow named Khadijah. The two married when he was 25 and she was around 40, thus providing financial and emotional support for Muhammad. The couple produced at least six children, but no male-child survived into adulthood. As a religiously devout person, Muhammad had surely experienced the diversity and divisiveness of religious people in his land, and he spent time meditating and pondering deep spiritual concerns. He sometimes wandered outside his home to meditate amidst the hills.

A SPIRITUAL QUEST

About 610 Muhammad's spiritual quest led him to meditation in a cave on Mount Hira. To devout Muslims, the story is heartwarming: A brilliant presence came to Muhammad and held before his eyes a bright cloth covered with writing which commanded three times that he recite what was written there. "Recite in the name of the Lord who created—created man from clots of blood," he was instructed by the angel Gabriel. At first, Muhammad doubted the nature of the revelation. Thinking he could be insane, he confided in Khadijah, who encouraged him to accept the experience as a true communication from God. Then he shared revelations with his closest friends and family, especially his wife, his cousin Ali, and his long-time friend Abu Bakr (the first convert outside of Muhammad's household). These sympathetic supporters became the first Muslims, meaning "people who submit" to Allah, which is Arabic for "the God."

Other converts came from the ranks of young people and slaves. Pressure was placed on the new converts to renounce this new religion and return to traditional polytheism; after all, the new teaching of a strict monotheism was viewed as a threat to the native religions and to the source of economic livelihood from the many tribes who made pilgrimages honoring the many deities in the Kabah. Islam grew, nonetheless, even making converts among the persecutors. Yet vilification and persecution continued, and Muhammad and approximately one hundred Muslim families finally left Mecca in 622 (a migration is called the *Hijra* or *Hegira*, meaning "flight") and established Yathrib, now Medina ("city of the prophet"), as the base of missionary operations.

During a trying time in Muhammad 's life, he lost both his wife Khadijah and his protective uncle Abu Talib, but soon afterward he experienced his famous "Night Journey" or "Night of Ascent" *(miraj)*. Muhammad had left Mecca and gone to Jerusalem. The story is told that while in Jerusalem Muhammad ascended from the biblical site of Abraham's sacrifice and Solomon's temple into heaven and encountered great prophets of the past, including Abraham and Jesus, and then he experienced the presence of God. For Muslims, this momentous event confirmed for Muhammad that he was still a true prophet and messenger of God. The narrative, whether taken as a literal event or as a vision received by the prophet, provides one of the reasons Jerusalem is a holy city to Muslims.

Muhammad preached his recitations. They were piously written down by his loyal followers, who also had memorized these recitations, later to be combined into the *Holy Qur'an*. Since then, Muslims have revered these scriptures in their pure, Arabic form as the final, infallible revelation of God's will for humankind.

Muhammad was a skillful leader who knew how to combine religious, military, and administrative strategies to unify the diverse tribes of Arabia. After several successful sieges and military victories against Mecca, he and his army took Mecca in 630 without a struggle. At the time of his death, Arabs were unified in one faith that their Allah was the one and only God and prepared to promote their religion by any means available throughout the Byzantine Empire.

Thousands of pages of history might be necessary to chronicle in detail the influence of Islam over the centuries since the death of its great prophet. Such panoramic history would take us from Muhammad's call through the rise of the Ottoman Empire that cut a swath that stretched from the Atlantic coast of Spain to the frontiers of the Far East. The empire engulfed what today includes Egypt, Iraq, Syria, and a great portion of North Africa.

Though this great empire was finally dissolved in the early twentieth century, Islam has been the ideological foundation for the development of a rich culture of achievement in art, literature, science, mathematics, medicine, and architecture. Muslim thinkers and scientists kept the lamp of learning aflame even during Europe's Dark Ages. Arab Spain, the cultural center of Europe before the Renaissance, produced some of history's brightest minds. As human history marched into the twenty-first century, Islam maintained its rapid growth throughout most sectors of the globe.

Throughout all this transition, Muhammad continues to be adored by Muslims as a sincere servant and prophet of God. Loyal followers over the centuries have praised him as pure-hearted, humble (he first resisted his calling to "proclaim"), honest, sensitive to the suffering of others, of sweet and gentle disposition, ready to help the poor and the weak, and beloved by all who knew him well. He is considered the ideal statesman, diplomat, judge, and also the model father, husband, kinsman, and friend.

Two Great Religious Leaders

The profound influence of Muhammad began around the Mediterranean and has fanned out from the nations of Eurasia to all parts of the globe today. Indeed, there are interesting similarities between Muhammad and Jesus, one an Arab and the other a Jew. Together, both are considered founders of the world's two largest religions. Two cities figured in the personal history of each—Mecca and Medina for Muhammad and Nazareth and Jerusalem for Jesus. Both religious leaders were concerned about social justice and the plight of the poor and disadvantaged. Each was an effective teacher who began a call to a new understanding of authentic faith with only a small, devoted band of disciples. Each called followers to a mission of converting others to the faith. Each respected the prophets that preceded him. Each had an experience of transfiguration. Both proclaimed the reality of a great day of judgment and an afterlife and that human destiny is determined by the way people live before God in this life. Each teacher spoke of both paradise and hell fire. And each had moments of questioning and temptation from which he emerged with greater strength and a deeper sense of mission.

Yet when Muhammad stands beside Jesus, there are also glaring differences. In fact, Muhammad's lifestyle scarcely compares to that of Jesus. There is no evidence that Jesus ever married or fathered a child. Not only did Muhammad marry, but he married several times after Khadijah's death; it is possible that he married some of his wives out of compassion, for widows of soldiers often needed financial support and legal protection. Interestingly, his favorite wife was Aisha, whom he married, according to tradition, when she was only nine years of age. And Muhammad lived thirty years longer than did Jesus.

Jesus taught so clearly that his followers must reject violence as a means of advancing God's Kingdom. In interpersonal relations, Jesus instructed his disciples to resist evil by turning the other cheek, giving the extra garment, or going the second mile. Most Christians are familiar with those passages in the Sermon on the Mount even though how many make a literal application of Jesus' directives on interpersonal relations or advocate a pacifist position in international relations might be questioned. Jesus sent his apostles on peaceful missions to enter the market place or go door-to-door to emphatically announce the good news, and then simply to "shake the dust" from their sandals upon confronting rejection and persecution. Jesus never took the life of another man or woman for any reason, nor did he ever counsel any of his followers to do the same.

Potential converts to the faith are urged to weigh the cost of discipleship. Following Jesus begins both in the mind and in the heart of the receptive listener, and then discipleship is fleshed out in daily cross-bearing. Jesus' conversion model sets the Christian faith dramatically apart from the methods of Muhammad and of Islam since its prophet's death. Islam has been militaristic since the earliest days at Medina, when it used the sword to deal with resistance from Jews and Christians. Muhammad himself raided caravans for their booty and exterminated the Jewish tribe of Banu

Quraiza after the Battle of Khandaq in 627. The Ottoman Empire—in which Muslim rule was established in numerous nations in Northern Africa, Central Europe and the Middle East—was spread and defended through military might. Critics of Islam claim that no nation has ever peacefully converted to Islam, but that each Islamic nation was brought into the fold under sword. Thoughtful Muslims counter that historical, cultural, and socio-economic factors were more decisive than military force.

SEEKING BALANCE IN THE HISTORY OF MUSLIM-CHRISTIAN RELATIONS

Many Christians, too, have been violent and cruel. Muslim intellectuals claim that over the centuries Christianity has been more violent than Islam. In the centuries of interaction between Muslims and Christians, few historical developments have had a more devastating and long-lasting negative effect than the Crusades. And what happened in the Crusades is less important in Muslim-Christian relations than how each side perceived this era of European-Middle Eastern history. Each side perceived the other as militant holy warriors whose fanaticism spawned numerous acts of barbarism. Muslims perceive the Crusades as an early example of the naked aggression and imperialism of the Christian West. And the general Western mind thinks of the Muslims as instigators of the aggression, that the sole purpose of the Crusades was to liberate Jerusalem, and the Holy Land from infidels, and, finally, that European Christendom triumphed in this long struggle.

Reality was much different (see chapter 22 on Holy War). The Crusades were launched by Pope Urban II, aided by secular Christian rulers, for purposes that were as much or more economic and political than religious; and while the Christian soldiers seemed to be succeeding in their mission at first, on balance the Muslims prevailed. Whatever else might be drawn from this sordid history, the Crusades certainly reveal a crimson stain on the pages of church history. So we must not speak of *jihad* without also speaking of Christendom's dark history of violence in the name of God. What a disgrace that during these Crusades western Christianity betrayed their Master's highest ideals of non-violent love, mercy, and forgiveness!

The popular images of Islam today include hijackings, suicide bombings, improvised explosive devices, hostage taking, bombings, and holy war against the West in general. Those who point to the unspeakable violence by Islamic terrorists around the globe in order to make a strong case against Islam may neglect to place names such as Timothy McVeigh and Terry Nichols in the same category of terrorist violence and cruelty. And what about Eric Rudolph, accused of bombings in abortion clinics, gay nightclubs, and the 1996 Olympics? Does it not make as much sense to refer to these heinous criminals as "Christian terrorists" as to employ the term "Muslim terrorists" to those who plant or discharge explosives out of their supposed devotion to Islam and who recite *Qur'anic* verses just before detonating explosives in a suicide mission? Violent terrorist acts constitute a perversion and betrayal of both and Islamic teaching.

Though some of his disciples would have thrust the interests and strategies of political power and national independence upon him, Jesus told Peter to put his sword into its place and clearly rejected violence and force as means of advancing God's kingdom (Jn. 18:36). Though there are varying interpretations of the role of the sword and warfare among Muslims, there is no denying the place of the sword both in advancing the cause of Islam and also maintaining their ranks. The first Caliphs, the spiritual leaders of Islam, were also brilliant military leaders. When Christendom has resorted to violence and cruelty against innocent people, the gospel of Christ did not inspire these terrible acts, nor was the cause of Christianity advanced by them.

Clearly, Jesus renounced force and embraced the way of love. When Jesus was asked which was the greatest command, he said it was to love God with all one's heart, soul, and mind (Mt. 22:37). He always spoke of God as a loving Father. Love was not a strategy of ducking away from enemies—it was and remains a way of redeeming life! The teaching of Jesus, especially in his Sermon on the Mount, fleshes out the meaning of this powerful love in the lives of his disciples. His moral teaching is the very heart of Judeo-Christian ethics. Islam has always advanced a strong legal and moral code for its adherents and contends that its teaching should be the law for all citizens in a Muslim political society. On the other hand, one seldom encounters claims about great ethical teaching rooted in divine grace and love from the followers of Muhammad!

Christians who take Jesus' words seriously as well as understand the political realities of today's international climate will advocate something more, perhaps something different, than military force in defeating terrorist extremism. The much-publicized "war on terror" is a clash of ideals and ideas that in the next several generations will be waged in the hearts and minds of the world's citizens. Resolution will come more by understanding, empathy, peaceful dialogue, negotiation, and compromise than rather than by force and violence.

Devotional Reflection

Has it been worth our time to place Muhammad and Jesus side by side? Given vast millions who are Christians and vast millions who are Muslim, the answer is clearly affirmative. Christianity and Islam agree on many points, including the conviction of each that its faith must be a missionary religion. Followers of these two great religions possess a common starting point for fertile dialogue in that both Christians and Muslims passionately proclaim belief in one God. Both religions concur that this Supreme Being has revealed himself through human language placed in writing to his human creation. Each agrees that truth is supreme. And with the Jews, Christians and Muslims constitute the spiritual children of the patriarch Abraham.

Christians and Muslims, however, see truth as revealed in different sources—in Islam in the *Qur'an* as recited to Muhammad, and in Christianity through Jesus Christ. For Christians, Jesus does not simply *reveal* the Word of God. Jesus *is* the Word of God. Through the *Qur'an*, God broke into human history through a word that is written, but, through Jesus Christ, God broke into history through the Word who lived and taught truth as a human being! More simply, in Christianity the Word became human flesh; in Islam, the Word became a book

In Christianity, Jesus' life, teaching, and death on the cross were perfect for moral direction, spiritual counsel, and atonement for sin; in Islam, the untranslated *Qur'an* is the uncontaminated Word of God and Jesus did not die on the cross. In Islam, God is great, but remote; in Christ, God drew near. Regrettably, though Muslims accept the vast majority of the Bible's teachings and narratives, they deny and reject two cardinal Christian doctrines: Christ's claim to divinity ("Jesus is human, so how could he be divine?") and the Trinity ("Allah is one, so how could he be three?"). And these two doctrines make all the difference in the world!

On the other hand, there is so much that followers of Jesus could learn from the followers of Muhammad. Muslims remind us that good and evil matter, and, that while God's wrath and vengeance are realities, God's mercy and compassion emerge far greater. The *Qur'an* presents life as a comparatively brief but immensely significant opportunity to prepare for a day of reckoning and an eternity that is concretely and vividly experienced. Each of us alone is responsible for one's own fate. And Muslims remind us of the sacred nature of God, the sanctity of God's name, and the immense value of spiritual discipline and daily prayers to God during various times of the day.

Finally, who can argue against the bottom line of Islamic theology—submission, or surrender, to the totality of God's will brings the deepest peace. Always remember that surrender is a process, not an event. Surrender is a wholehearted "yes" to God.

Prayer: Father God, we thank you for the vital role in history played by Muhammad in proclaiming to people of his generation that you are essentially *one* God and not many. We thank you for those devout Muslims throughout history who have reminded us that you are both holy and sovereign and that your name must be reverenced. We thank you for the numerous contributions of Muslims since the time of Muhammad in the sciences and arts. Even more, we thank you for revealing yourself in the person of your Son, Jesus. We ask that all inquiring Muslims simply look at Jesus—fairly, openly, and patiently—as he is depicted in the gospel narratives. And we humbly ask that those who follow your Son as Lord and Savior and those who look to Muhammad as your last great prophet and to the *Qur'an* as your last revelation will pursue peace and seek genuine dialogue for the purpose of understanding you, your will, and the cultures of the world more completely. Through Jesus, the Prince of Peace. Amen.

15

The Perennial Issue Every Worldview Must Face

W ho would argue with the basic principle that pain serves valuable purposes in our lives? Most of us would not question what Christian author Philip Yancey calls "the gift of pain" when that pain gives us warnings and lessons protecting us from even greater harm and injury. Pain is not fun, but often serves good purposes. It warns. It teaches. It protects. It facilitates growth and development.

The basic issue is not simple physical pain, for it is much larger—it includes unspeakable evil, unrelenting pain, and intense human suffering. To be honest, not only might unbelievers mock Christians for their faith in a personal God, but Christians may unintentionally mock unbelievers by reducing their arguments against a loving God to a straw man, a much weaker version of their main argument, that is much easier to knock over, all to the applause of those believers who know already they are correct.

How much easier it is to explain the discomfort and pain of someone standing too close to the fire or who inadvertently brushes up against a hot stove—that quick experience with pain stirs a reflexive withdrawal that protects the skin from severe burns. On the other hand, what is the purpose served by being trapped in a burning building and having one's body incinerated and reduced to a pile of unrecognizable ashes? And how perplexing to explain unspeakable pain and suffering when they are caused by the evil acts of seemingly ordinary people! No critical thinking person would attempt to place the sensation of burning one's hand on a hot stove in the same category with the experience of suffocation in a gas oven at Auschwitz; the former serves as a warning mechanism to prevent a worse injury and the latter serves only as a tragic illustration of the unspeakable horror that one human can inflict upon others.

No thinking person can avoid this issue. And this may be the most perplexing enigma that every worldview must face. Every worldview, not simply the Judeo-Christian worldview, must come to grips with evil and suffering. It is perhaps less recognized that this same problem exists in eastern religions, though teaching about the origin of actual suffering and evil is more difficult to find. In eastern religion, *karma* is easily understood as a form of payback for one's deeds; it might be thus inferred that whether one suffers from an accident, a disease or illness, or violence, one has, in some sense, brought it on oneself. In essence, you deserve whatever happens to you.

Nor can the depth and breadth of evil and suffering be discounted with simplistic explanations. A worldview without a realistic answer to the enigma of evil and suffering is so unlikely to gain wide acceptance. Before attempting to offer definitions and establish categories, let's concede that evil and suffering constitute a mystery that will never be fully understood by thoughtful Christians, least of all those who have been victimized most by evil and suffering.

EVIL IS A REALITY

Denial of evil would be difficult to maintain in light of such historical figures as Rome's Nero, who persecuted and murdered Christians with a variety of methods which entertained him and his cronies; the Soviet Union's Joseph Stalin, dictator from 1929 to 1953 whose purges of political dissidents sent 20 million to their deaths by various means and who started the Great Famine which killed millions of Ukrainians; Adolph Hitler, Germany's Nazi dictator in the 30s to the mid-40s whose quest for world domination led to World War II and whose genocidal policies during that war constituted the Holocaust and the deaths of six million Jewish men, women, and children; Pol Pot, Khmer Rouge leader whose killing fields of Cambodia claimed the lives of 1.7 million; Idi Amin, Uganda president from 1971 to 1979 who ordered the execution of thousands of Ugandans; and Slobodan Milosevic, Serbia president from 1989 to 1997 and Yugoslavia from 1997 to 2000 who was responsible for deaths of more than 200,000 people in 1992-95.

The current generation certainly knows of Saddam Hussein, Iraq president from 1979 to 2003 whose use of deadly bio-chemical agents against the Kurdish people of his nation and ordering the execution of 148 Shiite Muslims deemed to be enemies established his dubious reputation as one of the world's deadliest and greediest dictators; he was dubbed "Butcher of Baghdad" by friend and foe alike. These political dictators met their demise in a number of ways, with Hussein being tried and convicted by an Iraqi court and then hanged in late December 2006—a fiasco that seemed more like sectarian revenge than retributive justice. And then there is the wholesale carnage of the killing fields of near genocide in Africa that brought little more than news briefs to American citizens—first in Rwanda of the mid-90s and in the Sudan, 2005-07 and continuing.

The name that nearly all Americans have uttered as almost synonymous with extreme terrorism is Osama bin Laden, believed to be the mastermind behind the terrorist attacks on the U.S. on September 11, 2001. Three years later, the most hunted terrorist in the Middle East became Abu Musah al-Zarqawi, wanted for a series of gruesome, high-profile atrocities in Iraq. Al-Zarqawi was a former petty criminal from Jordan who became the symbol of a murderous insurgency. His group made a specialty of kidnapping foreign nationals and beheading them on videotape. In a familiar tableau, the terrorists pronounced the death sentence on their blindfolded victim, then savagely sawed off his head. Consider that most people would not deem these terrorists to be insane, but fanatical extremists who are otherwise sane and rational. Al-Zarqawi eventually met his fate also in 2006 through U. S. firepower, another confirmation of Jesus' very sensible proverb that "all who live by the sword shall die by the sword" (Mt. 26:52).

Let us not imagine that the atrocities of wartime are committed solely by "the other side." Many Americans may cling doggedly to unshakable belief in their nation's innocence of ordinary evil. Vivid accounts of the massacre of the My Lai village in Viet Nam, to cite one illustration, expose this belief to be without foundation. In this generation's war, Abu Ghraib prison was an environment of squalid submissiveness enforced by wardens against prisoners of war—Iraqi prisoners were stripped of clothing and stacked in a human pyramid, strung up and blindfolded as though they were about to be hung, or leashed like vicious dogs. All kinds of explanation are deployed to deny or discount evil in our own ranks—this was war-time; the victims deserved their fate; this was another nation and another religion; the shameful acts of humiliation were an exception and not the rule; the guilty were punished, and so forth. But what gave rise to My Lai and Abu Ghraib is rooted deep in the history of sinful humanity, shame, and guilt.

As if these examples did not suffice to underscore the reality of evil, most of us have heard of the evil acts of individual U.S. criminals such as Ted Bundy, a former law student executed in the electric chair at a Florida state prison on January 24, 1989. Bundy was convicted of the sadistic murders of several women, including a twelve-year-old girl, two women in a Florida State University sorority house, and may have killed as many as one hundred women over the six-year period prior to his arrest. Timothy McVeigh planted explosives that blew up the Murrah federal office building in Oklahoma City in April, 1995, killing 168 people, including a number of young children which he heartlessly dismissed as "collateral damage." Jeffrey Dahmer lured seventeen men into his apartment under the guise of friendship and hospitality and murdered them, actually eating flesh of some of his victims. Susan Smith, a young South Carolina mother, strapped her two young sons into their car seats and rolled her Mazda Protégé with its most innocent passenger load into a nearby lake, and then reported to authorities that she had been carjacked and her sons abducted by an African-American male. And more recently, in April 2007, a deranged Virginia Tech student named Cho Seung-Hui went on a murderous campus rampage that tragically claimed the lives of 33 victims.

The first decade of the twenty-first century provides little hope that the new century will be any less violent and bloody than the previous century. How foolishly naïve it would be to conclude that modern humanity is becoming more enlightened and advanced in interpersonal relationships and international justice! At the center of evil, at least from a Christian perspective, is the stark reality of sin. Further, evil people possess a number of character defects, but the one common thread trait among them is an utter inability to empathize with their victims and feel compassion for them.

Two Kinds of Evil

Western philosophical thought has distinguished between two kinds of evil: moral and natural. "Moral evil" refers to all those terrible deeds for which humans are morally responsible. We might think of moral evil as the deliberate infliction of pain and suffering upon another person or group of persons without any moral justification; additionally a person doing evil often inflicts this unjustifiable pain and suffering on others without any sense of remorse or regret and, in fact, may take delight in such evil. The study of ancient civilizations will provide almost innumerable examples of moral evil that one person or one group perpetuated against others, and, to be honest, the Old Testament narrates occasions of barbarism and terrorism inflicted by men and women.

"Natural evil" includes those terrible events that happen in nature such as hurricanes, tornadoes, floods, earthquakes, droughts, volcano eruptions, diseases, and epidemics, just to name a few bigger calamities. The Christmas tsunami of 2004 that hit the Indian Ocean rim of nations, drowning several hundred thousand adults and children and changing the lives of their surviving relatives forever, raised serious questions about God in the minds of millions. Some would likely be uncomfortable applying the word "evil" to natural disasters which are part and parcel of the laws of the physical universe, while others gravitate to the opposite extreme of contending that all evil is essentially moral evil with the devil brought in as the cause of natural evil.

To offer an analogy: A wayfarer is traveling alone to what he hopes will be a better place to find a job and a place to live. As he travels an old road covered with dirt and gravel that winds its way through the hills, a major rainstorm descends upon him, slowing him down and soaking him with water. He happens upon an abandoned shack on the steep side of one hill and is able to enter, find relief from the storm, and lie down for rest. As the hours pass, the relentless rains and water run-off erode the foundation of the shack, and it slides off the side of the hill, collapsing on the man and killing him. That is *natural* evil. Let's imagine another wayfarer takes refuge in the same shack, but a vicious thief breaks into the shack, steals his money, and stabs him to death. That is *moral* evil.

Does Evil Disprove God?

The philosopher Epicurus of ancient Greece (341-270 BCE) first raised this paradox about God: "Is he willing to prevent evil, but not able? Then he is impotent. Is he able, but not willing? Then he is malevolent. Is he both able and willing? Whence then is evil?" Some strong believers (theists) are willing to concede that the "atheologians" (those who argue against the existence of God) retain only one arrow in their quiver, an argument for disbelief in a personal God. Let's structure this argument with three propositions affirmed by the Judeo-Christian tradition:

1. God is all powerful (his powers include omniscience)
2. God is perfectly good and compassionate.
3. Evil exists.

The "atheologians," those making a case for atheism, contend that the above schema is not simply a paradox about God, that it is an implicit contradiction containing propositions that are starkly contradictory. If God is perfectly good and compassionate, then why does he allow evil to exist? Could it be that God is not totally powerful? Could it be that there are some realities that grieve God but that, regrettably, he can do nothing about?

Perhaps God is all-powerful, but is God actually good and compassionate? To claim that God is not all-goodness would be a most serious charge to level. If we remove this quality of divine benevolence from God, leaving God with mere power and all knowledge and nothing more that is divine, then why would we want to worship this God? God surely cannot do evil and remain God!

Does God Need Our Defense?

If there is an all-powerful and all-good personal God and his thoughts and ways are superior to ours as human beings, then we will certainly not understand all of God's ways. Yet this does not mean that we shut down our minds and walk away from one of the greatest intellectual challenges. Surely God does not need our defense any more than he needs anything from mere humans in order to be God. God does seek a relationship with us that must surely be authentic and honest as well as spiritual and loving. While God has no need to learn about us as human beings, we may perpetually be open to truth and insights about our Heavenly Father.

A temptation exists to be indifferent to evil as an issue, especially evil we have not experienced first-hand, since that relieves us of responsibility of grappling with profound paradoxes. Why not summarily dismiss the entire issue by saying that no one can fathom God's mystery? In the final analysis, evil may be a problem for those whose tolerance for mystery is minimal. Issues do not go into seclusion simply by ignoring them. Our defenses must be ready.

The main defense of God's nature in the light of evil and immense suffering is the *free will defense*, referenced in early medieval times by St. Augustine (354-430 A.D.). This free will defense adds a fourth premise to Epicurus' paradox: God has created human beings with radical freedom, and it is logically impossible for God to create free creatures and guarantee that they will never do evil.

There are only two ways that God could have prevented the human race from falling into grievous sin. One would be by depriving us of free will in the first place, thus making us either animals living by instinct only or puppets whose every move is controlled by a higher power. Such deprivation would mean we humans are not really humans—moral freedom is part and parcel of any meaningful humanity. The other way would be to create us as angels who live in a sin-free heavenly environment and are not capable of sin. So, as humans we are free to choose between good and evil acts. For certain, a wide range of factors in our physical and social environments influences our moral choices, but we are ultimately responsible for our own moral choices.

So, while God created free human beings he could not guarantee that they would never abuse that freedom and do evil. Could God have created a world in which humans enjoyed partial freedom but were spared the terrible consequences of the worst evil they commit? Certainly an omnipotent God could have created other worlds, but, can we agree that this particular world possesses a high ratio of good to evil? Aren't there far more random acts of kindness than there are random acts of violence? Might this world, though far from perfect, be the best physical environment that an omnipotent, omnibenevolent God could logically create?

A second line of argument is the *theodicy* defense, an attempt to justify the ways of God before humankind. Apologists endeavor to show that God allows temporary evil in order to bring about our greater good. Yes, maybe we could imagine a world that is a total island paradise, where people live as long as they like, where no one could make a wrong choice and where no one could possibly harm an insect, much less another human being, and where everyone could eat, drink, and be merry as much as one desired with absolutely no negative consequences.

This world, however, is a place of "soul making," which gives us the opportunity for discipline and developing moral character. If our world were some "play pen paradise," there would be no use for education, exploration, discipline, diligence, honor, commitment, integrity, courage, love, kindness, compassion, and forgiveness— none of these virtues would make sense if no one could perpetrate any physical or emotional harm to others or self. We know reality all too well. Our world is not a Playboy mansion-type hedonistic romper room. Our world is a tough world environment where ideas and ideologies clash and people fight, injure, and even kill others. This is a world where human error occurs—whether in design, technology, or human performance—so that planes and automobiles crash or a massive bridge over the Mississippi River collapses. This is a world with no guarantees about the future.

Jesus Confronts This Perplexing Issue

Biblical texts do not skirt this perplexing issue. In fact, Jesus faced it head-on. Once he was asked if the victims of one of Pilate's massacres of Galileans had deserved their trauma because of their own sinfulness; and in the same discussion Jesus mentioned eighteen tragic deaths of innocent people due to the collapse of a tower (see Luke 13:1-5).

The most memorable occasion in which Jesus faced the issue was when a man who was blind crossed the path Jesus walked with his disciples (the story is told in John 9). Surely Jesus had answered all kinds of questions for his closest disciples, and it is quite understandable that they would ask him about the reasons for this man's blindness—"Who sinned, this man or his parents, that he was born blind?" Everyone would concur that such a severe disability created both physical limitation and emotional pain. Behind the question was an unstated assumption that some powerful force had punished this poor victim because of his own sinfulness or that of his parents. Jesus completely surprised his followers by dispelling the widely held conception that human suffering is arbitrary punishment for someone's sin, and he pointed them to an opportunity for demonstrating the power of God in the man's life.

Devotional Reflection

The Judeo-Christian worldview depicts a powerful and loving God who grants us freedom, but allows us to assume both the deep joys and the terrible risks of being human creatures. God created us in his image, but knows that through human choice or neglect that the image can be so marred as to be unrecognizable as divine imprint. The abundant life of joy is the lifestyle Jesus offers, though, admittedly, that life seems so elusive at times.

The Christian faith presents a loving Father with such amazing love that he is able to enter empathetically into our deepest hurts and pains. This Father awaits the time in which he will wipe every tear from our eyes and put an final end to death, mourning, pain, and grieving—all will be destroyed with the old order (Rev. 21:3-4). In the interim, spiritual development requires obstacles and the opportunity to fail as well as succeed.

As we speak about the senseless evil lurking in nuclear threats, suicide bombers, serial killers, gang rapists, and child abusers, we must not be blinded to evil we allow to seep into the brokenness of our relationships with both God and fellow human beings. How much easier it is to recognize the evil in the impersonal criminals whose pictorial images are aired on the evening news than to recognize the more personal, subtle deeds that wound others, even those we profess to love deeply and care about immensely!

The cross may once again be the ultimate answer to the perennial enigma about life. The central message from the cross is that Jesus did not seek to avoid evil and suffering, but he endured it. Through Jesus, God himself entered the entire human experience, from the smallest pain in the carpentry shop when a hammer hit his hand to the deepest physical and spiritual agony when Roman nails were driven through his hand. The cross of Jesus—not Auschwitz, not the killing fields of Cambodia, not the Gulag Archipelago—symbolizes evil at its worst. The cross also symbolizes God's love and mercy at its best. The cross of Christ is God's final answer to the problem of moral evil and deliberate sinful choices.

Prayer: Dear God, so often we are perplexed by the human toll taken by both the moral evil of vicious individuals as well as by impersonal tragedy and natural disaster. Surely you want us to seek understanding, explanations, and wisdom from the toughest of life's experiences, but even more you want us to trust you with the ultimate answers to life's most puzzling experiences. May our faith not falter during hard times, and in tragedy and disaster may we discover deep blessing in reaching out to survivors. In the name of Jesus, who seeks the spiritual survival of us all. Amen.

16

Pantheism—Default From Divine Revelation

Most certainly you have visited some sites of scenic beauty and wonder. Perhaps you, like me, have visited Niagara Falls or the Grand Canyon. You may have visited the Great Smoky Mountains, the Rocky Mountains, or even the Swiss Alps. You likely have watched the sun rise or set over an expansive, blue ocean or enjoyed the pure white sand and turquoise water fully embracing a Caribbean island. Likely you enjoy watching a full moon rise heavenward through clear skies early in the evening. Surely you have your own special places in nature somewhere near your residence. For me, the experience of walking on a trail high above Radnor Lake or along the serpentine trail in Warner Park, both in the Nashville area that I call home, provide experiences that are both spiritual and emotional as well as physical.

When you visit those sites in nature, what comes to your mind? Consider three possibilities: First, perhaps no special thoughts come to mind. Maybe you just view these sites as elements of nature and places to retreat from the world of computers and cell phones and the hubbub of daily routine. Or, second, maybe you consider these not only as places to retreat to or take a vacation, but the scenery is valued as a special manifestation of the incredible design and handiwork of a Creator God. A third response is the conviction that the natural world contains not simply places of beauty to remind us of God, but that all the universe, including the plain ordinariness of many places actually *is* God.

Most of us would likely endorse and experience the middle response cited briefly above, seeing beautiful scenery in our natural world as blessings given to enrich and

enhance aesthetically our sojourn on earth. You might even affirm that you feel closer
to God while in certain habitats of his natural world than you do in any other setting.
Some have claimed they feel more spiritual taking a walk in the woods or spending
hours on a lake on Sunday morning than in a worship assembly of the church. And it's
not simply what we see in the great outdoors. Those experiences which seem to transcend human language—smelling a fragrant flower, stroking a hand over a dolphin,
feeling the warm embrace of a very best friend, observing the birth of a first child
or even the first grandchild, making love to one's life-time mate—may be properly
viewed as both precious and sacred.

Does it seem strange to you that the third view, the doctrine that the natural world
is God, has roots that extend far into history with humans' first experience in religion
but also is as contemporary as today's most recent New Age publication? This doctrine
is part and parcel of pantheism, and today continues making inroads into all kinds of
forums and institutions, even into some mainstream churches. Many college students
accept pantheism in some form and they express this doctrine in different ways. "We are
all part of God and we all have some divinity within us, and divinity is anywhere one sees
goodness and beauty," is typical wording from many young adults. Even some liberal
Christian churches speak of "re-imaging" God, denouncing any chauvinistic or patriar-
chal notions of God, elevating nature, and offering worship to "our mother, Sophia."

"GOD IS EVERYTHING AND EVERYTHING IS GOD"

Pantheism is the belief that "God is everything" or "everything is God." Monotheism declares that everything was created by God and that a singular, supreme God
stands apart from his creation; if one could remove the universe from God, God would
in no way be diminished. Pantheism emphasizes the fundamental unity of all things.
Each person is as much God as God is God.

The doctrine that "everything there is *is* God" is a succinct definition of absolute monism. Do not oversimplify pantheism and simply think of it as the "worship
of nature." *Pan* is from the Latin meaning "all" and pantheism is the overarching
worldview that God and the material world are one. A modified version of pantheism
claims that "God is the reality or principle behind nature," and it is sometimes stated
as "God is to nature as soul is to body."

This concept is not easy for Christians to grasp, admittedly. In contemporary
times, it is almost a religion by default from the bankruptcy of atheism or agnosticism. The atheist must conclude that we have in the universe all there is; and that there
is nothing beyond what we can see or touch or smell—no unseen Creator God, no
Redeemer Savior, no life beyond our immediate time and place. Death is therefore

the stark finality of individual existence. Atheism is a doctrine of the dead end street. And agnosticism boasts of its humility in not knowing answers while providing no hope and reassurance for some of life's ultimate issues. What doctrines of despair! Of course, there are many who build their philosophies on these assumptions of chance and nothingness—for example, communism, secular humanism, materialism, and secular existentialism.

Millions are clearly uncomfortable with the "death" of God and the despair and hopelessness when any sense of immortality is lost. These people want to live spiritual lives and honor moral goodness. Yet, they are also all too conscious of the vacuum in their lives by fatalistic dogma, and they seek some doctrine that will account for the sense of awe and wonder as they look at the universe and give it some meaning. These seekers still retain the words "God," "divinity," and "transcendence," but employ them in a different sense or meaning from understandings within historic orthodox Christianity. Clearly, "God" to pantheists does not refer to a personal, transcendent Divine Being who is separate from the universe, who created the universe, who maintains moral character, who has revealed much of his will for the human race, and who seeks fellowship with his created human beings.

EASTERN PANTHEISTIC MONISM

In pantheism, "God" is identified in some way with the universe as a whole or with some part or aspect of it. In Eastern religious thought and philosophy, monism is the dominant feature. *Monism* is the belief that the basic essence of the entire universe is one. God is One in the sense of being a oneness without duality or differentiation. God is beyond distinctions, including distinctions between persons and between good and evil.

Pantheism is clearly taught in Hinduism. In this ancient religion, Brahman, or the Universal Spirit, is the closest word to "God." In the *Upanishads* he is described as the one Divine Being "hidden in all beings, all-pervading, the self within all beings, watching over all works, dwelling in all beings, the witness, the perceiver, the only one, free from all qualities. He is the one ruler of many who (seem to act, but really) do not act; he makes the one seed manifold." In the *Bhagavad Gita,* the Brahman speaks to Arjuna through Krishna, one of the most popular deities within the Hindu religion: "Listen and I shall reveal to thee some manifestations of my divine glory...I am the soul, prince victorious, which dwells in the heart of all things. I am the beginning, the middle, and the end of all that lives...And know, Arjuna, that I am the seed of all things that are; and that no being that moves or moves not can ever be without me...Know that whatever is beautiful and good, whatever has glory and power is only a portion of my own radiance...Know that with one single fraction of my Being I pervade and support the Universe and know that I AM."

Though Hinduism may provide the most persistent commitment to pantheism throughout the centuries, some version of this doctrine has thrived on all continents and in all centuries. Ancient animists believed that each object in nature possessed its own god or spirit. Pantheistic monism is the foundational worldview undergirding the Hindu Advaita Vedanta system of Shankara, the Transcendental Mediation of Maharishi Yogi, and the views in Herman Hesse's popular novel *Siddhartha*. Buddhists have seen deity as *nirvana*, or abstract void, though otherwise have shared with Hindus many aspects of interpreting the world; they have contended that the world can be accepted, appreciated, and valued; the cause of suffering is not the world but each individual's attachment to it.

Many serious thinkers have combined philosophy and pantheism. The Stoics of ancient Greece were pantheists. Attacking the popular polytheism of their culture, they insisted there is but one Sacred Being, which they called Logos; there is no perfect translation of Logos into English, but the term generally means Reason or Ultimate Word. The Stoics were realists and they also taught that each human is a spark of this divine Logos. In a sense, paradoxically, the ancient Stoics were quite "New Age."

In the seventeenth century, the Dutch philosopher Baruch Spinoza (1632-1677) introduced pantheistic ideas into western philosophy. Some twentieth century theologians have been influenced by Eastern religions and pantheistic concepts. One of the most influential theologians in modern times, Paul Tillich (1886-1965) described God as "Being Itself" rather than "A Being." Tillich challenged his students to forget everything traditional that they had learned about God and perhaps even the name "God." "The God who is a being is transcended by the God who is Being itself, the ground and abyss of every being."

New Age Pantheism

If these quotes seem abstract and esoteric, perhaps they are. New Age doctrine, by contrast, is quite clear and understandable. Sometimes that doctrine is simply and clearly stated as "God is all; all is God." The central doctrine of the New Age regarding God is that everything is fundamentally divine because everything flows from the divine Oneness that is existential Substance—the essential Reality—that is beneath all things. New Agers characterize this oneness as a force or an energy that can be called the Cosmic Mind or Cosmic Consciousness or even the Universal Self, True Self, Higher Self, or Deep Self. Their practices aim at getting in touch with or harnessing this fundamental energy. The benediction of blessing that a New Age disciple might offer is a declaration from the movie *Star Wars*: "May the Force be with you."

Interest in nature and ecology points to a significant source of New Age spirituality. The theme of the "planet" as a living being filled with divinity and concern for the environment as a common heritage and the subsequent call for "planetary transformation" has united this movement. To their credit, many New Age disciples seem more devoted to proper stewardship of the earth and its natural resources than are the majority of mainstream Christians, whom most New Agers view as materialist and consumerist. Most New Agers celebrate the beauty in nature, appreciate what is natural, seek to undo the damage they believe society has inflicted on the planet, work to conserve its resources for future generations, and link the welfare of their lives with the well-being of the earth. Who can fault them for this specialized ethic of ecology? Clearly, this ethic cannot be dismissed or discounted as insignificant.

Pantheism has much that appeals to thinking and sensitive persons. The doctrine can unify all thinking and feeling persons in an appreciation for what the entire human family shares in nature. This doctrine elevates all of nature and discourages our treatment of any moment in time or any element in nature as being trivial and mundane. Living in a world in which so much of humanity fails to respect human rights, a world in which nations and factions continue to wage war and perpetrate violence and evil, a world in which greed and materialism are granted a free reign that cancels respect for other human beings and the environment, pantheism seems healthy and therapeutic. Yet pantheism must be taken seriously as a formidable opponent of the basic foundation of Christianity.

Is There Heresy in Pantheism?

Pantheism has always been foreign to the Christian tradition of the West for good reason. As Christians we accept the biblical account that God created the heavens and the earth and that God exists above and beyond the physical universe. This is the very meaning of transcendence. Most of all, pantheism is a cruel thief robbing God of moral character and personality and then reducing God to Oneness--a sheer undifferentiated, impersonal, abstract unity. How can one pray confidently to such a deity? How could one feel loved and accepted by divinity? How could one find divine grace after having committed a terrible mistake? How does one find the power to live a more abundant life? Where does one find a moral example worthy of imitating?

The first words of the Bible begin with a crucially important declaration: "In the beginning God created...." and then lists the general entities which this omnipotent God created. The first two chapters of Genesis underscore the supreme importance the

Hebrew Scriptures give to nature. The recitation of the many entities that God created, ranging from the highest heavens and the depths of the sea, leaves absolutely no doubt—all elements found in the universe are created by God and cannot be gods themselves.

Much like a persuasive prosecuting attorney making his case that God indicted the whole world for sin, the apostle Paul in his treatise to the Roman Christians focused on the crucial failures of both Gentiles and Jews in his epistle to the Romans. For so many in the Greco-Roman world, Paul contended, their sin was intuitively *knowing* there was a transcendent God, but refusing to acknowledge that Supreme Being. And the manifestation of that sin of rebellion by the Gentiles was their worship both of the Creation and even of idols of familiar creatures as substitutes for worshiping the Creator. In claiming to be wise, "they worship idols that are made to look like humans who cannot live forever, and like birds, animals, and reptiles...they did what they wanted to do...they gave up truth about God for a lie, and they worshiped God's creation instead of God, who will be praised forever" (1:23-25). In essence, Paul says the Gentiles were guilty of, among other serious unrighteousness and moral misconduct, practicing pantheism.

And, yet, are the beauties of nature special? Of course! Genesis reports that God looked upon all that he had created and pronounced everything good. No painting or photograph can fully capture the majesty and beauty of the rich variety of God's creation. And God teaches us valuable lessons through all his mighty deeds and works. Just as Jesus employed the imagery of nature in some of his best-known stories, thus all of life and the world constitute God's classroom to which we are invited to learn about him and one another. The Psalmist spoke clearly of the heavens declaring the glory of God and the firmament manifesting his handiwork (Ps. 19:1). The very best of nature says something very special about God, but the best of nature is *not* God personally.

Pantheism has strong appeal, to be sure. When it is integrated with other New Age doctrine, there is no real evil, only ignorance. There is no serious sin that alienates one from a personal, loving God—only correctable mistakes that keep one from measuring up to one's full potential. Both New Age doctrine and pantheism can set the morality bar fairly low—conserving gas and water and not littering our parks and highways constitute a good start. Active concern about global warming could be the next step. All important concerns, to be sure, but, as C. S. Lewis once noted, this is the religion that people can fall into quite naturally, apart from divine revelation.

When your computer programming is completed, programs run according to a pre-set coding for such specifications as margin, font, and point-size, and unless you make deliberate changes from the programmed format your work will be performed in a "default" mode. For people who want to feel spiritual and live good moral lives and believe there is something bigger and better beyond themselves, on the one hand, but then reject divine revelation and the notion of a personal and holy God who wants to draw humanity into righteous relationship with him, on the other hand, the religious default mode is pantheism. This "default" is designed to make us feel good about ourselves. The default is also designed to drive us to appreciate anything in nature, whether human nature or physical universe, that strikes us as beautiful or valuable.

Devotional Reflection

As Christians we may be reminded that "the earth is the Lord's and the fullness thereof" (Ps. 24:1) and that all of us are stewards of this great gift of a physical universe.

God's relationship with nature is likely far deeper and far more complex than any of us can comprehend. Just as a painting reflects the creative skill of the artist or a composition reflects the writer or musician, the universe in many awesome and wonderful ways reflects the power and glory of God. And nature's awesome power, astounding complexity, and amazing beauty convince us that the highest feats in human achievement and design pale by comparison to God's handiwork.

Look all around. We are truly living in an art gallery. Every shade and hue of color is found in fascinating combination somewhere on earth or in the sky. To climb a mountain peak in Yosemite or to scuba dive into the clear waters off the coast of Belize, to see colorful tropical birds or the foliage in a Central American rain forest, to drive through a painted desert, to visit the Swiss Alps or a golden meadow with Wyoming mountains in the background—who could deny our travels around the globe are free admission to a grand museum of incomparably exquisite art? Creation is God's classroom.

Just as a movie director can place oneself into one of the scenes of the cinematic production, the Creator painted something of himself in all his creation. And though there will never be an opportunity to meet the artists and sculptors of ancient Greece or Rome or of the Renaissance, nor even likely we would come to know personally popular artists today, such as Thomas Kincaid, we are invited to know and maintain a relationship with the Grand Artist of the universe through knowing his Son.

While we may heartily sing the classic hymn "This is My Father's World," sadly, the world's community has not always been a worthy trustee of the earth's bounty and beauty. Humanity's reliance on fossil fuels, the spread of cities with their urban sprawl, the destruction of natural habitats for both residential neighborhoods and farmland and over-exploitation of the oceans are all destroying Earth's ability to sustain the quality of life as we know it. And the United States is among a handful of nations who leave the biggest "ecological footprint" by spending nature's capital faster than it can regenerate.

The greatest cost of the American way of life is passed off to the remainder of the community of nations. With less than six percent of the world's population, the United States consumes more than a third of the earth's resources and is responsible for the biggest share of its environmental pollution. In generations ahead, populous nations such as China and India may rival the USA as the world's most polluting nation. A 2007 study by a consortium of the world's leading scientists concluded that global warming, though the severity and possible future scenarios are debated, is indeed an accelerating reality and that human beings and their lifestyle choices constitute the major causal factors. Our life support systems are in jeopardy.

God—humans—nature! These three are meant for each other. Thoughts about God and nature must not stop at shallow sentimentality. Not only are we called to a proper doctrine of God and nature, but we are also summoned to a morally responsible trusteeship of all God's blessings. Answers and solutions for environmental issues seldom come easily, but that does not absolve our responsibility to cherish and protect all God's bounty. To do nothing is to side with the cultural status quo.

Prayer: Creator God, we rejoice in the wonders of your creation—the mountains, the oceans, the rivers, the hills, the streams, the sky, the trees, the flowers, the rocks and cliffs, and especially the schemes of design and color found in nature. With the Psalmist, we proclaim, "How great are Thy works, O Lord." May we always see your loving heart and your creative mind as we appreciate nature. And, O Lord, move us beyond appreciation to a wise stewardship and careful preservation of your creation, so that generations to come may also appreciate its beauty and sing your praises. Bless this land, O great God, and deepen our appreciation for it and bless our efforts for its preservation. Through Jesus. Amen.

17

Reincarnation—
Reality or Ruse?

The sign on the wall of an obstetrical unit in a big hospital declared: "The first two minutes of life are critical." Some wise person added a quip below: "The last two are pretty dicey as well." Another has quipped: "Nobody gets out of this world alive."

The reality of our death may be the most sobering thought we will ever consider. Truth is, of course, most of us are able to repress any thoughts about our departure from this world until undeniable evidence of our mortality rocks us between the eyes. Perhaps we have a close scrape with death. Maybe a best friend dies most unexpectedly. Maybe there is the sudden loss of a close family member. Death, then, becomes a subject we cannot ignore. As we think about death, another crucially important question emerges: "Is there really life after death?"

Next to the idea of God as an eternal Supreme Being who controls our destiny, the idea of life after death is the greatest idea that has occurred to the human mind. Yet the idea of immortality is a rather abstract concept. What is the nature of the life we experience after death? Will we be born to die again? What will be the nature of existence—in some body or in spirit form only? And whom can we trust as an authority on this subject since there is so little data and it's not exactly something we can find answers for in a science laboratory?

Various worldviews answer these questions in different ways. And it comes down to which view of afterlife makes the most sense and which authority on the subject we trust the most.

ANCIENT WORLDVIEW

The ancient worldviews incorporated much diversity about human origins and destinies, but most accepted the idea that all humans possessed both earthly and spiritual dimensions. A prominent theme in ancient religions is that humans were created to serve and honor the gods. Stories about the failure of humans to achieve the purposes of their creation are common. Many ancient religions taught that humans survived death and that life in the hereafter was much to be desired; other traditions taught that humans survived as joyless ghosts.

The Greeks spoke of the afterlife as an existence in the shadowy land of the dead *(Hades)* beneath the earth from whence no one returns. The Egyptians, Inca, and Aztecs saw death as a passage to eternal life. Some of these religions had several heavens or realms of the dead and one's social status determined the eternal location. The Egyptian journey to celestial immortality was facilitated by the *Book of the Dead*, a collection of rites, formulas, and spells inscribed on tombs and coffins to be recited by the soul on the journey in the hereafter.

The notion of *reincarnation*, that the spirit of a human being leaves that body upon death and enters another body, received wide acceptance in the ancient world. Socrates made an argument for immortality, and Plato, his best-known student, believed that the human soul survives death and can be reborn. As we cross the Atlantic to reflect on the religions of the Americas, we find that belief in reincarnation was widespread; the soul of the departed would be reborn as a child within the tribe. The cycle of the soul was not immediate for it might well happily experience an indefinite stay in a happy hunting ground.

THE HINDU WORLDVIEW

The *Upanishads*, religious dialogues composed over a period of several hundred years beginning about 900 B.C.E., compose a major part of the religious heritage and teaching of Hinduism. The *Upanishads* were an inquiry into the meaning of the individual self and the relationship of the self to the underlying reality of all. The self, called the *atman*, is distinguished from both the body and from the individual identified by name and form. The *atman* is subject to continuous rebirth in the cycle called *samsura*, a prospect interpreted as a form of eternal bondage. Every action, called *karma*, performed by an individual produces an effect, also called *karma* or the karmic result. That effect is like a seed that eventually bears fruit in the present life or in a future life.

Karma is not fate. One's current plight and status in life is the direct result of one's own action in this life and in previous lives. There is a direct cause and effect link between past behavior and current plight, just as your early morning indigestion is the consequence of the previous night's overindulgence in poorly selected menu items. The Hindu doctrine of reincarnation assumes that humans have at one time or another existed as a lower form of life, such as an animal, insect, or possibly a plant. Hinduism also recognizes grades of human life, from exceptionally affluent, pleasant, and free down to painfully limited and degraded. Rebirth can move in either direction.

According to Hindu doctrine, this process continues unceasingly unless one is fortunate enough to achieve the ultimate goal of liberation, a release from the endless of *samsura* cycle of rebirths. The *atman* becomes one with the underlying reality of all called *Brahman*. Then, there is no separate self to be reborn. One has achieved immortality, a deathless state called *moksha*, meaning the freedom from rebirth.

The faithful Hindu seeks to end the separation of the individual self with Brahman, the underlying reality of all. This illusion of separate identity is the cause of rebirth. Systems of yoga teach practitioners to conquer desire by asserting control of the mind and body. The *Bhagavad Gita*, the best-known Hindu text and composed in the 100 C.E. to 400 C.E. period, emphasized two paths to liberation from cycles of rebirth: the disciplined performance of duty without any self-serving regard for the favorable fruits of action and the offering of every action and the entire self to Krishna in love. For a Hindu to accept duty (*dharma*) means to live one's life in accord with one's social class and one's stage in life. Interestingly, no practices can be said to be universal for all Hindus. Families and social roles are different from various classes. There are many ways to be a faithful Hindu.

The Buddhist Worldview

Buddhism is a major reform version of Hinduism, and the Buddha accepted the Hindu idea of *samsara*, believing that birth follows death. He rejected the notion of a soul, an unchanging spiritual reality, but he accepted the concept of rebirth. Like the Hindus, he saw the cycle of rebirths as a prison to be escaped. The Buddha came to be less pessimistic than many in his old religion, for he believed that a righteous person, regardless of the person's caste, could achieve escape within one's lifetime from suffering rebirth. Furthermore, it was not necessary to follow the Hindu scriptures, the priests, or the rigors of asceticism. By concentrating on the Four Noble Truths, a woman or a man could attain release from suffering in this life.

And how can an individual be reborn if there is no soul? Buddhism holds that while there is no soul the important elements of personality that provide the essence of an individual can re-unite and thus continue from one lifetime to another. Buddhism

offers the analogy of a flame passing from one candle to another; the candles are separate, but only one flame passes between each candle.

As within Hinduism and Jainism, the principle of *karma* is crucially important to
Buddhists. In Hinduism and Jainism, *karma* works automatically. It clings to the soul as
it passes from life to life in reincarnation. Fidelity to duty and good deeds bring blessings,
such as higher birth, wealth, and intelligence; bad actions produce karma that brings
the opposite, including even rebirth into animal and insect life-forms. Understanding
the impact of *karma* within Buddhism is a little more complicated, but it is believed to
accompany and affect elements of the personalities that reappear in later lifetimes. The
goal for the Buddhist is escaping the cycle of change and reincarnation and eventually
reaching *nirvana*, an indescribable existence that marks the end of rebirth.

Despite minor differences in doctrine, the concept of rebirth has been a powerful
one in the major religions of the East. The Jains believe that spirits are constantly being
reborn in various forms. A spirit can move itself up and down the scale of rebirth,
as well as free itself entirely from this cyclical chain. Jains traditionally believe that
superhuman beings exist in realms of the universe above the earth and that they are
subject to *karma* and change. When the *karma* that brings rebirth to gods runs out,
according to Jainism, these deities will be reborn in bodies on earth. The goal is to
become liberated spirits and subsequently experience a state of total freedom. And
thus, whether one is Hindu, Buddhist, Jain, or, most likely, some adherent to any other
eastern religion, one is a living being, existing as a cluster of innumerable *karmas* from
the timeless past, persisting in the present as the contemporary manifestation of a
vast, long-flowing river of *karma*. And that river will keep flowing through eternity.

Popular Acceptance in the Contemporary World

The idea of reincarnation has made resurgence in many new religious movements, such as New Age and Scientology. Some popular New Age authors have discussed their beliefs that they experienced adventures in some glamorous former lives
such as royalty or as a loyal knight for a great king. The New Age worldview does not
allow for humans being burdened with a serious sin problem, thus any talk of salvation is meaningless. And Jesus had to die on the cross because there was so much bad
karma on the earth at the time that the planet was in danger of self-destruction. Much
like the doctrine of Eastern religion, New Agers believe that reincarnation must continue until the soul reaches perfection, eventually leading to one's uniting with God. In
the doctrine of Scientology, every human being in his or her true identity is a *thetan*,
an immortal spirit that goes from one body to another through reincarnation over tril-
lions of years of existence.

On today's university scene, many students accept reincarnation as reality. To some, reincarnation seems to explain child prodigies wherein special pre-schoolers can perform classical music flawlessly, solve challenging math problems, or easily master a difficult foreign language. For example, Mozart wrote a sonata when he was four and an opera when he was seven. Do we attribute such amazing performance by children to an accidental group of genes or to the possibility of some "carry-over" from a genius of past generations?

Others see life in a former body as the only way to explain the phenomenon of *déjà vu*, the sense of having been to a place previously even though your logical self knows you are visiting a location (maybe a new place on the globe) for the first time. And why is there only a one-way immortality? Why have people in the West readily accepted the idea of a life *after* death, but discarded the idea of a life *before* birth? And rather than a person losing identity in so many reincarnations, some argue, our true identity will not be lost any more than a good actor loses personal identity by playing many roles and wearing many costumes over a lifetime. How intriguing the arguments from speculation!

Can a Biblical Case Be Made for Reincarnation?

The Christian message clashes mightily with this ancient Eastern doctrine. The Judeo-Christian worldview is rooted first and foremost in biblical teaching. And the teaching of Holy Scripture is clearly against the doctrine of reincarnation—or is it? The vast majority of Christians reject reincarnation as taught in Eastern religions. The anonymous author of Hebrews in the New Testament informs us that all human beings have an appointment with death and that immediately following cessation of human life is judgment before God (9:27). The doctrine of reincarnation seems to violate common sense and basic educational psychology—how can one be reincarnated to learn lessons to live better in another body if the person has no definite memory of his or her former life (or lives)? The doctrine of reincarnation also denigrates the value of the body. Rather than seeing the body as a gift from God capable of pleasurable experiences, the body is viewed negatively as a prison for a soul seeking liberation and as an instrument of bad behavior.

On the other hand, what might we make of the fact that literally billions of people over the centuries have believed that reincarnation does occur after the death of a woman or man? Quite possibly, over the many centuries of history there have been more people who espoused the notion of reincarnation than people who accepted the Christian doctrine of resurrection of the body into a transformed, immortal body. Would it not be unspeakable arrogance on the part of Christians to dismiss an idea without examining it when innumerable people in the East since the sixth century B.C.E. have clutched the idea tenaciously?

Back to our question: can any Scripture in the Bible be marshaled in support of reincarnation? Surprisingly, yes, though let's clearly state at the outset that the evidence is both scant and circumstantial. Jesus nowhere affirmed reincarnation. On the other hand, some point out, Jesus nowhere denied it. On an occasion where Jesus asked his disciples, "Who do men say that the Son of Man is?" The answers of John the Baptist, Elijah, and Jeremiah were thrown out (Mt. 16:14). Is it strange that Jesus did not reply, "Don't be talking nonsense!"? On another occasion, Jesus seems to identify Elijah and John the Baptist as the same person (Mt. 17:9-13). On still another occasion, a man born blind was brought to Jesus with the question, "Master, who did sin, this man or his parents that he was born blind?" (Jn. 9:1). If this man could possibly have faced the consequence of his sin and yet had been born blind, then would not the sin have been committed in a previous life?

Those who search the Bible for clear evidence that it teaches reincarnation or accepts it as reality will come up empty-handed. The Bible is an immense collection of religious material covering numerous subjects and composed and compiled over many centuries by many authors. The ancient worldview outside of Judaism and Christianity easily accepted reincarnation of souls as fact. And yet the Bible neither accepts nor discusses the topic. The two or three incidents we have cited may be simply idiomatic expressions understood more easily in first century Palestine than in twenty-first century America. John the Baptist did indeed exemplify the courage and prophetic boldness of Elijah. And Jesus did also exemplify the prophetic courage and forthrightness of Israel's best-known prophets. Striking comparisons and analogies can be drawn from leaders in any field, and they constitute slender threads to hold the weighty doctrine of reincarnation or transmigration of individual souls into new bodies.

THE HOPE WITHIN A CHRISTIAN WORLDVIEW

The exact nature of the afterlife will forever remain one of the greatest mysteries of human existence. There is little attempt by biblical writers to describe life after death. It is "being with the Lord," and "departing to be with Christ which is far better" (1 Thess. 4:17; Phil. 1:23). And the precise order of events slated to occur after a person dies has been the subject of many a book, sermon, debate, and printed pamphlet.

The Christian concept of life after death is one of joyful anticipation and hope. We have one life to live. Though we are not born as sinners, inevitably we make some wrong moral choices. For some of us, our wrong choices are grievously hurtful to others and ourselves. Our need is a moral and spiritual transformation, becoming a new person.

And thus we are "born again," a vivid metaphor that means we have made a decision to forsake all that was sinful in our past and inaugurate a new beginning in our lives. Compared with the holiness of God, our sins are hurtful enough to earn God's death penalty. Yet, by his grace we are given salvation that we do not earn. Entrance into the glory of heaven and God's presence is not earned by our good deeds, however virtuous or commendable—such admission is a gift granted to those who entrust their lives to Jesus as God's Son and follow his teaching as his disciple.

For the Christian, there is no cycle of birth and rebirth. One is not born with a body that bears the penalties for sins and misdeeds in a former life. Our individuality is a reality, not a cruel illusion. There is but one "new birth." And especially for those who have been marred in sinful behavior, broken relationships, and harmful addictions, this new birth carries such a positive connotation and is much to be desired. As we have noted in historic Eastern religions, the cycle of rebirth is a degrading and frustrating phenomenon from which to be liberated. In Eastern teaching, one has no choice about reincarnation. A person can move backward as well as forward on the wheel of rebirth, but the soul is bound to the revolving wheel through *karma*

In biblical teaching, clearly an individual can refuse to be born again. There is no compulsion about God. Our Father in heaven will not have conscripts in his heavenly abode. If people choose to turn their backs on God and push past the cross of Christ, which he allowed to be erected as a barrier to stop people from going to their own destruction, then he permits all of us to go "to our own place." And heaven is not simply a place of peaceful emptiness as in *nirvana*. Deliverance for the Christian is not deliverance *from* life—it is deliverance *into* life, life in the presence and fullness of God. Revelation, the last book in the Bible, does not depict heaven in terms of the Islamic view of a sensuous paradise where a person's every physical appetite will be satiated. By contrast, heaven is an environment quite unlike anything we have ever experienced in terms of both eternal rest from earthly concerns and eternal praise and fellowship with the Father.

The Christian worldview inspires a different vision about life. For some, a Christian commitment inspires a life of sacrificial service to others—in schools, public service, hospitals, health care facilities, churches, and foreign missions, just to name a few areas. For many others, commitment to Christ means simply living and working as "salt" and "light" in one's family and in careers and professions. Some religious people join causes such as saving the environment, fighting poverty, or saving the "unborn" from abortion. And the good deeds which are done by the Christian—such as giving drink to the thirsty and food to the hungry, clothing the indigent, visiting convicts who are incarcerated, and ministering comfort and support to those who are sick—are done simply because such service was the ministry of Christ and because Christians truly care about other people (see Mt. 25:31-46).

By contrast, those living under the illusion of a wheel of rebirth and reincarnation may be "called" just to get through life and on to the next life, or indeed to "renounce" this life and live in anonymity and austerity in hopes of a better existence the next go-around. The Roman Catholic sister known as Mother Teresa, and not a Hindu guru, was the one who established hospitals for the dying on the streets of Calcutta. One insight into being a Christian is that the Spirit of Christ dwells within the only physical body we will ever possess (Col 1:27; Rom. 8:9), and that indwelling drives us to invest ourselves in the same ministry that Jesus began some twenty centuries earlier.

Devotional Reflection

Life! That is exactly what we all desire and what seems so hard to discover. Isn't every worldview about living in some way? Whether a person is resigned to a life of mere survival or determined to obtain the proverbial "good life" or the "self-actualization" at the pinnacle of psychologist Abraham Maslow's triangle, we are all reaching, scurrying, or burrowing in order to obtain life of some type. We build businesses, get jobs, create communities, set goals, form family units, seek recreation, and save for our advanced age. We do it all in the name of building a life.

Yet, the greatest, deepest dimension of life is the spiritual one. How interesting that Jesus never once made the claim, "I have come to bring you a new religion." Jesus entered our human realm of existence to bring us life—an abundant life (Jn. 10:10). He assured that he constituted life and those who are united with him then share in his life. And eternal life begins in the "here and now" for the followers of Jesus, for "eternal life" is not about length of life but about depth and quality of life.

Trusting that God gives us life through Jesus means we need not demand some architectural blueprint of heaven's dimensions or some virtual reality experience on the distant shore. All the eloquent sermons, all the stirring poetry, and all the traditional hymns that speak of heaven in terms of real estate or weather conditions cannot begin to capture the essence of a life God prepares for those who open their hearts and lives to his grace.

And it matters not whether we can answer everyone's questions about immortality. We are not called to refute claims about reincarnation or any other tenet of various religions. We are invited to embrace life as God chooses to grant it.

Prayer: Dear God, we acknowledge you as the source of life and that you sent your Son so that we could experience life in great abundance. We thank you for the gift of human life and for all the rich meaning and joy this life can bring to us. While life can also bring us great pain and agony, we thank you that we need not worry about repeating lives of drudgery over and over again until some century we just may get it right. Thank you for your grace that spares us from the compulsion to perform endless good deeds and gives us life now and an even greater measure of eternal life in a world without end. Through Jesus. Amen.

18

Practical Religion in a Fortune Cookie—Finding Rhythm, Balance, and Presence

B usy. Hectic. Stressful. Rat race. Just trying to stay ahead. Out of kilter. Out of sync. Running on empty. Continual quest for the American dream. Swimming with the sharks. Trying to keep my head above the water.

Surely you recognize these words as describing life in the USA in this twenty-first century. Some of these words or expressions may apply to your own life. Sometimes we may wonder if there is much within the Bible that can give us specific counsel in dealing with some of our stresses in the business and professional world and within our family life and personal relationships. And it surely seems unlikely that any teaching or insight from the ancient Eastern worldview can offer anything practical to an individualistic, high-energy, high-tech, competitive western society. Or is it so unlikely?

Let's reconsider the ancient sages from the East. If the word "sage" is new to you, let's apply the term to men and women who address how we live and who combine religious inspiration and extraordinary insight into the human condition. The root word for sage is the Latin *sapiens*, meaning "wise." We may just find that these Eastern sages, though living centuries ago, understood the human condition better than many people today. Much of their wisdom, especially that of Confucius, has been compressed into brief statements printed on narrow strips of paper and inserted into fortune cookies.

If we remain attentive and wise, we just may find more practical religious doctrine in fortune cookies than in the ever-flowing opinions of popular preachers. And at least our quest here will provide the opportunity to introduce some philosophers and teachers that we have not yet discussed.

The Tao

China honors two sages as founders of its religions. Lao-Tzu, who lived in the sixth century B.C.E., is the more mysterious sage of the two. Legend holds that he was a bureaucrat known by a nickname variously translated as "Old Master," "Old Boy," or "Old Philosopher." As an old man, Lao-Tzu had become so disgusted with bureaucratic life that he quit his position to pursue virtue in a friendlier environment. The keeper of the Han-Ku Pass recognized him and urged him to compose a book before he totally withdrew from social life. Honoring this request, Lao-Tzu produced the small (5,000-word) book known today as *Tao te Ching* or *The Classic of the Way and the Power (Virtue)*. After the *Analects* of Confucius, the *Tao te Ching* is the most influential book in Chinese history and is claimed to be second only to the Bible in the number of translations available in English. Lao-Tzu's teaching and writing perhaps preceded the enlightenment of Siddhartha Gautama. Confucius (551-479 B.C.E.) is the more widely known sage and is thought to have been a contemporary of the Buddha.

For our western minds, the *Tao* (or *Dao*; we may use these terms interchangeably) seems too vague and obscure. *Tao* means "way" or "path." Indeed, *Tao* cannot be precisely defined or named. It is the mysterious, impersonal, cosmic power present in all human experiences. *Tao* is also understood as the source of all existence, the way or path of the universe, the principle of all things, even the moral law. Is this great Chinese sage attempting to identify the God of the Judeo-Christian worldview? Regardless, the sage comes to deal with the force and unchanging dimension of nature more than with a personal deity. *Dao* is seen as the "Mother" of all living things and Daoism requires a response of the whole person. Meditation and contemplation provide quiet and effective ways of intuiting the "way" or "path."

In ancient Eastern cosmologies, all events and elements are perceived as harmoniously interconnected. Heaven is not radically separated from earth. There are two opposing forces that continually interact. *Yin* is weak, negative, destructive, and dark; *yang* is positive, strong, light, and constructive. Heaven *(yang)* and earth *(yin)* exist in perpetually harmonious balance. "Equilibrium is the great foundation of the world," Confucius once declared, "and harmony its universal path." The *Tao te Ching* focuses on this harmony of opposites within the peaceful flow of the *Tao* (or *Dao*). Beneath phenomenal changes in the natural order, there is a relentless flow or movement that may not be visible or fully grasped, but it influences the process of changes that can be observed. The way of true *Tao* is a peaceful harmony of opposites.

CONFUCIUS

Whether called Master King, Kongfuzi, or Confucius, this great Chinese sage is definitely a historical figure who, over the process of centuries, became a legendary hero. As a young man he was a teacher who sought high political office so that he could enact governmental reforms. As he observed widespread social decline, he promoted reform based on benevolence, custom, and the cultivation of high moral standards. Despite his failures as a political reformer, Confucius is still acclaimed as one of the great teachers of all time. Students of philosophy have drawn comparisons of Confucius with Socrates—both were humane, witty, complicated, confident, modest, diverse in intellectual interests, and committed to human dignity and welfare. Each disliked hypocrites; each liked to challenge students. The wisdom of Socrates is found in many of the dialogues of Plato and a collection of Confucius' conversations is found in the *Analects*, the single most influential book of Asian philosophy.

Confucius possessed a fundamental belief—humans by nature are good. Despite the fact that this public servant/teacher was surrounded all his life by neglect of education, discord in families, social injustices, and cruel acts of inhumanity, he still believed in the basic goodness of men and women. And how can humans learn to behave with moral goodness? In answering this question, Confucius added a second great principle: every society needs a model human being who will set a noble example for others to follow. Confucius called this model a *junzi (chun-tzu)*, which translators into English call "gentleman" or "superior man." Even here, the meaning may not seem specific. From Confucius' teaching, we can know that the moral role model, the *junzi*, is just the opposite from a person who is petty, selfish, narrow-minded, contentious, or aggressive. This philosopher believed in transmitting the very best in traditional culture to future generations.

Confucius believed in the power of meaningful relationships. He believed the principle of harmony should rule the home, the society, and the empire. He spoke of the famous "Five Relationships" between superior and inferior persons—ruler-subordinate; husband-wife; elder brother-younger brother; elder friend-junior friend; and father-son. There are proper and appropriate rituals and conduct in each relationship. In essence, it is the quality of being a genuine human being to all other human beings in our lives. The proper man and woman seek the good of others and of self and keep every relationship within balance. This balance is the way of *chung-yung,* the *Golden Mean*, and is translated as moderation, normality, and the universal moral law. Students in moral philosophy may remember that Aristotle of ancient Greece made the Golden Mean the central standard for establishing moral virtue between the extremes of excess and deficiency.

The excellent role model acts in compassion for others at all times. He always seeks the good of others as well as self. Tsu-kung once asked Confucius, "Is there a single word which can be a guide to conduct throughout one's life?" And the Master said, "It is perhaps the word *shu*. Do not impose on others what you yourself do not desire."

Confucius was clearly a teacher in political philosophy and applied ethics. Though he has been venerated in China and elsewhere for generations, we must not think of his work as religion. Though he believed in heaven and spoke of praying to heaven, he actually spoke little of heaven and even less of a higher power. Confucius enjoyed religious rituals and participated in worship, but his devotion was directed toward humanist ideals and love for Chinese classics. In the *Analects* we are told "the Master did not talk about marvels, feats of strength, irregularities, gods." When he was asked about serving ghosts and gods, Confucius said, "Until you can serve men, how can you serve the ghosts?" And when asked about death he said, "Until you know about life how can you know about death?"

Lao-Tzu and Confucius Standing Beside Jesus

When Lao-Tzu stands beside Jesus, what do we see? Though these men lived several centuries apart, both were great teachers of an Axial period of philosophy—a time frame of several centuries in which the greatest ideas of all time emerged and around which all other great ideas began to rotate (referenced with more explanation in chapter 3). Both great teachers stood in opposition to the popular cultures of their day, but only with Jesus did this opposition take a toxic turn. Lao-Tzu's wisdom urged disciples to see Ultimate Reality as some vague, impersonal entity requiring resignation and accommodation; Jesus declared and demonstrated that Ultimate Reality was intimately personal and gracious. Both call for a self-forgetfulness that allows the Spirit (God's Spirit in one case and the *Dao* in the other case) to move through individuals and develop stellar virtues we may never have imagined. While Lao-Tzu spoke of the Way and the need to be in harmony with the Way, Jesus claimed to *be* the actual Way to eternal life and to the Father. Interestingly, one of the most frequently employed names for the first century disciples of Jesus was "the Way."

Lao-Tzu and Jesus would surely concur that there are various compelling forces and emotions in our lives that must be harmonized. Jesus could share joy and laughter at a wedding feast and could weep at the gravesite of a beloved friend. He could show compassion for a woman who had been humiliated by a group of self-righteous adult males because of her embarrassing sin, and he could level righteous indignation against the social injustice and stubborn recalcitrance of certain Pharisaical religious leaders of his generation. Both great teachers would concur that there is a sense of paradox about life on a higher plane. Jesus spoke paradoxically about those wanting to become great by first living as servants; that those who seek to gain the entire world can lose it; that those who strive to be first shall be last. The apostle Paul spoke of the message of the cross being foolishness to those who think themselves to be wise. He also spoke of God producing spiritual strength through human weakness. Sometimes it is only through weakness that God's grace and power are experienced (2 Cor. 12:10).

Just as the Old Testament books of Proverbs and Ecclesiastes are considered wisdom literature of the ancient Hebrews, so the *Tao te Ching* is considered part of the wisdom literature of ancient Asians. Lao-Tzu and biblical writers would surely agree on the need for rhythm in the flow of our lives. While we do not seek negative experiences that produce pain and sadness, these learning experiences compose reality that must be harmonized with good and positive experiences. Life must be embraced in its totality. The author of Ecclesiastes reminds us of the cyclical flow of human and social experiences in our lives:

> There is a time for everything,
> And a season for every activity under heaven:
> A time to be born and a time to die,
> A time to plant and a time to uproot,
> A time to kill and a time to heal,
> A time to tear down and a time to build,
> A time to weep and a time to laugh,
> A time to mourn and a time to dance,
> A time to scatter stones and a time to gather them,
> A time to embrace and a time to refrain,
> A time to search and a time to give up,
> A time to keep and a time to throw away,
> A time to tear and a time to mend,
> A time to be silent and a time to speak,
> A time to love and a time to hate,
> A time for war and a time for peace. (3:1-8)

And when Confucius stands beside Jesus, what do we see? Of course, we see two of the greatest teachers who have ever lived. Confucius has influenced the Eastern world almost as much as Jesus has influenced the Western world. Actually, all three teachers we have compared in this study attracted their own second-generation disciples who wrote the words of their masters and shared their messages. Jesus, of course, gave his great commission to all his disciples to carry the gospel into the entire world, teaching and baptizing those who were brought to faith; the narratives of four evangelists who told the story of Jesus were accepted into the New Testament canon. Chuang Tzu (369-286 BCE) developed Taoist thought in a text that might actually predate *Tao Te Ching*. Mencius (372-289 BCE) incorporated Confucius' teachings in his own book that became completely accepted as orthodox Confucianism.

Both great teachers spoke of heaven, though Jesus spoke of heaven in terms of his Father's abode while Confucius treated heaven as something of a personal deity Jesus spoke of salvation from humans' sins, whereas Confucius did not label human failure as sin. Both saw the potential for goodness within all human beings. Both knew the reality of personal and social evil, and both were concerned with instruction in good morality and ethical teachings. Nowhere in Confucian thought is there support for the Christian concept of the essential fallen human nature or the pervasive influence of sin in all human thought and behavior.

While Confucius emphasized the need for good role models, Jesus himself served as the ultimate role model for his followers; the apostle Paul urged Christian disciples to be "imitators of Christ." Both Confucius and Jesus taught their disciples to be eager to learn. Jesus spoke of himself as being truth, and the Confucian tradition had already emphasized the imperative for learners to follow truth wherever it might lead. Jesus and Confucius taught the virtue of compassion.

And both great teachers taught that basic, common-sensible moral criterion that considers the needs and feelings of others and which has become known as the Golden Rule. The essence of this moral rule addresses the question, "How will my action affect the other person?" While Jesus offers a more positive rendition of the Golden Rule, the Confucian version, interestingly, is stated in negative terms: "Do not do unto others what you would not wish done to yourself." Some ethicists have even argued that the Confucian rendition, *shu*, is a more realistic moral rule that helps followers to consider actions from the other person's viewpoint.

Devotional Reflection

We began this chapter with reminders of the hectic stress and anxiety so many of us face. We attempt almost impossible balancing acts among our responsibilities in careers, family, education, and some semblance of a social life. Still within an Eastern worldview, we move over to Buddhism to conclude with *tathata*, meaning "thatness," "thusness," or "suchness." Even those English words are invented, of course, for a literal translation of *tathata* seems impossible. The concept is crucially important, however, for our time and our culture.

Tathata represents the concept that reality is revealed in each moment that we savor and cherish relationships, beauty, change, and patterns. Because each moment is not the same as any other moment, each good moment can be observed and appreciated as it passes. And each difficult and challenging moment can be observed for what lessons that moment teaches us about ourselves and life in general. No good moment and no good relationship should go unappreciated. And no pain or failed relationship should pass without learning a new lesson or reinforcing an old one. *Tathata* suggests that we can see wonder in everyday life. We know that we are experiencing "thatness" or "suchness" of reality and say to ourselves, "Yes, that's it; that's the way things are; this moment will never happen again." And at that moment, we acknowledge that life is both richly meaningful and vulnerably fragile.

Even simple, everyday occurrences reveal the nature of reality. We may experience "thatness" or "suchness" on the first crisp drop in temperature after a long, hot summer. Or it might be when random elements come together, such as a group of deer suddenly appearing at sunset while you are hiking with a friend on a nature trail. Or it may be the moment you see a humming bird hovering near a bird feeder or a butterfly landing on a flower petal.

Tathata is experienced as your heart is touched and eyes become misty when you witness a group of soldiers returning home from foreign combat soil and being reunited with their loved ones. It might be experienced as you witness the birth of a new baby, especially if that new arrival is your own child or grandchild. It is experienced when you watch that child or grandchild being baptized into Christ, taking first communion, performing in a musical recital or a school drama, competing in an athletic event, or being honored for academic achievement. It can be experienced when you are sitting beside a beloved relative or devoted friend when that person passes from this life into eternity. Obviously, some moments are so sobering they are best observed with prayerful silence.

The Christian believes that God can make each significant moment a special event in the mosaic of our lives. An old, familiar saying provides an appropriate conclusion: The past is history and cannot be changed. Tomorrow is a mystery and there are no guarantees. Today is a gift from God—that's why it's called the present!

Prayer: God, our Father, thank you so much for the lives of great teachers who have wielded such great influence for good for so many centuries. We know that truth can emanate from many sources, but that all truth is your truth which you have placed in the hearts and minds of many men and women. May we heed the counsel of the sages, while never forgetting that the fear of the Lord is the very beginning of wisdom. Through Jesus, our world's greatest role model and greatest teacher about you. Amen.

19

Continuing Story— Symbols, Rituals, and Ceremonies

T he lights were dimmed or turned off, except for the lights above the baptistery. A minister wearing waders stood in waist deep water and extended his hand to a woman or man who moved to the center of the watery tank. As a pre-schooler, I, along with some of my peers, crept up toward the front of the assembly to catch an unobstructed view. The minister raised his hand and ritualistically announced to the whole congregation the authority and purpose of the immersion that followed immediately. To my young mind, such baptisms, along with observing the believers partake of the Lord's Supper, were the most intriguing experiences in a church house. The power of something ritualistic and symbolic was so great that I began a joyful anticipation of the time in which I would be old enough to personally experience both baptism and regular communion.

The power of rites can be used to mark momentous occasions, such as holidays, births, marriages, and deaths. Thus, obviously, rites may be based on calendars or rites of passage within the human life cycle. Weddings and funerals, birthday celebrations, graduations, all serve to state or reinforce a story and the expectations that are to be met after the ritual has concluded. A wedding marks the union of a man and woman. A funeral provides an occasion for mourning the loss of life, honoring the value of life lived for whatever space of time, allowing friends to comfort the bereaved, and bringing closure to the deceased one's existence on earth.

The Role of Symbolism in Worldviews

Worldviews present concepts of reality, and most speak of the sacred. Yet worldviews are so varied in their teaching and many of the teachings express a deep complexity. The most profound concepts within a worldview or religion are inextricably connected with symbols that express them. We all know the function of a symbol as something that stands for an object, being (human or divine), or concept, and its use is intended to elicit an appropriate response. A symbol is fairly concrete, universal, and often ordinary, but can be employed to express something of great complexity and intensity. Clearly, worldviews and religions express ideas and insights symbolically.

One of the greatest blessings of being human is that we are able to engage in symbolic behavior, and our use of symbolism can be simple and almost elementary or it can be intricate and sophisticated. Perhaps the earliest religious concepts and insights were first communicated through the symbolic images of the sacred that are represented in cave paintings in the late Paleolithic cave systems; given the paintings are prehistoric, meaning that no writing explains them, we may not know for certain if they express religious or aesthetic concerns. Because religious and other worldview concepts involve the supernatural and intangible, they cannot help but be expressed symbolically. Symbols point beyond themselves to something else. They transcend the barriers of a single language, offer a message that can be instantly communicated, and often cut right to the deepest emotions of the worshiper, seeker, or student. Over the course of sacred history, a great repository of religious paintings, pictures, and literature has been built.

A rite is a solemn or ceremonial act. Ritual is the observance of rites or a system of rites. In religion, rites are usually believed to have been established in some way by the deity being worshiped, either by direct instruction, by example of a respected role model of the faith, and/or by the needs of the worshipers. The rituals, feasts, and holidays in any worldview constitute a powerful, sensory experience for keeping alive the beliefs within a faith community and bind the members to one another and to cosmic meaning. In contemporary Western cultures, handshaking may be the simplest ritual that involves little emotional meaning or commitment other than a desire between two people to be congenial instead of apathetic or hostile. In earlier generations, men would tip their hats, soldiers would salute, women would bow or curtsy, and even babies and toddlers are taught to "wave bye-bye." The earliest Christians were instructed to practice the "holy kiss" among their greetings with each other, thus imparting a deeper degree of mutual warmth and affirmation.

In the broadest sense, ritual is simply repeating an action that has some kind of significance beyond the action itself. Rituals are practiced in every human community, thus fostering social cohesion. The abundant political rites and rituals in our culture are familiar to most of us. The recitation of the oath of office by the newly inaugurated chief executive, usually in January following a national election (and occasionally following the untimely death of a predecessor), constitutes a ritual watched around the nation and much of the western world. Independence Day, each July Fourth, is a special national holiday that celebrates the nation's independence as colonies from a mother country and the founding of a new nation. The international Olympics are also conducted quadrennially, and they are also opened and closed with much colorfully elaborate pomp and ceremony. And perhaps the most familiar seasonal ritual in America is Thanksgiving.

Let's appreciate worldview rites and rituals as part of a grand story in which people are drawn to be participants. In fact, rites and ceremonies facilitate the narrating of stories. Most historians and philosophers will call these grand stories myths. A myth certainly need not connote deliberate deception by those who share it. A myth is a "bigger than life" story in which grand lessons are taught and deep mysteries of the world are communicated. The historical reality and details of the story are insignificant compared to the central lesson to be passed on to future generations. One cannot imagine a loving father taking his young children to a performance of the *Lion King* and, then, upon exiting the theatre, immediately asking them, "Do you think that story is really true?" So much truth and insight are shared through the power of myth. Most religious language is richly poetic and metaphoric in nature, and the stories are not verifiable in the same sense that scientific hypotheses are tested.

As we survey some of the major rites, rituals, and symbols throughout history, we may be struck with both the rich variety in style but also with the similarity of symbols representing the cherished concepts of the world's various faiths. Water, for example, is used in all kinds of religious rituals; fire and ashes can be infused with special meaning. And our globe is dotted with hundreds of sacred places and sites—natural phenomena such as mountains or rock formations or human constructions, all of which inspire a sense of awe in the devout pilgrims who visit the sites. After all, the master symbols of religion are not always intended to provide information for outsiders as much as to inspire commitment and devotion among believers.

Tribal Sacred Symbols

There have existed, perhaps, thousands of tribes, each with its own sacred stories and rituals. And the phenomenon is not simply historical—tribal and shamanic religious practice (recall that the shaman was a tribal religious leader, often viewed as a medicine man or woman) continues in our time and on every continent. The majority of these tribes identify a strategic struggle between the powers of good and evil, and both forces are symbolized in a variety of ways and dealt with in a variety of rituals. Remember that religions which cannot rely on the published and written word find artistic expressions in rites, rituals, chants, dance, statues and other artifacts to be highly significant in maintaining their faith and capturing the stories of their tradition.

Totemism, the use of animal figures that are revered for their symbolic meaning, is common to the various tribal societies on all the continents. These cultures go back to prehistoric times, but still exist today in areas where education and urbanization have not penetrated. These tribal societies are led by shamans (usually a male), who are expected to interact with supernatural forces on behalf of the tribe; the role is not unlike a priest in other religions. The shaman relies on visions for spiritual direction, and his drum—traditionally festooned with colorful symbols of the forces he may encounter in the spirit world—aids him in entering ecstatic trances. The shaman's ritual may also include use of a decorative rattle. Tribal spiritual and ritual leaders typically don symbolic clothing for their ceremonies, once again, not unlike leaders in other religions. There is much variety here and it is all too easy to stereotype tribal people and their leaders. All the drums, masks, rattles, statues, and other objects that are important in tribal religions may seem to us as curiosities to be collected and placed in anthropological museums, but we should appreciate their importance to the tribal cultures that produced them. They represent the human quest to probe the mystery of human existence and life beyond ordinary boundaries.

Tribal religion honors the power of the natural world, especially animal life. Among some African tribes, the speed of the antelope represents the elusiveness of the spirits. Because Native American hunters and fishers depended on the generosity of animals and fish, they honored their prey; offending the prey could bring starvation. These earliest Americans esteemed highly the birds, but have especially revered the eagle as the natural master of the sky; feathers were symbols appearing among all peoples of the Americas. The bear is respected for its strength and ferocity. Chickens can play a visible role in the healing ritual of an African medicine man or woman.

These totemic figures may be symbolically displayed in totem poles, constructed with carved representations of the spirits that are important to the tribe in hierarchical order. Great mountains and monumental rock formations have symbolized sacred powers and concepts. Many of the tribal religions teach that the spirits of ancestors are ever-present in the world and demand respect and homage from their descendants. All tribal traditions incorporate regular performances of ritual ceremonies and each component in the ritual possesses deep significance in the expression of their most sacred beliefs.

Mediterranean and European Symbols and Rituals

Ancient peoples of the Mediterranean and European societies were also awed by the forces of the natural world which impacted their everyday lives, but they went further in developing a rich pantheon of deities which controlled both nature and one's personal destiny. Many of the deities of these civilizations were envisioned as leading fascinating lives and their religious symbolism personified their most dominant traits. These deities, it was believed, controlled all-important aspects of daily life.

Little wonder that the creator-sun god Re was the chief deity of the ancient Egyptians—the sun was the dominant force of nature for Egyptians. The pharaohs esteemed themselves to be divine sons of Re. Symbols of the great legend of Osiris and Isis—an intriguing story of murder by drowning in the Nile River, dismemberment and scattering of parts, a recovery of body parts, and the birth of a son named Horus who would avenge his father's death and become a pharaoh—also figure in the more prominent Egyptian stories. The Egyptian sphinx, with its pharaoh's head and lion's body, symbolized protective authority. The pyramids likely symbolized a great cosmic mountain and served as sacred burial sites that safeguarded the bodies and treasures of the society's most revered leaders.

Ancient Greeks were quite creative in developing a rich mythology of their gods. After his defeat of the Titans, Zeus reigned supreme over a host of other deities. And the Romans were content to adopt the Greek pantheon virtually wholesale and simply changed the names to reflect their own preferences. The artists of the ancient Greco-Roman world depicted their deities in an idealized human form. Sculpted depictions of the deities were placed in specially consecrated temples for public worship. The stories of the deities were performed on stage in public theatres, and, in a sense, the productions might be viewed as worship services. The Greeks often combined images of animal with the human. The goddess Athena was frequently depicted in the company of a serpent, the symbol of wisdom; the owl, with ability to see in the dark, symbolized the power of wisdom to penetrate the darkness of ignorance. Athena planted the first olive tree, thus rendering it sacred, and she became the patron goddess of Athens, site of the Parthenon, which is also dedicated to her.

The early northern Europeans, much like Native North Americans, sought to live in close harmony with the natural environment. There was a mysterious, sacred quality to the natural features all about them, especially the forests. Evergreens were especially venerated. Norse mythology featured both a cosmic tree, an evergreen ash called *Yggdrasil*, and a cosmic battle. Thor was the mighty sky deity and warrior with his chariot pulled across the sky by goats and with hammer in hand that symbolized the angry producer of thunder ("the Hurler"). The Celts were awed by the abundance of the natural world and this inspired many of their sacred beliefs, symbols, and ceremonies. They were influenced both by the conquering Romans as well as by Christianity, but the original Celtic cross (distinguished by the circle that surrounds the arms of the cross) is an ancient representation of the dynamic solar wheel.

Megaliths (literally, "large stones") and ancient stone circles could symbolize spiritual meaning. The most spectacular of ancient British stone monuments grouping is located at ancient Stonehenge, in Wiltshire, England. How incredible to imagine how many men and how much time were required to drag each of the huge upright sarsen stones across the countryside and place them in proper position for use as a calendar, a clock, and, most likely a temple for worship of the sun! To be fair, no more incredible than to imagine the construction of the pyramids of ancient Egypt.

Asian and Indian Subcontinent Symbols and Rituals

Some of the most colorful, diverse religious symbolism emerged from the faiths which began in the Indian subcontinent and Asia. These faiths—including Hinduism, Buddhism, Jainism, Sikhism, and Taoism—presage a major transition away from the worship of nature and the reluctant acceptance of the forces of nature and mysterious deities to deep conviction about individual spirituality and internalization of sacred beliefs. There is similarity and sharing of sacred beliefs among these religions and, thus, also a sharing of religious stories and symbols.

The rich, complex system of Hinduism first emerged from a blending of native Indians' religious beliefs and practices with the religious beliefs and practices of conquering Aryans, nomads from the area of Persia who arrived in the Indus Valley thousands of years ago. And the system developed over many centuries of Hindu religious history. Sacred Hindu symbols connected with this trinity (*trimurti*) include the conch shell and solar disk of Vishnu, the trident of Shiva, and the white bull, Nandi, the embodiment of male potency. Hindu depictions of deity seem unlimited in creativity, imagination, design, and color. For example, a human-elephant form symbolizes the Hindu god Ganesha, patron of prosperity and learning. Hindu temples are typically dedicated to one or more deities and are elaborately adorned with symbolism both inside and outside the structure. The cow has been sacred in Hinduism for its valuable role in providing nourishment by its milk and as a symbol of feminine fertility and motherhood. The process of meditation is intended to raise energy through the seven charkas, symbolized as wheels or lotuses. During meditation, specific mantras—phrases of power—should be chanted, and no sound is more sacred or powerful than that of *Om (Aum)*, the primal symbol that heralds the cosmos. The earnestly-sought ritual of being cremated along the banks of the Ganges

River is rooted in the expectation of purification and the enhancement of one's life and status in the next reincarnation.

The worldviews and religions of China and Japan are rich in story, ritual, and symbolism. The dual nature of the universe is symbolized by the yin/yang circle, an image of harmony and interdependence surpassed in recognition, perhaps, only by Christianity's cross and Islam's crescent moon. The Taoist founder, Lao Tzu, is depicted as an elderly wise man who bears a scroll of the *Tao Te Ching* text and riding a water buffalo. In Chinese religion which holds the natural world as sacred, many birds, animals, and plants possess symbolic significance, and jade is associated with immortality. In Japanese religion, fans are regarded as protecting against evil spirits. Mount Fuji (Fujiyama) is the sacred center of the Japanese world and is guarded by the goddess Sengen-Sama.

Buddhism is rich in symbolism that is centered in the Buddha himself and in the principles he taught his followers. The legendary component of Buddhism begins with the narration of the birth of Siddhartha Gautama from the side of his mother, Queen Maya, after a white elephant, carrying a lotus, entered her side. Because Buddhism emerged from Hinduism, the two religions share some symbols; both Hindus and Buddhists, for example, venerate the white elephant, the former for its association with Ganesha. The Buddha's body is often depicted in sculpture and art in a meditation posture, perhaps seated on a lotus throne in the shade of the *bodhi* tree. Elaborate Buddhist images are found in depictions of *bodhisattvas*, compassionate servants who forego nirvana to remain within the cycle of *samsura* (rebirth) in order to help others. Zen Buddhism emerged in Japan with emphasis on spiritual truth encapsulated in the natural world and expressed in the Zen garden, highlighting both nature and meditation. Tibetan Buddhism has numerous symbolic expressions, though the best known one to westerners is embodied in the person of the perpetually reincarnated Dalai Lama (the current one having been exiled from Tibet by the Chinese since 1951, but has discovered a notable career of touring, writing, and speaking).

SYMBOLS AND RITUALS OF RELIGIONS OF THE BOOK

Turning from the plurality of deities in the world all about them, Judaism, Christianity, and Islam worship and serve only one Supreme Being. These religious faiths have been called "religions of the book," for each claims to be founded on, and directed by, a divine revelation from God that was placed in written Scripture and read, studied, and revered by subsequent generations. The term "scripture" is an English word derived from the Latin *scriptura*, meaning "a writing." Scripture is thus a written text, though many sacred texts are collections and editions of stories circulated for centuries in oral form. Keep in mind that most scriptures were handed down orally for many generations, even centuries, before leaders in the religious communities ordered the stories composed in written form for practical purposes. A clear exception is in traditional Islam that specifically teaches the *Qur'an* was dictated to Muhammad without any preceding "oral tradition." (Remember that in the Christian practice, the Bible is rarely treated with the same sense of awe as the *Qur'an*, because Christians look to Jesus as the ultimate Word of God and believe that he embodied divine incarnation when walking amidst humanity.)

Numerous other common experiences are shared by Jews, Christians, and Muslims. All look to the patriarch Abraham as a great father and leader of their faith, considered by all to be the true model of faith and devotion. (They also look to Adam and Eve as, whether literally or figuratively, the first and prototypical human beings.) The moral and spiritual aim of life in all three religions is the restoration of human wills to harmony with the divine will of God. Followers in each great tradition have suffered periods of persecution because of commitment to the faith of their fathers; that persecution included discrimination, cruelty, expulsion, exile, and efforts at extermination. Their sacred stories, rites, and rituals served the purposes of maintaining communion with the one true God as well as keeping the faith alive in the younger generations during the darkest days of each religion's history.

Judaism

The Old Testement is filled with the stories of how the Jews used rituals and symbols to maintain the cherished covenant relationship with Yahweh, their God. In the Genesis narratives, God arched the sky with a rainbow for Noah and his descendants to remember a covenant with all humanity that he would never again destroy the world with a cosmic flood. As a symbol of the covenant God made with Abraham and his descendants as heirs of Canaan (Israel), God commanded that every male be circumcised. The people of Israel continually offered a variety of burnt offerings and other sacrifices to Yahweh; the sacrifice of "pure" animals and birds was a meaningful dimension of Jewish ritual through the centuries until the time of Jesus.

The written name for God as revealed to Moses is one of the most profound Jewish symbols, a tetragrammaton of the Hebrew letters YHWH (with vowels added it becomes "Yahweh"). When the Hebrew nation was wandering through the Sinai wilderness en route to Canaan, the presence of Yahweh was symbolized in the Ark of the Covenant. The Ark was also a repository for the tablets of the Decalogue contained in a gilded wooden box and surrounded by a pair of golden cherubim that symbolized God's love. Once Israel settled in Canaan, the grand temple for worship rites and rituals was built by Solomon in the City of David. When Israel was conquered and led into exile, the traditions of worship and education were maintained in local synagogues. Since ancient times, the most familiar symbol within the great faith of Judaism is the six-pointed Star of David, a symbol which has adorned decorations, publications, clothing, uniforms, and flags throughout the illustrious centuries of Jewish history. As a symbol, the Star of David has many complex interpretations. In modern Israel, the Western Wall possesses meaning far beyond the fact that it is the only part of the Second Temple that was left standing by the Roman Titus, who destroyed Jerusalem in 70 C. E. For centuries it has been a gathering place for lament by practicing Jews for past losses (hence, the "wailing wall") and prayers for the present and future blessing of Israel. Modern pilgrims of both Judaism and Christianity wedge written prayers into the crevices in this massive wall.

The major Jewish festivals celebrate various historical events in their history. The *Sabbat* (Sabbath, from Friday sundown to Saturday sundown) is the weekly observance of communal worship and shared faith that occurs in both the synagogue and the home. The traditional purpose of the Sabbath was a compassionate one: to grant to everyone, including slaves and animals, regular rest from labor. The twelve-month lunar year begins with *Rosh Hashanah* (the New Year) celebration; it recalls the creation of the world and begins by a month of daily blowing of the *shofer* (a ram's horn). *Yom Kippur* (Day of Atonement) falls on the final day of a ten-day period of penitence that is intended to bring reconciliation and restoration between humans and God and among humans; it is the most sacred day of the year and has been traditionally honored by prayer and fasting and as a time to seek forgiveness. *Sukkot* (Festival of Booths) is an annual eight-day fall festival and entails thanksgiving for nature's bounty. *Hanukkah*, the Feast of Dedication, is an early-winter festival of joy. *Purim* celebrates the deliverance of the Jews from a Persian oppressor as narrated in the book of Esther. The *Bar Mitzvah* ("son of the commandments") is celebrated with a ceremony signaling a boy's turning thirteen, his knowledge of Judaic tradition, and willingness to keep God's commands. The *Bat Mitzvah* is an equivalent status reached by girls and thus appropriately celebrated.

Undoubtedly, the best-known Jewish festival is *Pesach* (Passover) which celebrates the exodus of the Israelites from Egyptian bondage. Its most profound feature is the *Seder* (order of worship) conducted in Jewish homes. The *Seder* continues the story of God's gracious deliverance from slavery so that each generation may relive the Exodus experience. A rich, diverse symbolism narrates that story: special prayers, declarations, unleavened bread (*matzah*, the bread of affliction); bitter herbs (signifying enslavement); a nut, apple, wine and cinnamon mixture (reminders of the mortar they mixed); salt water (symbolizing tears); green herbs (representing spring); and roasted bone of a lamb (recalling the blood of the Pascal lamb on their doorposts which identified the Jewish slaves and saved them from the tenth plague of Egypt). Two of the elements of this Passover feast, as most of us recall, made their way into a special commemorative meal for the Christian community.

Christianity

Christianity and Judaism share a common heritage, of course. Christians respect and study the biblical texts which they know as the Old Testament. Since they see Jesus as the long-awaited Messiah and Savior of the world, the symbolism of their faith is drawn first and foremost from the exemplary life and teaching of their Master, whose cruel execution satisfied God's justice in redeeming humanity. Christ's incarnation into a human body, which began with a thrilling birth narrative that combined the ordinariness of a stable for livestock with a glorious announcement by angels in heaven, is celebrated on Christmas Day, December 25. The white dove came to symbolize the coming of the Holy Spirit into Jesus' earthly ministry, confirming the divinity of Jesus as God's Son. At the death of Jesus, the lowly lamb, which symbolized physical weakness and moral innocence and had already played a central role in Jewish rituals, was then clearly identified with Christ.

Jesus himself gave two ordinances to his band of disciples. Those who accept the call to discipleship are initiated into the body of believers by water baptism. In Christianity the rite of baptism tells the story of Jesus reclaiming humanity from sin. A convert makes a confession of faith and expresses belief that Jesus is the Son of God. The believer requests to be baptized. His or her body is lowered into "a watery grave" symbolizing the death and burial of Jesus, paralleling the subject's own choice to die to the sinful life that was known, and is resurrected to a new life. The person is lifted out of the symbolic water grave, to live as a student of a Savior believed to be capable of resurrecting His disciples spiritually and, in God's own time, physically. Both spiritual and physical deaths are conquered by the power of Jesus. No small claim, to be sure! Christians believe that the angels in heaven are rejoicing around God's throne when the baptism ritual is observed here on earth. Surely, rejoicing on earth is a testimony to what they deeply believe when they witness such an event! And Christian worshippers might well lift their hands in praise and gratitude when they praise the Lord for such great salvation!

The other ordinance is a special commemorative meal that has been observed under the names "communion," "Eucharist," and "Lord's Supper." Jesus himself told his disciples the meaning of the two major symbols—the bread representing his body and the cup of wine, the fruit of the vine, representing the blood that he willingly offered in his death for the sins of all humanity. The regular observance of this special meal keeps the story of divine love and atoning sacrifice in the memory bank of each generation of Christ's followers. The "laying on of hands" was a common practice, likely drawn from the example of Jesus, when Christians commissioned others for a special mission or prayed for the healing of the sick.

A varied church tradition incorporated a wide variety of other symbols and ceremonies over the centuries and, in fact, church architecture typically communicates abstract messages. One of the earliest symbols was the fish, which identified secret meeting places of disciples in Roman catacombs. The early generations of Christians remembered that Jesus called his disciples "fishers of men" and the Greek word for fish, *ichthus*, is an acrostic of the Greek term, "Jesus Christ, Son of God, Savior."

Despite the utter simplicity of Christian symbolism and ceremony in the first several generations of church history, Christians of every major branch of Christianity have built magnificent houses of worship and developed elaborate symbolism and ceremonies. No center is more impressive, perhaps, than the church of St. Peter in Rome and St. Peter's Square. The first church of St. Peter was constructed by Emperor Constantine in the fourth century, but it suffered so many fires that a new basilica was ordered in 1506 by Pope Julius II. Michelangelo, the artist who also painted the ceiling in nearby Sistene Chapel, designed the dome. Christianity has inspired a wealth of paintings and sculptures, and Michelangelo's paintings are considered among the elite masterpieces of world art.

Islam

Traditional Islam maintains high respect for such religious leaders and prophets as Abraham, Moses, and Jesus, but Muslims contend that Muhammad was the final and truest prophet, the one who was the mouthpiece for Allah ("the God"). Muhammad, though an historic figure, is rarely depicted in Islamic art, which honors the Old Testament prohibition against "graven images." In recent centuries, some western illustrations of this prophet have been drawn and scenes from his life have been depicted. In honor of the ban on idolatry and graven images, Allah is never depicted in any form in Islamic art. The one theme that has inspired much Islamic art, architecture, and garden design is the theme of paradise. Paradise is both concrete and sensuous.

Perhaps the most popular story in Islam begins with the night journey of Muhammad, traveling on his human-headed horse *al-buraq* ("lightning") from Mecca in Saudi Arabia to Jerusalem's Temple Mount *(Haram)*. There, Muhammad ascended through the seven heavens into the presence of Allah. The grand mosque called the golden Dome of the Rock was built on this site between 688 and 691 and is not only one of the most sacred sites of Islam but also the most identifiable landmark for Jerusalem. The rock is said to bear the imprint of Muhammad's footstep. Medina. also in Saudi Arabia, is another special holy city in Islam. The most significant and sacred city is Mecca, where the cube-shaped *Kaba*, toward which Muslims face when praying, is located. Muslims believe that Allah instructed Abraham and his son Ishmael to erect the *Kaba*, which houses the black stone that Gabriel first gave Adam. The pilgrimage to Mecca is an annual ritual and Muslims are expected to make this visit at least once in their lifetime.

Muslim worship is filled with rich ritual and symbolism. Ideally, five daily prayers are offered at the mosque, a "place of prostration." Worshipers must purify themselves by washing before entering the mosque. Furnishings in the mosque are spartan, with a *minbar* (pulpit) for the sermon on Friday, the *kursi* (a stand for a copy of the *Qu'ran*), carpeted floor or prayer mats for kneeling and bowing in prayer, and sacred decorative art which incorporates the beauty of flowing Arabic calligraphy, abstract geometrical patterns, and floral arabesques. Although typically a prayer carpet is not considered an exhibition of religious art, the symbolic, stylized forms of prayer carpet constitute the artistic equivalent of stained-glass windows in Christian houses of worship.

Id al-Adha, the Feast of Sacrifice or the Great Feast, is the most important feast in the Muslim year. This feast occurs on the day when those on the *haji*, the pilgrimage to Mecca, have returned halfway and make a feast by sacrificing an animal (commemorating the time when Abraham was commanded by God to sacrifice his son, assumed in Islam to be Ishmael). And finally, the best-known symbol associated with Islam today is the *hilal*—the star and crescent—which represents Islamic themes of divinity, sovereignty, concentration, victory, and openness. The crescent moon is claimed to have originated among the grateful citizens of Constantinople (Istanbul) of the fourth century and much later became the symbol of the Ottoman Empire with the pole star with its five points being added around 1800.

Devotional Reflection

Storytelling abounds in rituals, and we need to ask ourselves what story is being kept alive, for what purpose, and what is the effect on both the storytellers and their audiences. To postmoderns seeking to communicate a message from God, the entire Bible is a continuous, if at times disjointed, story of God's abundant love and mercy freely offered to all of humankind. Some dimension of that divine love and grace may be found, either directly or indirectly, in every book in the Bible.

And what might be the leading symbol of all religious history? The brief survey in this chapter could only cite a relatively few of what surely would be thousands upon thousands of symbols, rites, and ceremonies among the various worldviews and world religions throughout history? Does any symbol stand high above others in terms of its meaning and in terms of its power, both in history and in individual lives?

For clues to answer this question, take a look at the architecture of the hundreds of thousands of meetinghouses of Christian people in the western world. Check the logos of Christian charitable organizations, such as hospitals and social agencies. Take note of religious jewelry. Give attention to the religious scenery and music of the Easter celebration. To the observant eye, there is a symbol that is omnipresent in the western world and can be found elsewhere within almost every nation of the world community.

The four gospel narratives tell the story of Jesus' trial, passion, and death so that we have many details, both large and small, on which to weave a composite, compelling story. More than anything else that Jesus ever reached to touch or anything else that touched Jesus, it is the cross on which he hung that has become both the leading symbol of Christianity as well as the most powerful symbol in the world.

Interestingly, those coming to an understanding of Christianity from a Hindu or Buddhist tradition, believing they have come to earth with an established karmic account, may conceptualize the experience of Christ's death on the cross not so much as a sacrifice for one's personal sin but a sacrifice for one's accumulated karmic debt.

Surely no story has evoked more introspection, more soul-searching, more humility and contrition before God, and more tears than the story of the cross. The cross is a symbol for a divine/human experience that happened as an unrepeatable single event in human history, and this event was intended to bless the whole of humanity. One nation or one party bent on destroying or conquering another nation or party must not adduce the cross as a banner or symbol of its militarism. The horrific execution of an innocent man on that Roman cross was simultaneously an event driven by the guilt of every human as well as the means of forgiveness and hope for every human.

Thus, we do not cling to that old rugged cross in some sentimental, maudlin way, but we acknowledge its power to transform lives. Search every worldview and every world religion and, while you will find courageous martyrs for their faith, you do not find the founder of any other faith willing to be driven to his execution for the sins of the vilest offenders before God. No other story could have driven the inspiration and dedication of countless disciples over the centuries who have risked their lives to confess their faith, built majestic cathedrals in which to worship, erected hospitals to facilitate healing, staffed schools to provide education, and organized agencies and ministries to meet every conceivable human and spiritual need. Little wonder we blissfully sing, "In the cross of Christ I glory"!

Prayer: Abba, Father! Your Son drew us to you and, with the Roman ritual of horror on the cross, rescued us from the penalty that your justice demanded. And by your power, Jesus came forth from the tomb! Father, help us to live rejoicing in the story of Jesus. Empower us by your Spirit to observe the rites and rituals that keep the story of Jesus alive in us, spread the victorious tomb tale to others, and rekindle it for those whose faith and passion have waned and weakened. In the name of Jesus. Amen.

20

What Kind of Sacrifice Does God Demand?

"Can any of you think of some example of where there has been a conflict between religious behavior and lawful behavior?" This was the question I throw out to any college or university class in ethics, hoping to stir students' thinking about the relationship between religion and the law of any nation or culture. The deeper issue questions the validity of what ethicists call "the Divine Command theory of ethics"—what God commands is always right and what he condemns is always wrong. While all kinds of examples could be given in answering that question, I remember especially an answer given by Helmut a few years ago.

"The best example I can think of is found in the Hebrew Scriptures," Helmut offered. Helmut was a bright adult student, born in Germany, raised as an orthodox Jew but later turning to reform Judaism, and completing his undergraduate degree. "I'm referring to the story of God commanding Abraham to sacrifice his son Isaac," Helmut continued. In fact, that was the very illustration I frequently cited to provoke students' thinking. "God tells Abraham to offer his son, and so he has time to think about it, and then Abraham ties Isaac up and is about to kill him and God intervenes and commands Abraham not to continue. Had Abraham killed his son, he could have been guilty, at least in modern times, of a criminal act of homicide, but had he refused to obey God, he would have been a sinful and disobedient man before God," Helmut concluded.

"How many of you have heard this story?" I asked the class. Almost every hand was raised in this diverse class of several Christians, a few Muslims, and one Jew. "And what do you think of this story?" I then asked. I was certainly expecting a class consensus on the way the narrative is told in Scripture: that God was testing Abraham's faith by giving the ultimate test and once God knew the answer—as well as Abraham knowing for himself the answer—the stunning command was withdrawn and an animal for sacrifice was readily available. Before anyone else could answer that question, Helmut—this very mature, self-confident, independent thinker—spoke up again.

"If I were Abraham, I would not have done it," Helmut asserted. "In fact, I would never have considered it. And, for that reason—and I don't care what the religious fundamentalists say—I'd say that Abraham failed the bigger test as a father!" I thought his answer was intriguing. He explained: "When God first commanded this terrible deed, I would have said, 'God, I do believe in you, I have maintained my faith in your promises from the very beginning, and I have left my homeland to follow your direction to a new area, and all that's well and good, but when you ask me to slaughter my only son as a sacrifice to please you, then you have crossed a line by asking me to do what no father could ever do to his own son—I refuse to do it.'"

There was a silence in the class. Some seemed stunned and speechless. Most were likely indifferent. And for just a few moments, I was at a loss for words, and simply thanked him for his candid and provocative comment. Then I confessed to the class that this Old Testament story had been a personal challenge of mine, too, but is truly worthy of our study, reflection, and even debate as to its meaning.

Blood and Bloodless Sacrifice

The concept of sacrifice is as old as human communal life and the study of the ritual of sacrifice throughout the centuries tells us much about worldviews. A blood sacrifice was an offering to a deity in a ritual context that involves the total destruction of the life of the offering.

While modern people may recoil at the entire concept of a blood sacrifice, its practice was an important, common feature of the ancient world. Its practice clearly began in prehistoric times and continued as common practice in almost all societies and cultures at least into the first century after the birth of Jesus.

Two kinds of sacrificial offerings were practiced in ancient times. One was the blood offering of animals and humans. Herein there could be a non-fatal self-wounding that would serve as a sacrifice of blood or a body part, or there could more likely be the killing of the sacrificial victim and offering of the sacrifice in honor of the deity. In all primal religions, the central purpose of the blood sacrifice was to effect a closer relationship between the human and the divine. The offering of each sacrifice was readily transferred through the spirit world to the deity, who then bestowed favor upon the worshiper. Blood seems always to have been understood by human beings as their life force, and no greater sacrifice could be offered the deity than that precious, life-sustaining fluid.

A second kind of sacrifice included a wide variety of bloodless offerings. A wide range of material offerings such as food, drink, grains and cereals, fruits, and flowers could be offered. There might also be drink offerings or libations in which blood or strong drink (likely wine) is poured out onto the ground. Sometimes these material offerings, along with animal sacrifices, were placed in the burial sites as food for the hereafter and even humans such as servants and soldiers might be sacrificed and buried with a master in order to provide service and protection in the afterlife. The status of the deceased determined the extent of the sacrifice in the death ritual, with nobles and kings typically receiving preferential honor.

The concept of sacrifice is inescapable in the Judeo-Christian worldview. The word "sacrifice," used both as a verb and a noun, is found over two hundred times in the Bible. In the ancient era in which some modern transfer of personal wealth through currency could hardly be imagined, the blood sacrifice of animals, especially the animal without spot or blemish, was the highest gift a person could offer Yahweh, the God of Israel. God as the Giver of all life did not need these costly gifts, but his people needed a continual reminder of the Source of life and their relationship to their Creator.

Jesus participated fully in the religious life of first century Judaism, and this involved the offering of birds and animals at the temple in Jerusalem. Going back to Old Testament times, the type of animal offered reflected the financial standing of the worshiper. The offerings among the Jews were made as atonement for sins. The high priest brought a young bull. A ruler brought a male goat, but a commoner could bring a female goat or a lamb. A poor person could offer two turtledoves or two young pigeons. A hand was laid on the offering as though the worshiper was identifying the offering with himself. The edible flesh could be taken by the priests for food and the other parts of the animal were consumed by fire. These offerings were conducted on holy days and the entire ritual must have been awe-inspiring for the ancient Jewish participants and observers.

Most likely these bloody sacrifices would not seem like an inspiring or reassuring way to worship today. In fact, without an orientation to the historical-cultural context of this style of worship, modern people could be offended and traumatized by the experience. And this ancient worldview must be understood to appreciate the New Testament doctrine of the sacrifice of Jesus, the Son of God, for the sins of humanity. Throughout the New Testament various writers speak metaphorically of Jesus' death in the context of these Israelite rituals of sacrifice and empathically identify Jesus as perfect Passover lamb who was sacrificed for the sins of humanity. Jesus even spoke of his own impending death as a sacrifice. The anonymous author of the epistle to the

Hebrews clearly places the death of Jesus within the context of historic Israelite ritual. The writer claims that, through the shedding of this one perfect person's blood, the perfect and all-sufficient atonement for all the sins of humanity has been offered.

HUMAN SACRIFICE

The study of worldviews presents the good, the bad, and the ugly in human history, and few phenomena seem any worse or any uglier than the practice of human sacrifice. The stark reality is that human sacrifice was widely practiced in most ancient urban societies. Human sacrifice was practiced sparingly in Greece, India, China, Japan, and many Middle Eastern countries, yet surely all citizens were aware of its practice.

In addition to God's amazing command to Abraham regarding his only son, there are other isolated references to human sacrifice. For example, the author of 1 Kings in the Old Testament reports that during the reign of King Ahab of Israel, the builder of Jericho sacrificed his firstborn under the foundations of the city and his younger son under the gates. Such a radical act presumably was intended to ensure protection and good will for the city. Some biblical scholars believe that infant sacrifice may have been connected to the offerings of first-born among livestock, hunts, and harvests.

The other most memorable Old Testament narrative with the story line of human sacrifice involves Jephthah, an Israelite who delivered his people from dominance by their enemies (the Ammonites), and who vowed to sacrifice to the Lord in exchange for military victory (his dilemma is narrated in Judges 11:30-38). Bargaining with God for some highly desirable outcome in a dangerous situation was not new in that time or any time since. What must have been horrifying for Jephthah, under the stipulation of his reckless and ill-conceived vow, was the obligation to sacrifice his own daughter as a burnt offering. Many Bible students, thinking it incredible that God would allow one of his devoted leaders to offer a human sacrifice, quickly point out that the biblical text does not explicitly state that Jephthah carried out his ghastly, ill-conceived vow. Their explanation is that Jephthah may have found an adequate alternative to killing his virgin daughter by consigning her to live a monastic life in recluse among sister virgins. The interpretive problem here, of course, is that this possibility is conjecture and, in fact, the text informs us that Jephthah "did to her as he had vowed."

CLOSER TO HOME

Director and actor Mel Gibson clearly captured an ugly reality of the Mesoamerican worldview in the action epic *Apocalypto*—the Mexica practiced human sacrifice on a scale unparalleled in all of human history. Though Gibson's movie depicts the ancient

Maya, the Aztecs were even more prolific in their practice of human sacrifice. The Aztec Empire has been called "extractive" by historians, meaning that following their massive military conquests the Aztec warriors demanded heavy tribute in human labor and material goods from the vanquished. Consequently, wealth of all kinds flowed into Tenochtitlan in what is now central Mexico.

Human sacrifice on a prodigious scale was the bloody centerpiece of the Aztec worldview and worship. The Aztecs believed the sun god Huitzilopochtli demanded human blood to sustain him as he waged war against the moon and stars each night in order to rise again the next morning, and it was their sacred obligation to provide the victims of this bloody sacrifice. The Aztecs saw their gods as being wounded to sustain the cosmic order, thus it behooved them to self-sacrifice to these gods—blood was the nectar of the gods, through human sacrifice and auto-sacrifice (self-wounding). To prevent drought, the Aztecs might sacrifice children or prisoners to Tlaloc, the god of earth-nurturing rain, and, who, it was believed, was pleased by the tears of all who were saddened. Also, the celebration of an important victory or the appointment of a new emperor or some important political leader would entail the sacrifice of hundreds and sometimes even thousands of humans.

Most of the victims were prisoners captured in battle. Young men, young women, and children were especially desirable as subjects for sacrifice. Every eighteen months, a greatly honored young man was sacrificed to Tezcatlipoca, the deity of human fate, but on special occasions all of Mexica (Aztecs referred to themselves by this name, and the name lives on as Mexico) practiced sacrificial bloodletting to demonstrate the depth of their religious devotion. Similar rituals were practiced among the Maya and Inca, the latter settling along the west coast of what is now South America.

No Hollywood screenwriter could write a script or describe a scene gorier than the actual realism of Aztec practice. The methods of total sacrifice were entrenched in gruesome tradition and carried out under the supervision of priests. The most conspicuous practice involved taking the victim to the top of the temple where a priest cut out the heart while it was still beating and offered it to the deities, and then the head was severed, later displayed on a large rack, and the limbs prepared and eaten in a sacred ritual at the base of the temple.

Could any religious practice become more ghoulish, more reprehensible, or more antithetical to the genuine sacrifice of praise to the living, holy God of Scripture? In our minds, we may think of Aztec and Mayan ritual sacrifices as surpassing in evil and immorality the deployment of sacred prostitutes in the Greco-Roman temples of the ancient Mediterranean world. Even the conquistadores from Spain as led by Cortes, none known for their respect for human life, found these rituals of human sacrifice so disgusting that it seemed mandatory either to convert the natives to Christianity or destroy them utterly.

The various civilizations of Mesoamerica made remarkable achievements in writing, calendar design, civil engineering, astronomy, and mathematics, and they have been favorably compared to the ancient Romans and Greeks in terms of achievements. So, their intelligence and creativity need not be questioned. The Mexica had also developed an extensive and complicated cosmology, that is, a doctrine of how the entire universe came into existence and was sustained through violent conflict in the unseen world. So much time, energy, blood, and emotion were poured into their rituals of sacrifice, thus it seems unfair to doubt this people's sincerity of beliefs or devotion to their gods. They certainly would have considered themselves to be highly religious.

More importantly, while the Aztecs, Mayans, and other Native Americans sacrificed more humans ritualistically than any other culture in history, this certainly does not mean they intentionally killed more people than any other society. A number of societies in history have systematically set out to destroy an entire race or ethnic population and this list would include the millions of Jews systematically killed by the Nazis during the World War II era; the millions of Russian dissidents ordered killed by Soviet leader Joseph Stalin, also during the mid-twentieth century period; the hundreds of thousands of Chinese killed by the Japanese in modern times. Historically, warfare involves the killing of innocent human life, whether intentionally as part of a war strategy, or whether as an unavoidable by-product of military strategy against an enemy armed force.

A Biblical Drama Both Dramatic and Confusing

Few if any biblical stories are any more dramatic and any more confusing than God's command to Abraham that he sacrifice his only son, the son he loved dearly and the son of his old age. The story is narrated in Genesis 22:1-12 and is the best known episode in this patriarch's life story. The Scripture informs us that God is testing the loyalty of Abraham. The next morning after God gives the command (and one might wonder how well Abraham slept that night before), Abraham and Isaac begin their journey to a mountaintop accompanied by two other lads. Apparently, Isaac was not aware that he was the one being offered until the time arrived for the sacrifice. Throughout the ordeal, the youngster is entirely compliant, poignantly asking his father only about the availability of a sacrificial lamb. After wood is placed on the altar and Isaac is tied down, Abraham raises his knife to stab his son to death and then next to light the wood for a burnt offering. Only then does an angel of the Lord call out a command to Abraham: "Do not lay a hand on the boy," the angel ordered. "Do not do anything to him. Now I know that you fear God, because you have not withheld your son, your only son."

Many entertain no serious ethical or religious concerns about this real-life drama. Others have found reason to find the story deeply troubling. Why would Abraham, who argued so effectively in defense of the residents of the wicked twin cities of Sodom and Gomorrah when God announced his plan to destroy them, remain tight-lipped when given a command to kill his child? The residents of those twin cities were largely strangers to Abraham, the exception being Lot and family, but Isaac was his own innocent and beloved "flesh and blood." Why did Abraham not cry out immediately, as Helmut suggested in my class, and exclaim: "My God, this is so wrong. No God should ever ask a father to kill his innocent child and no decent dad would ever consent to do so, no matter what the payoff will be."

Abraham's humble obedience has been explained in terms of his knowing what the outcome would be. As he separates from his servants for the last leg of the journey up the mountain, he reassures them with a simple statement: "We will return." But if Abraham knew that God would either step in and "stay" the sacrifice or would later raise Isaac from the dead, could the command serve as a real test of faith and loyalty? We certainly cannot know Abraham's thought process during the entire ordeal. Yet, given the trauma that both father and son must have endured, it's fair enough to say that this was a true test. It's sensible to argue that Isaac's faith in his earthly father was just as great as Abraham's faith in his heavenly father. Though Isaac's eyes may have been filled with tears, he was not rebellious toward his father's mission. And did Abraham consult with Sarah before making his journey to the mountain for sacrifice? After all, Isaac was her son, too, and presumably she loved and cared for him as much as did her husband Abraham.

Yet one final interpretive dilemma cannot be dismissed: if an omniscient God knows every thought and motive of every person, why would this God choose to put Abraham through this hellish experience just to discover if his servant would honor and reverence him? If concrete evidence were needed by God, would not Abraham's willingness to leave his home country and travel for the first time to a new land, his rejection of idol worship to serve one Supreme Being, his acceptance of divine promises and longing for a blessing from God that would stretch for many generations, his pleading like an eloquent defense attorney on behalf of any righteous residents of Sodom and Gomorrah, his long patience for an heir (though not without limits) during Sarah's infertility—would not sufficient evidence of the patriarch's faithfulness already abound?

Some may contend these concerns are easily answered and for others they will always be problematic. Clearly, the Hebrew Scriptures intend to teach Israel a lesson to remember for posterity and the author of Hebrews wants the Christian community to be inspired by the same lesson: no matter what Abraham truly believed would be the outcome of this trip to the mountain or what parental emotions or ethical principles he was compelled to suspend for this one situation, he had no choice but to demonstrate his faith in the God on which he had literally committed his own life decades earlier. When Abraham accepted the call to follow the one true and living God, not only did he abandon the polytheism and idol worship among all his peers, but his clean break with the past was so complete and irrevocable that he would obey this God even when compliance seemed senseless and heartbreaking. Perhaps Abraham needed to comprehend the depths of his own commitment to God more than God needed any additional evidence of the patriarch's loyalty.

So significant was this obedience, so inspiring was this biography of one remarkable man's life, that the fully obedient life of Abraham constitutes the centerpiece in the evidence the apostle Paul employed centuries later to Roman Christians. Paul argued that this same God considers us righteous simply because of our faith and trust in him alone. Perhaps, also, God was teaching the Israelite nation and then later the Christian community that being a devoted follower of the true God often means sacrificing what is most precious. Some Jewish rabbis have made that application, pointing to the forced displacement and separation of their nation's parents and children during the trauma of the Crusades, the Inquisition, and, more recently, of course, in the Holocaust. Regardless of how this ancient story is read today, no one can read it seriously and not be challenged both to think and to feel!

Devotional Reflection

Abraham's command from God to sacrifice his only son is, arguably, the most dramatic story in the Old Testament documents, but it is not the most dramatic story in the entire Bible. Another story of human sacrifice shares much of the same dynamic, but eclipses it by far. And life stories that combine self-sacrifice, costly commitment, moral integrity, and undaunted courage always constitute the most dramatic, most inspiring, stories.

Someone has said that if it were not for sin and human failure, the nation's newscasts and newspapers would go out of business. That's an overgeneralization, of course, but certainly a good part of what makes the lead stories or the headlines each day is either an act of sin or the consequences of sin, either individual or societal. But sin is far too serious and far too complicated to leave to social analysts, newscasters, journalists, talk show hosts, pundits, and late night comedians. Sin is an offense against the God who created all humans for his pleasure and purposes and calls us to live holy and righteous lives. Sin creates a breach in our relationship with a loving Father.

How does God repair this breach in the divine-human relationship? How can God forgive human sin? And how is fellowship restored? God took dramatic action. Out of compassion he voluntarily entered the world in human flesh to provide a living, breathing example of how he wants us to think, to feel, and to act. And, then, this God, appearing in human flesh and wearing the name Jesus, allowed himself to be crucified on a Roman cross. The story of the cross permits us to gain deeper insight into how desperately and intensely God loves his children. While God thoroughly despised the human sacrifices made to idols, especially when Israel imitated that pagan practice, he allowed his own Son to be sacrificed for the human race.

And thus, God, like Abraham, was the Father of but one son. And while God stayed the poised hand of Abraham from sacrificing his only son, God must surely have turned his face away when his only son was cruelly flogged and executed. The doctrine of atonement ("at-one-ment") is so huge and so complex that New Testament writers and theologians over the centuries have been compelled to use a variety of analogies and metaphors to describe it. Bible scholars use terms such as "substitutionary atonement," "redemption," "justification," and "propitiation," words that may convey no meaning whatever to most people. Others have described an angry God who could only be appeased by some innocent person's intense suffering. Still others have spoken of a "ransom theory" that portrays the human race as held captive by Satan until a mighty payment in innocent blood could be made.

What is foremost in this story? The emphasis must surely be the voluntary suffering of Christ and concomitantly on the self-giving of the gracious and compassionate God who wants no man or woman to be lost. God, in his boundless grace and mercy, having irrevocably determined to redeem the human race, became himself our Redeemer in the person of his only Son. And Jesus was not simply a helpless victim in this dramatic turning point in human history—he freely chose to perform the most loving act that one person can offer for friends by laying down his life for them! The story of Jesus' life, death, and resurrection is the core feature in the greater story of God's desire to reach sinful humanity and restore an intimate relationship.

The concept of sacrifice is crucially important in the Christian worldview and in Christian doctrine. Obviously, there is no divine command for God's people today to offer a blood sacrifice, neither human nor animal. Yet when we respond to God's grace by offering to love him and our fellow humans with all of our heart, mind, soul and body, the depth of this transformed life-commitment can only be described as "living sacrifices" and our deepest worship as "sacrifices of praise."

Prayer: Thank you, God, for demonstrating the power of sacrificial love in history and for your Son who was unreservedly willing to lay down His life for all of us when we were the least deserving of such a gift. Grant to us the courage to make the sacrifices needed to effect the peace, mend brokenness, heal the wounded, and save the lost and dying we encounter in life's journey. We dearly appreciate the love of Christ and ask these requests in his name. Amen.

21

How Shall We Live?

"This country would be a whole lot better off if it were truly Christian and not just filled with a bunch of Sunday Christians only!" Thus spoke a rather indignant member of a Bible class in a church I recently attended. In my sometimes argumentative mind, I thought, "I wonder if there are Arabs in some Middle Eastern nation saying, 'This country would be a whole lot better off if it were truly Muslim and not just filled with a bunch of Friday Muslims only.'" Or could some Jews in a synagogue in Israel or elsewhere be saying, "This country would be a whole lot better off if it were truly Jewish and not just filled with a bunch of Sabbath Jews only"? Regardless, it is clear that most people connect one's religion with "doing." Jesus was once asked, "Teacher, what good deed must I *do* to have eternal life?" (Mt. 19:16). The same question in one form or another has surely been asked by all great teachers and philosophers.

All human beings possess the image of God. This is one of the most important beliefs within the Judeo-Christian worldview. This presence of God's image within us explains why human beings are capable of reflecting on God and life itself, reasoning, loving, establishing intimacy with others, and committing to some cause. It also means we are capable of making moral decisions and engaging in moral (and immoral) behavior. It also means we are capable of asking deep questions. A non-human animal such as a dog or horse lives by a pattern of instinct and naturally eats certain kinds of food and both reproduces and cares for its young according to instinctual programming. As humans we ask much deeper questions than any nonhuman animal could possibly imagine: From what source did we originate? Who created our world? Where are we headed? What is life all about? How should we behave?

One of life's most important questions was asked simply by the Jews when forced into exile and feeling the consequences of their choices: how shall we then live? (Ez. 33:10). The major worldviews offer answers to this vital question. Proponents of each worldview are deeply aware of human deficiencies and the reality of evil. How much are their answers to these answers alike? What is the connection between worldviews and ethics? Is there such a thing as a universal moral principle or are all moral rules relative to an historical or cultural context? Do humans need an all-wise, creator God to give them worth and dignity? Should ethicists give as much attention to how people treat animals and the environment as to how human beings should be treated?

These questions are crucially important and they are raised only to reinforce the fact that worldviews play a significant role in moral philosophy. All ethical philosophy, moral rules, moral reforms, and moral crusades are rooted in some kind of worldview. We all look to a worldview with its values and beliefs to affirm what is morally right, true, and important. As we proceed we can only provide a general sketch of some worldviews and offer a few observations and insights. In fact, we have already frequently touched on moral rules and lifestyles in the various worldviews through this study.

HINDUISM

Hinduism is an umbrella term covering a wide variety of religious beliefs, practices, and moral rules. The development of this religion can be traced back in India at least to 2000 B.C.E. Hindus begin with the guidance from the *Vedas*, the earliest of preserved Hindu sacred literature. The *Upanishads* began as oral traditions that were preserved in writing between 800 and 300 B.C.E., and the religious lessons of this tradition were taught by the gurus, whose thoughts and insights led students to believe they had been illumined by the gods. The gurus over the centuries have asked their students questions, probing the meaning of life. (See chapter 17 for a discussion of the inexorable law of karma in Hindu doctrine.) The ethical implication of *karma* is obvious. Hindus have the opportunity to live more ethically so that the next embodiment of the soul will have a higher status and a better life. Morality can be subordinated to the quest for an improved human experience. The paths to deliverance from this continual cycle of rebirth *(samsura)* can be useful knowledge, the yoke of work or faithfully discharging caste duties, disciplining the body and mind through correct postures and breathing, and devoted love for God. Each path is a different form of yoga.

Hinduism has a rigid moral code. *Dharma* emphasizes duty, embracing both extensive social and religious obligations. Freedom comes through being true to oneself. The family is a sacred unit of creation. Wives and husbands should be loyal to each other. They should assume responsibilities for bringing children into the world, educating them in spiritual and secular matters, and providing for their physical needs. The younger generation should care for the older generations. Hindus must do no harm to other people or their property. They must give special assistance to holy people who have renounced material comfort and pursued the spiritual nature. Compassion must be demonstrated to all humans and all animals, especially the cow which is a symbol of all living things and supplies milk and manure used for fuel. Kindness should be shown to all people. After all, God is not transcendent but the essence of divinity (the Brahman) which flows through all human beings.

SHINTO

We cannot say precisely how long the people of the islands of Japan have worshiped *kami no michli*, the way of the gods. For many centuries B.C.E., the Japanese have honored spirits of sacred persons, places, and heaven and earth. To the *kami* of these places people brought gifts of vegetables, fruit, and wine. The islands of the Japanese were special creations of the deities *(kami)*. Mt. Fuji and other mountains, as well as the ocean, were viewed as sacred. And Shinto was concerned with the Japanese people rather than humanity in general.

The Shinto ethical system was largely concerned with devotion to family and country. One must not be selfish when the greater good of the nation, the family, the school, or even a business organization is at stake. Honor is an important concept. An individual is never isolated and must always consider acting honorably toward everyone in his or her social environment as well as toward the nation and one's ancestors. One must do her or his best in every endeavor. A Japanese woman must honor her husband and children and be willing to die to protect their honor; a court lady must be devoted to the aesthetic traditions of art, music, and literature.

The code of the bushido, the feudal warrior or knight, has intrigued both Japanese and foreigners for centuries. The code, with deep roots in this ancient religion of Shinto, emphasized absolute loyalty of the knight to his lord. The warrior was expected to demonstrate courage, loyalty, devotion, and justice. Should he fail in his mission, the code required him to commit *hara-kiri*, ritual suicide.

CONFUCIANISM

Confucianism is one of the main schools of philosophy in China and the rest of the Asian world. This philosophy incorporates a holistic worldview with perspectives on politics and political institutions, family life, social ethics, the scholarly pursuit of knowledge and wisdom, and a way of ordinary life. Confucian ethics paralleled the emergence of Greek virtue ethics around the same period in ancient history. In both systems, the goal of the moral life is to cultivate a virtuous character; virtues are character traits that translate into human excellence. Confucian ethics emphasizes a number of ethical responsibilities an individual honors in one's relationships, such as toward the family or the government. The results of the good ethical life will be personal happiness at the individual level and a well-ordered, harmonious society at the social level. For Confucius, good manners were important, too, and were expressed in genteel courtesy, filial piety, loyalty, benevolence, and righteousness. This great philosopher believed in "the Way of Heaven" as sincerity and urged his followers to practice moderation and consideration of others. (For more insight into the ethics of Confucius, see chapter 18, "Practical Religion in a Fortune Cookie.")

Daoism

Daoism (Taoism) represents one of the two most important schools of philosophical thought emerging from the Chinese tradition (Confucianism, of course, being the other). The earliest Daoist sage was Lao-Tzu and his *Tao Te Ching* is the central text of Taoism, a slim text which has inspired over a thousand commentaries. The central concept of *Tao* or *Dao* is "the way" or "the path." "The Way" cannot be given a definite description and must remain nameless. The concept of Yin-Yang is crucial to understanding Daoism: nature consists of two opposite but complementary forces that appear in a number of different guises. Each entity in nature makes sense only in terms of its opposite. The chief ethical challenge is not to act in ways that are contrary to nature. In other words, let nature take its course. Free yourself from desires for things that go beyond what is necessary. Excesses in food, drink and clothing must be avoided. The one who truly understands these concepts is the sage. (For more insight into the doctrine and ethics of Daoism, once again see chapter 18, "Practical Religion in a Fortune Cookie.")

Buddhism

For millions of eastern people living in nations such as Japan, Sri Lanka, Burma, Thailand, Laos, Cambodia, and Vietnam, Buddhism is a religion. However, its founder, Siddhartha Gautama, would have insisted that he definitely was not a deity and that his philosophy embraced life, metaphysics, and ethics. Gautama's quest was to understand the nature of reality and discover rules of conduct with the overall purpose of diminishing suffering. Gautama is now referred to as "the Buddha." There are several varieties of Buddhism, and, according to one school of this philosophy, anyone who reaches the ultimate level of enlightenment becomes the Buddha ("the enlightened one").

The ultimate problem for humans is suffering. Suffering is caused primarily by ignorance of the impermanent nature of the world and ignorance about the nature of human beings. We cannot assume that the world and its contents remain permanent, nor can we assume that somehow suffering can be avoided. The Buddha offered a doctrine of the Middle Way which contains Four Noble Truths, detailing the nature of suffering, and the Eight-fold Path. The latter specifies how we must live to attain release and it encompasses the main facets of daily existence, prescribing the right outlook, the right resolutions, the right speech, the right acts, the right livelihood, the right endeavor, the right mindfulness, and the right concentration through meditation. The law of *karma* is very much alive in Buddhism. Each thought and deed have an impact on the universe that carry over from one lifetime to another, just as one candle lights another candle and this one lights the next candle. The goal of morality is emancipation from rebirth.

Buddhism has taught high respect for all forms of life. No living thing should be harmed; consequently, most Buddhist monks avoid eating meat or fish and many laypeople follow this disciplined example. Most certainly Buddhists advocate peaceful relations between people and nations. In their personal moral code, Buddhists shun theft, injury to others, sexual immorality, and drunkenness. (For more about Buddhism and its ethical philosophy, see the earlier chapter 11, "When Buddha Stands Beside Jesus.")

JUDAISM

Throughout their history, Jewish people have maintained a strong conviction about the existence of one God, a Supreme Being who was far superior to the unworthy gods worshipped by their non-Jewish neighbors. This one great Being, Yahweh, had chosen Israel alone to be his special people. This one personal God has created all male and female humans in his divine image.

The concept of covenant is vital to understanding Jewish ethics. A covenant is a contract and a bond, but it is no ordinary contract or bond where money is paid for services rendered. The bond is a special relationship; the contract is enhanced by a high degree of emotional commitment and loyalty among the covenanting parties. Faithfulness to Yahweh was manifested by the code of laws which had been revealed at Sinai. Humans are responsible. They are answerable to God for their conduct, a principle emerging from the first narrative in Hebrew Scriptures. They can obey or disobey God, serve God or reject God—they must only bear the consequences!

For the ancient Hebrews, the Ten Commandments encapsulated the essence of what the people were required to obey to keep faith with Yahweh. Most of the commandments were prohibitions against certain immoral acts against another person in the covenant community. The first four commands safeguarded the exclusivity of Yahweh, protected both his image and his name, and called for all people as well as beasts of burden to observe a special day of rest (the Sabbath). Additional instructions, such as commandments regarding diet and circumcision, were mandatory for practical reasons which may be unknown to contemporary readers; however, these supplemental directives granted Israel a sense of identity as a special theocratic community in the ancient world of nations and tribes. Altogether, the Hebrew tradition of the Torah cites 613 commands, 248 positive and 365 negative.

The Hebrews could keep their part of the covenant by living a consecrated life. They did not, however, view God's law as arbitrary restrictions upon their freedom. Instead, their good pleasure and honor was to obey Yahweh's commandments, not out of fear of punishment, but out of deep gratitude for his liberation and lovingkindness *(chesed)*. To state it succinctly: the primary ethical principle of the Hebrew Scriptures is the imperative of obedience to the will of God. Jewish ethics were not concerned with human reason, honor, happiness, power, or reaching human potential, but only about divine will and purpose. Because God had acted decisively in history and had performed mighty acts of deliverance and protection for the Jews, he assumed the right to speak and command.

The law given through Moses required the Hebrews to demand strict justice but also to demonstrate kindness among their fellow citizens. As centuries passed, the Hebrews became lax about their covenant relationship with Yahweh. At times pride, immorality, idolatry, and exploitation of the weak and poor corrupted the basis of the Jewish community.

Through the eighth century B.C.E. prophets the greatest ethical ideal was developed among the Jews of the Old Testament era. Through their sermons and their writings, these courageous and inspired men preserved the best in the ethics of the early Hebrews, and they even raised moral standards to a higher level. Amidst widespread practices of social injustice and exploitation of the poor and weak, the Hebrew prophets protested passionately against the corruption of religious practice and dereliction of duty.

The chief contribution of the later Hebrew prophets to moral philosophy in general is simple yet profound: there is a vital connection between genuine religion and ethics. A corollary to this rule was evident to prophets such as Amos and Hosea: the most magnificent worship assemblies to God and the most elaborate religious ritual can never substitute for justice and compassionate service to those who need it most. Such prophetic passages as Amos 5:21-24 and Micah 6:8 leave no doubt about what God expects from those who claim an intimate, spiritual relationship with him. The eloquent prophetic utterances against social injustice, neglect, materialism, and hypocrtical religion have been just as needed and relevant in affluent nations in modern times as in ancient days.

When we step back to view the entire Hebrew panorama (the old analogy of "not being able to see the forest for the trees" comes to mind), it might help us focus less on the seemingly innumerable "do's" and "don'ts." Indeed, the Hebrew Scriptures (the sacred writings that Christians and even many Jews call the Old Testament) are also filled with general exhortation: feel this way, think that way, be a third way. God was truly concerned with forming character more than he was concerned with ritual purity. Deeds were important, of course. Among the greatest saints, such as King David, the Torah and its constant study and meditation delighted the soul. But the heart, the disposition and motivation, was of utmost importance.

Like other great faiths, Jewish ethical thought has developed over the centuries through pious scholars, rabbis, and wise people, all the while never abandoning its traditional roots in the Torah. Modern Jewish morality is not simply personal, but is concerned about joyful, healthy life in both family and community. Since the Holocaust, Jewish thinkers have wrestled with the concept of a revised understanding of the concept of "chosen people." The major branches of Judaism (Reform, Orthodox, Conservative) have taken different interpretations of the relevance of some of the ancient ceremonial, cultural, and ritual commands. These branches are in complete accord on the greater, weightier matters of the ancient moral law—loving God with the totality of one's being, committing to social justice and personal righteousness, and assuming responsibility for one's life and witness in the world.

CHRISTIANITY

The Jesus one encounters in the synoptic gospels (Matthew, Mark, and Luke) organizes much of his teaching around the concept of the kingdom of God. Many scholars, as well as some noted and thoughtful citizens such as Thomas Jefferson, have attempted to praise Jesus' ethical doctrine while discarding his theology, as if his ethics were the pearl of great price to be extracted from an outer shell of Jesus' doctrine about God and his reign. No such separation is possible, however. The reign of God was a mighty concept that impacted the whole of human existence—what a person valued, how a person thought, how a person felt, how a person treated all others, how a person related to enemies, and even how a person communicated. The lasting result of his lifestyle for the faithful disciple was an abundantly rich and joyfully fulfilling lifetime experience.

The Sermon on the Mount is the greatest single discourse in Christian ethics located in the New Testament canon. Though relatively brief by modern standards,

Jesus candidly laid out the directives in thought and action for those who earnestly sought the kingdom of heaven. This sermon, sometimes called the Magna Carta of the Christian Faith, poignantly describes the character revolution necessary for kingdom preparation and kingdom discipleship. Authentic discipleship transforms ordinary people into extraordinary ones—men and woman of purity, mercy, justice, forgiveness, compassion, peacemaking, piety, humility, endurance, and spiritual devotion who courageously think and act against the cultural grain. These disciples are the people who are equipped in heart and soul to be sources of enlightenment and preservation in the larger political and social environment in which they live.

The Sermon on the Mount seemingly presents an impossible ethic. At least in human terms. It presents an ideal for life in the kingdom of God. It presumes a sacrificial commitment to Christian discipleship. Even still, is it possible for ordinary men and women to measure up to such a radical ethic? To divorce religious devotion from any self-serving motive? To endure persistent and unrelenting persecution? To love one's enemies, even to pray for their welfare? To remain totally pure in heart? To find blessing in persecution? To shun the temptation to stockpile and trust in your material blessings? To give no thought about your next plate of food or drink of water? To practice unconditional love? To be perfect as God is perfect?

These questions may lead us to consider the Christian ethic an "impossible possibility." This phrase is vague enough, to be sure. Let's think of the "impossible" in terms of attaining complete perfection by human effort alone. And let's think of "possibility" in terms of attaining perfection through a process of maturity ("sanctification" in the language of Christian theologians) by the direction and the strength of the grace and Spirit of God. Clearly, Christian ethics are meant for Christians.

The ethic of Jesus is manifestly an "ethic of inwardness." Morality is an inner experience: not an overt act as much as a state of the heart. Not coincidentally the Sermon on the Mount opens with the beatitudes, declarations which pronounced God's blessing on those who have espoused an inwardly-driven, counter-culture lifestyle. The Beatitudes list the traits of Jesus' ideal moral character and personality. In this sense, Jesus' ethic is similar to the ancient Greek virtue ethics which contended that there is more to morality than doing the right thing. Both Jesus and the Greek philosophers emphasized *being* over *doing*, character over duty.

The basis of the Christian ethic is loving concern. This *agape* is the "bottom line" in dealing with people in all kinds of difficult situations, whether with the stranger who is mugged and robbed and left to die along the highway or with the younger son who demands his inheritance and promptly wastes all of it in decadent living. Jesus' concept of the Fatherhood of God expanded the brotherhood of all people, thus making us all neighbors of one another.

Christian moral philosophy has developed over two thousand years of church history and been applied to every conceivable ethical dilemma, many of which were unheard of by the earliest Christian authors. Augustine (354-430) was an early thinker and writer who argued that the source of sin was a rebellious will. In the medieval days, the monastic movement emphasized seven deadly sins: pride, envy, anger, sloth, avarice, gluttony, and lust. Thomas Aquinas (1224-1274), perhaps the most prolific theologian-ethicist of the centuries, developed the natural law doctrine—sin is human conduct that violates God's natural law and sound reason. The Reformation era brought several great theologians to the forefront of Christian thought, each making practical application to the moral life.

While Christian leaders have long debated the relationship between the church and society, some activists became involved in abolishing slavery, improving working and living conditions of the poor, protesting racial discrimination, fighting poverty, and protesting war. The U. S. presidential election of 2004 clearly indicated a great divide between large factions of Christians, often referred to as the "religious right," and other Christians and members of American society over issues such as abortion, stem-cell research, and homosexual rights. By the mid-term election of 2006, the political power of the "religious right" seemed diminished by rising concern about peace in the Middle East, the environment (population growth and global warming), and international justice and there were divisions in the 2008 primary campaign over which candidate best represented its interpretation of Christian values.

ISLAM

The Islamic faith provides a great illustration of the Divine Command theory of ethics—what God commands is right for everyone and what God condemns is wrong for everyone! Within a century after Muhammad's death, the Islamic world had already become larger than the Holy Roman Empire ever became. Since the Enlightenment in modern Europe, the West has maintained a strict separation of church and state, but in nations where a large majority of the population is Islamic the separation does not exist and the state has the obligation to uphold and support the growth of the Islamic law (the *Shari'ah*).

Islamic faith touches all of life, as clearly taught by the Five Pillars of Islam: (1) profession of faith that there is no god but Allah and that Muhammad is his messenger; (2) participation in *salat*, five periods of prayer each day though there is special value to praying in a mosque, especially on Friday at noon; (3) an obligatory tax called *zakat* to the needy; (4) a fast during from dawn to sundown in the month of Ramadan; (5) a pilgrimage to Mecca, the *Hajj*, once during one's lifetime. These are acts even the simplest Muslim can understand and practice. The Muslim community (*ummah*) and Muslim cities were built around a mosque, a symbol for a community centered on Allah. An individual separated from community and family is an anomaly in Islam. All Muslims regardless of race, residence, nationality, or economic status should strive to be one. Islamic faith touches all of life, and the virtuous Muslim respectfully submits to Allah's will always even though humans have individual free will. Perhaps the worse sin is forgetting Allah's commands.

There is no isolated code of ethics in the *Qur'an* as one finds with the Decalogue or Sermon on the Mount within the Bible, but sections of the Islamic holy book give specific commands. Islamic social ethics include giving not only to beggars but to a common treasury from which funds can be drawn to support the welfare of everyone in the community, even slaves and strangers. A loyal Muslim's personal ethics entails abstinence from certain harmful behaviors: adultery, gambling, drinking alcohol, stealing, lying, and usury. Believers must not eat pork. The faithful Muslim must not be an aggressor; however, when an injustice is done or the faith is threatened, fighting to avenge wrongdoing is required. The Muslim must be committed to justice, but justice is tempered by forgiveness, integrity, and truthfulness.

In modern states, marriage is typically between one husband and only one wife. Islam has permitted a man to wed four women simultaneously if he can support them adequately and treat them equally. This permission was viewed as a humane measure to provide security and protection for single women. Divorce is viewed as a last resort for handling marital conflict, yet divorced men and women may remarry. Historic Islam demanded an elaborate system of laws governing a Muslim's relationship to slaves and concubines. Slavery, of course, has ended and polygamy has declined for a variety of reasons.

The role of women in Islamic practice has intrigued westerners, some of whom have considered their status and rights (or lack of them) as barbaric. The popular stereotype of a Muslim woman is that of a mysterious female hidden behind a veil with only her eyes, the bridge of her nose, and hands uncovered and whose life is completely controlled by an oppressive male, either husband or father, in her life. In past generations, Muslim women have helped to usher in changes in their legal and social status in the moderate Islamic states. Whether westerners accept Islamic premises, the goal of Islam has been to provide protection of women from men and other women and to improve the status of females. The *Qur'an* instructs Muslims that Allah intended women to be honored as helpers and companions for their men.

One basic Islamic premise: women are by nature weak and should not be allowed to make major decisions lest they be swayed by emotions. The seductive nature of women means they can arouse desire in many men unless they are required to be veiled, segregated from males, and forced to be dependent on their husbands. For traditional Muslim women, sexual sin is a more serious offense than any other because it reflects on male relatives. Women should be treated properly at all times and never abused. In more progressive Muslim nations, women now possess rights to education, employment income, to inherit and own property, and to self-expression. There is also variety in styles of clothing and grooming. The rise of the late Benazir Bhutto to Prime Minister of Pakistan, despite her tragic assassination, provides an example of what women can achieve in a Muslim-dominated nation.

A final note: of all the major worldviews and world religions, Islam in particular suffers from a serious public relations problem. Islam is often linked to extreme terrorism and other forms of violence: taking of hostages, hijackings, suicide bombing, car bombing, beheadings, assassinations, and the continuing specters of Osama bin Laden and other terrorist leaders. Many Americans may stereotype Muslims as violent, fearless fanatics who hate Christians and any other religious groups as infidels and would sanction terror as a mission strategy to spread the Islamic faith by sword and dynamite. Just as Christianity or any other major religion with much complexity and a long history can attract violent fanatics, thus can Islam (a point made in some detail in chapter 21 on holy war). Critical thinkers distinguish reality and stereotypes based on fear.

Does Islam attract a greater share of violent, fanatical followers than any other worldview? Any reasonable answer to this question would require a patient analytical journey through complex doctrine and long, entangled history of western nation-states with Arab nation-states. Despite some obvious, well-publicized inconsistencies and failures emerging from fanaticism and extremism, the strength of the Islamic ethical system lies in the straightforward simplicity and clarity of the moral dictates (every Muslim can understand the rules) and the emphasis on worship, benevolence, and wholesome living.

HUMANISM

To state humanist moral philosophy as succinctly as possible: Humanism recognizes the value and dignity of persons and seeks to better the human condition. Human beings are self-sufficient to run their own lives and need no outside direction from divine sources or religious authoritarianism. Humans are the primary source of meaning and value. Humanists may reach some of the same conclusions on ethics and develop the same moral standards as forwarded by the wisest religious ethicists, but these conclusions and standards are reached without an appeal to divinity, sacred texts, or other religious authority.

The roots of humanism run deep in Greek virtue ethics—especially with Socrates, Plato, and Aristotle—and in the Italian Renaissance that turned to the human figure in art and to the classical literature of Greece and Rome which celebrated the human adventure. A case can be made for theocentric humanism, with humans having been created by God and inherently possessing God's image, but most humanists think of themselves as secular. The ancient Greek philosopher Protagoras gave the secular movement its best-known quote and motto: "Man is the measure of all things." Socrates' admonition, "Know thyself," gave an early push toward a humanistic philosophy, and Confucian humanism has been for the East what Greek humanism has been for the West.

Humanists contend that rational answers and solutions to all the moral issues and dilemmas that humans face can be found first and foremost within the process of intelligent human reasoning. Humanist moral philosophy must be rooted in reason, informed by science, inspired by art, and motivated by compassion. There is no need for divine revelation of any kind, even if such revelation exists. Humanists would insist that sacred scriptures are largely, if not exclusively, the creation of ordinary mortals and only the genius and insight found in these writings have resulted in their collection, canonization, and reproduction over the centuries. Moral rules emerge from the best philosophy and judgment of human beings and must reflect good common sense. A moral rule is right, not because God commands or condemns certain behavior, but is inherently right because the rule squares with sound reasoning and human experience. So many traditional moral rules are judgments and reflections of historical and cultural contexts in which they were formulated.

We must not stereotype and criticize humanists as worldly people calling for the abandonment of moral principles or ethical rules. Humanists do not seek to undermine traditional institutions such as family and government. They may argue more varied moral positions and grant more personal freedom in the moral decision-making than do religious ethicists. The fact of moral disagreement among individuals and cultures raises the question of whether there are actually any objective or universal moral principles. Many humanists today will say, "Don't force your value system on me," or "Who am I to judge?" or "Morality is all relative." Ethical relativism is one of the most popular moral theories among university students.

Obviously, the worldview of the secular humanist is at odds with a Judeo-Christian worldview that begins with God—his moral nature, his actions in history, his divine revelation, and his moral commands. A critique of this popular approach to ethics from a Christian perspective is important. First, the fact that intelligent people often disagree over morally correct action does not by itself negate the possibility of independent, universal moral principles. And if morality is ultimately a matter of one's own reasoning and feelings, neither we nor anyone else can be mistaken about what is right or wrong in human conduct. To illustrate: my persecution and terrorizing of certain students on campus because of their color of skin, their gender, or their sexual orientation could never be morally condemned, in fact might be morally commendable, so long as I have "reasoned" that my action was justified to teach my victims a lesson.

Many humanists are indeed wise and intelligent and they attempt to be kind and fair. In their compassion and generosity some humanists put many religious people to shame. Some have taken a stronger stand against the rank ethical subjectivism that justifies racism, sexism, or other discrimination, than many who contend for a religious basis to ethics. We may remember, however, that occasionally powerful leaders have "reasoned" their way into justifying persecution, even genocidal policies such as the Holocaust. We are left with crucially important questions for which science has no objective answer: Is there a Supreme Being who gives his created humans moral rules? Could not reason be informed by divine direction and the wisdom of the ages? Can there be an absolute moral code without a belief in a holy and just God? And can men and women be good without God?

Worldviews and Ethics

For centuries, wise and intelligent people have thought long and hard and written extensively about the meaning of life and how we should live with one another and with God. Perhaps because of the basic moral law of God inherent within intelligent and sensitive men and women, these ethical systems have far more in common than they have differences. With little exception, these religious and ethical systems have emerged entwined—each with sacred texts, sacred ritual, sacred narratives, religious experience, and religious conviction to undergird and highlight moral instruction. Clearly, religious commitment and spiritual devotion provide major motivation for people to develop moral attitudes and make moral decisions in a responsible way.

One virtue illustrates the commonality of religious ethical doctrine. Compassion is a foundational virtue for a truly decent society, though not always a popular virtue. Sometimes compassion gets reduced to some sentimental "soft spot in one's heart" when seeing a television special about people starving in a third world country or thousands of children orphaned by the December 2004 tsunami that hit the Indian Ocean rim of nations or even seeing dogs and puppies that have been dropped off at the humane shelter. All the great religions summon their followers to some form of compassionate action, perhaps because a compassionate response can be costly and may not come naturally. More than simply "feeling sorry for someone," it is feeling *with* others and acting selflessly on their behalf.

In all eras of Judaism, adherents are called to social justice for the poor, the disadvantaged, the widowed, and the orphaned. Confucius taught his disciples to practice the habit of *shu*—practicing eminent fairness by not inflicting behavior on others that they would not want inflicted on themselves. Confucius and Rabbi Hillel (30 B.C.E. – 10 C.E.) asserted a negative form of the Golden Rule: Do *not* do to others what we do *not* want done to ourselves. The Buddha also taught a form of the Golden Rule, challenging his followers to transcend the limits of self-interest and egotism. Jesus taught and modeled compassion on numerous occasions; he instructed his followers to leave judgment to God, love their enemies, and shun retaliation against those who inflicted harm.

The apostle Paul reminded the Corinthian church that a faith that moved mountains was worthless without genuine love for others. And, finally, one vital message of the *Qur'an* is that those who submit fully to Allah must not accumulate a private fortune. They must share personal wealth fairly in order to create a just and decent society where everyone is treated with respect and dignity. And Jesus taught that the practice of love and compassion is a willful decision that can be costly, for if we love only those who love us then no real effort is expended and no character growth occurs.

Yes, there are many worldviews, but we live in one world and we have many neighbors. The message of the greatest of worldviews is that the welfare of our own group depends on the welfare and good will of everyone else. We are woven into an inescapable web of mutuality. Whatever affects one group directly impacts all groups indirectly. We must be respectful and tolerant, even when personal, deep conviction means we do not agree. And we must learn to live together in peace and harmony as brothers and sisters or be prepared to perish together as rebels and fools.

Devotional Reflection

A dynamic highly unique in worldviews resides within the Christian concept of ethics—God's grace toward us. Christian ethics may be called "therefore ethics." When one reads some great ethical passages (the great New Testament texts such as Matthew 5, 6, and 7, or 1 Corinthians 13, or Colossians 3, or Ephesians 4, to cite a few) one does not sense that the inspired directives are absolute commands to be followed with meticulous legalism. Instead, these Scriptures describe how a loving, caring child of God and disciple of Christ will typically act and react in a truly exemplary manner in all one's relationships. They describe how moral excellence at the highest level, what educational philosopher and psychologist Lawrence Kohlberg called "post-conventional morality," can be fully developed.

God takes sin seriously. And yet, God bestows abundant grace through his Son to any at our lowest moral ebb. No other worldview can present this same incredible message. No matter how many terrible deeds one has done and no matter how much harm against others one has created that can never be recompensed, the Father's grace can reach the worst sinner and even make that reclaimed sinner the best saint. God loves unconditionally and saves by his abundant grace, *therefore*, we live a certain way. Our performance of right acts and good deeds is not intended to build heavenly credit, but provides a concrete way to say, "Thank you, Lord, for your grace and your deliverance!"

Prayer: Father God, thank you for your amazing grace that rescues our hearts, souls, minds and bodies from the desperate situations we have placed ourselves in. We want to say "thank you" by living the life your Son modeled while on earth. Empower us by your Spirit to become all that you have called and equipped us to be. Save us from the pitfalls of loveless legalism and impossible perfectionism as we apply your commands. Just as we have received your grace, may we model and mediate that same grace to others you have placed along the way in our journey. Through Jesus. Amen.

22

Holy Warfare—The Dangers of Religion

When Saladin stands beside Richard the Lion-Hearted, what do we see? Richard the Lion-Hearted, the handsome and temperamental king of medieval England, has been the romanticized subject of several books and movies. The son of Eleanor of Aquitaine, queen of France and England, he is considered today as a paragon of chivalry, an astute war strategist, a military hero, an unrelenting warrior who, after one battle, ordered the 16,000 captured enemy soldiers beheaded within full view of their own armies. And Salah-al-Din or Saladin? He was the sultan of Egypt and Syria of whom most may know little or nothing. For sixteen months, Richard and Saladin fought as fierce enemies across the parched plains of the Holy Land in the Third Crusade of a holy war.

The Crusades played a vital part in western medieval history. With the beginning of the eleventh century, "Christian" Europe was surrounded by nations considered by Christians generally to be heathen and infidel. For centuries, the great Muslim states had dominated the Mediterranean, firmly implanted in Spain, Sicily, North Africa, and the Middle East. Now it seemed time for the European Christians to become aggressors in defense of their values. Italian merchants began to open regular trade across the Mediterranean with the Middle East. Holy war seemed necessary to drive the infidels or unbelievers out of territory considered sacred by Christians.

The immediate impetus for the Crusades came when the Byzantine emperor, Alexis 1, asked Pope Urban II for assistance against the Seljuk Turks, who were Muslims. The pope envisioned a great opportunity for papal leadership. In 1095 he stirringly addressed the clergy, knights, and poor people of Europe at the Council of

Clermont and boldly declared a holy war of liberation. The pope called for an end
to pointless feudal fights between knights, and urged a battle against Muslim Turks.
Then he called for a march to Jerusalem to liberate the tomb of Christ and other sacred
relics from Muslim control.

Pope Urban's masterful rhetoric touched almost every emotion—remission of
sins, protection of their land until they returned, and the hope of plunder. "All who die
by the way, whether by land or by sea, or in battle against the pagans, shall have immediate remission of sins. This I grant by the power of God with which I am invested,"
he declared. Now, the pilgrims were given permission to bear the sword. At the end of
his appeal, Urban was given chants with one voice, *"Deus hoc vult!"* ("God wills this!").
The response was immediate and far-reaching. Preachers, Peter the Hermit being the
most famous, spread this call to arms throughout Europe.

What motivated the pope to make such a bold summons? Perhaps Urban was demonstrating that he, not the emperor, was the real leader of international Christendom.
And what motivated the clergy, both priests and prelates, the nobles, feudal barons,
knights, merchants, and peasants to don the cloth cross which signified that they were
pledged to the crusade? Most crusaders were not merely seeking land and wealth.
Crusading was a frightening, grim, and dangerous enterprise. Surely the motivation
was mixed.

In the medieval worldview, knights saw their duty as fighting for Jerusalem just
as peasants were taught to fight for the rights and wishes of their feudal lord. Deeply
pious saints were also keenly aware of their personal sin and feared eternal damna-
tion, and here was immediate opportunity for atonement. Just as a man fought for
his lord against feudal enemies, how could that man demonstrate his devotion to God
more convincingly than by fighting against God's enemies, the infidels who had defiled
Christ's sepulcher? The crusaders were convinced that God had called them to arms
through his representative, the Pope, and they answered gladly. For the adventurous
knights who seemed to thrive on fighting, here was an enterprise where fighting and
slaying were honorable.

THE FIRST TWO CRUSADES

Preparation and organization for the crusade required several months. In the
spring of 1096, five armies of approximately 60,000 soldiers accompanied by hordes
of peasants and pilgrims with their wives and children set off to Jerusalem—a super-
pilgrimage! Sadly, many of the crusaders died on the perilous journey through Eastern
Europe. The first divisions struggled toward Constantinople, the great center of
Christianity in the East, then through Asia Minor where they captured Nicaea, and

then to Antioch in northern Syria, where they bogged down in a long battle. After Antioch was captured in 1098, much of the crusading host proceeded down the Palestinian coast, evading well-defended coastal cities.

When the Crusaders finally arrived in Jerusalem in the summer of 1099, they found that the city was protected by a wall and would be heavily defended. The Franks, as they were referred to by Muslim foes, were not accustomed to besieging the stone cities of the East, cities with higher walls than most cities in Europe. After building two towers or "belfreys," a soldier was able to break into the city from one of these towers and the other crusading soldiers soon followed. For three fierce days in July, the blood-thirsty Crusaders systematically slaughtered about 30,000 of the Muslim and Jewish inhabitants of Jerusalem. For the victims, there was no sanctuary from the brutality. The streets literally ran with blood of men, women, and children. Few Muslims or Jews escaped the sword. Even some resident Christians were executed. When the massacre was complete, the Crusaders celebrated in the church of the Holy Sepulcher with tears of joy running down their faces. Meantime, the Christian Crusaders' brutality horrified the Muslim world.

After most Crusaders went home, the Crusader Kingdom of Jerusalem was established; Godfrey of Bouillon, a spiritual man of great courage, was chosen as leader. Godfrey possessed the humility to declare he could not wear a crown of gold in the city where his Savior had worn a crown of thorns, and he accepted a modest title of "Advocate of the Holy Sepulcher." Soon, the Crusaders promulgated a law banning Jews and Muslims from Jerusalem, and even the local Christians were expelled on suspicion of complicity with Islam. Godfrey's brother Baldwin succeeded him to the throne and assumed the title "King of Jerusalem." Under Baldwin's leadership, the Crusaders conquered Caesarea, Haifa, Jaffa, Tripoli, Sidon, and Bierut.

After the first Crusade, the Muslims had been divided and dispersed, but slowly they began uniting. Meantime, the Kingdom of Jerusalem was experiencing division and conflict between those Franks (those of European descent) who had been born in Palestine and understood the Muslims' point of view and the newcomers from Europe who saw no reason to tolerate religious diversity. In November 1144, the Muslims conquered the Crusader city of Edessa, thus emboldening the Muslim world. Muslims remembered the *Qur'anic* teaching about *jihad*—while war is abhorrent, sometimes believers must fight a war of self-defense to preserve their faith and values. News of the Edessa disaster led to the organization of the Second Crusade. Moved by the preaching of St. Bernard of Clairvaux, Louis VII of France and the Hohenstaufen emperor, Conrad III, led large armies to the East in 1147 where they accomplished little or nothing. The Second Crusade was a failure for European Christians.

Saladin and Prudent Mercy

Almost a century passed since the Christian conquest of Jerusalem before a leader strong enough to unite the Muslim Middle East appeared. Divisions among Christians living in Palestine deepened in the next generation, while on the other side the Turkish leader Saladin was uniting both Egyptian and Syrian Muslims under his rule. Saladin and his army marched through Palestine, conquering one town after another, until he reached and camped out on the Mount of Olives above the city. He surely thought of the desecrated shrines on the Haram and of the cross that Christian crusaders had placed atop the Dome of the Rock. To Saladin, this was sacrilege he was called to avenge.

In September 1187, Saladin initiated his attack on the western gate of Jerusalem. Three days later, an entire section of the wall had fallen into the moat with only an inner wall holding the Muslims back from leveling the same measure of savagery as the Christians from Europe had given his own people in 1099. Thus why should Saladin show any mercy?

An emissary from the besieged city of Jerusalem was sent to beg Saladin for mercy. The emissary Balian offered a desperate plea. He reasoned with Saladin that the hopelessly out-matched Christians had nothing more to lose and would kill their own wives and children, burn their houses and possessions, and pull down the Dome of the Rock, before coming out to meet Saladin's army. Even then each Christian soldier would attempt to kill at least one Muslim before he died.

Saladin consulted his advisors. For 88 years, European invaders had occupied the Muslim holy city. Christians had profaned Islam's holiest sites. The al-Aqsa mosque had been stripped of precious metals in the candelabra and other furnishings and then used to stable horses. Pieces of the holy rock from which Muhammad was said to have ascended to heaven had been chipped away to sell for profit in Constantinople. But unlike the Christian king Richard, the victorious Saladin agreed to demonstrate mercy and compassion on his enemies. He forbade acts of vengeance. A token ransom was arranged for the thousands of residents. The sultan kept his word. Not a single Christian was killed. And Saladin was moved to tears over the plight of poor Christians who were held as prisoners of war because they could not pay the modest ransom; hence large numbers were released.

The Third Crusade was a reaction to the fall of the Holy City in 1187 to Saladan's forces. All of Europe was ablaze with calls for revenge to be exacted in a new crusade. Three major monarchs reached agreement to lead their forces in person: King Richard I of England, Emperor Frederick Barbaroosa of Germany, and King Philip II Augustus of France. Thus the trio of monarchs and their armies set out to re-conquer Jerusalem. Imagine how compelling the pope's message of salvation and earthly glory must have been to draw the three most powerful kings of Europe into sailing east and leading armies of knights and peasants.

The entire episode became a tragicomedy. The crusading kings were of different character and were natural enemies, jeopardizing the entire military campaign. Barbaroosa drowned while swimming in a river. Philip eventually returned home to France. Though Richard was both daring and reckless, he was unable to translate those traits into ultimate victory. The truce between Richard and Saladin gave the Franks control of some outer territory along the coast and the right of free entry for pilgrims going into Jerusalem. Saladin began a building program in Jerusalem and also invited the Jews to come back to Jerusalem, their holy city from which they had been almost entirely excluded by the Crusaders.

Indeed, when Saladin stands beside Richard the Lion-hearted, he stands much taller in moral character. Saladin does not receive much ink in the historical narratives of the western world, but the Muslim commander looks more like the caring and compassionate carpenter from Nazareth than does the highly touted Christian king of England. And he has served as a role model for several Muslim political leaders over the centuries.

The Crusades and September 11th

There were later Crusades, but they accomplished little. As the decades passed, the westerners were unable to hold the lands they had won in the East, for the crusading spirit was declining. Repeated calls to defend or rescue the Holy Land from infidels were answered with ever-diminishing enthusiasm. Europeans were more interested in the rising power of monarchies in their own nations and the development of the commercial middle class. While western historians once spoke of eight distinct Crusades, from the Muslim worldview the Crusades never truly ended and were resumed every time the Franks, or some western nation, exerted some control over a nation in the Middle East. Before the medieval crusades, the Muslim societies possibly constituted the strongest, most vibrant civilization on the globe, but the crusader victories and the accompanying onslaught and destruction shook their confidence and deepened religious differences.

Fast forward to September 11, 2001. This date will go down in history as a day that dramatically changed the entire world. While the majority of Americans may know little about the Crusades, the terrorist attacks against the United States on this infamous date are indelibly etched in their memory banks. When Osama bin Laden declared his own *jihad* against the western world in 1998, he accused America of "[spearheading] the crusade against the Islamic nation." And in a taped message released to his followers in 2001, bin Laden promised that the world would "see Saladin carrying his sword, the blood of unbelievers dripping from it."

Are the Crusades of the medieval era and the terrorism of 9/11 linked? Let's not yield to temptation to consider the terrorism of 9/11 as an isolated event. The horror of that day was only one vicious strike in a long-running jihad against the West. Subsequently, "jihad" and "jihadists" now carry strong negative connotation in the minds of most Americans. Consider, however, the terms "crusade" and "crusaders" became the ultimate curse in Muslim countries. Meaningful dialogue is only possible by first understanding the historical context of differences as well as associated meanings of language used in communication.

THE GOOD NEWS AND THE BAD NEWS

Both the Crusades and contemporary radical Islamic terrorism provide horrifying illustrations of the dangers of religion. Christianity and Islam have glorious yet violent histories and leaders of neither religion can exclusively claim, at least historically speaking, the moral high ground. Some Christian people have committed some terrible deeds, and some Islamic people have also committed some terrible deeds, each using their religion as justification for discrimination, persecution, and violence. There are passages within both the Old Testament and the *Qur'an* that can be easily adduced by demagogic leaders and fanatics in justification for violence against "enemies of the faith."

The legitimate purpose of religion is to transform the faithful into healthy and whole individuals, enabling them to find practical answers to life's deepest questions, to cope with loss and the fear of death, and to live in positive, moral, and joyful relationship with other people. Religion possesses tremendous power to bring immeasurable blessing to those who truly believe and commit their lives to a cause greater than themselves. Religion that functions properly in wholesome and healthy ways is anything but "dangerous!"

Each religion serves as a repository of the information, concepts, doctrine, and moral rules that a given culture or faith community has deemed to be crucially important. Ideally, religion is intended to foster deep reflection and genuine humility--not easy certainty. Religious warfare is fighting about boundaries. The boundaries may be literal or metaphorical. The most devout of each religious faith who are unflinchingly convinced their doctrine is right may well fight to protect the boundaries which insulate the true believers from the enemies who seek to destroy that faith. Religion becomes dangerous when it is used to mask self-interest and justify humans' most selfish pursuit of power and possessions. Religious wars are fought for "good" reasons—spiritual soldiers are totally convinced they are guarding their faith against invading destroyers.

Obviously, worldviews do not simply meet in a library or clash on the pages of a textbook—worldviews get "fleshed out" in assembly halls, streets and highways, on waterways, in airways, and on battlefields. People will die (and kill others) for their religion; after all, their identity and spiritual survival are at stake. Little wonder that religions have been involved in most of the bloody and uncompromising disputes in recent times—the Middle East, Northern Ireland, Bosnia, and the Sudan, just to cite a few areas where failure to compromise led to bullets, bombs, and bloodshed.

No single world religion possesses a monopoly on distortion or abuse. All religions justify war and selected killing in some circumstances, most commonly in self-defense. The temptation to "baptize" our most selfish ambitions and most evil deeds with the covering of religious justification is part and parcel of humans' unredeemed, carnal nature, and it matters not whether one is Jewish, Muslim, Christian, or claims any other religious commitment or affiliation. There is a "jihad" faction lurking within the nature of every narrowly conceived religious faith that wars against international justice, civil decency, basic human respect, and social cooperation.

FUNDAMENTALIST TRADITION AND MINDSET: FOUR GENERAL TRAITS

"Fundamentalism" is a term most westerners associate with Christianity. We might pine for the days when "fundamentalism" conveyed the connotation of a Christian community fervently committed to the basic truths of Holy Scripture, such as the divinity of Jesus as the Son of God or the authenticity of Scripture as God's Word. The term no longer holds such a positive meaning, yet the phenomenon of fundamentalism in a negative sense is found very much alive in all worldviews.

Fundamentalism is not in itself a religious belief. Nor is it limited to any single religion or family of religions. In fact, there are fundamentalist political groups as well as fundamentalist religious groups. When religious and political groups abandon the grand themes that bring social justice, peace, unity, and healthy relations among followers and begin focusing on marginal issues, these distracting preoccupations draw attention to the differences between "us" and "them." Policies of exclusion are then advocated and practiced.

Fundamentalism has emerged in each of the major monotheistic religions during the twentieth century, and its strength has led many western observers to speak in grandiose terms of the "war on terrorism" as a "battle of the monotheisms" and even "a clash of the civilizations." In the latter, the forces of modernity that are the enlightened, democratic societies of the West are defending themselves against the archaic, barbarous, autocratic, and intolerant societies of the Middle East.

Fundamentalism is better described in this context as a way or style of holding particular beliefs, a mindset the late American historian Richard Hofstadter called "the paranoid style" in American political and cultural life. For example, every fundamentalist movement, no matter what the religion or political ideology, is fearfully convinced that the modern secular and cultural establishment wants to destroy it. With an "under siege" mentality, fundamentalists are fighting modernity and all that it represents. While fundamentalism is not inherently violent, most fundamentalists see themselves as remaining loyal to their faith and values in a socio-political environment that is increasingly hostile and inherently threatening to their survival.

Fundamentalism is driven by four major characteristics: First, fundamentalists contend that their religious stories, symbols and sacred texts are *literal* truth rather than interpreting them in pedagogical, metaphorical, and/or allegorical terms. Religious fundamentalists have a very specific, explicitly detailed body of beliefs, and all the beliefs in the system are highly important (some might say equally important). Christian fundamentalists take a highly literal reading of biblical statements and narratives. A literal reading of Genesis 1 and 2, for example, trumps any explanations and insights from physical scientists about the origin of the universe and human life.

Second, fundamentalism tends to hold its unique beliefs as *absolute*. These beliefs are unchanging; they are true for everyone and at all times. Furthermore, those beliefs are held with utter certainty. Fundamentalism usually sees itself as completely incompatible with any form of relativism. The middle ground and all shades of gray are eliminated. And fundamentalists see themselves as being absolutely right on the important issues, and all who disagree are absolutely wrong. After all, God is reflexively on their side and in support of all their positions. Little wonder that fundamentalists tend to be fanatical. An anonymous Mr. Dooley once offered a satirical definition of a fanatic: "A fanatic does what he thinks th' Lord wud do if he only knew th' facts in th' case."

Third, fundamentalism tends to be *intolerant* of those who do not agree with its beliefs. Tolerance is, of course, a matter of degree. In milder cases, this intolerance emerges only when its dogmas are directly challenged. Two ideas typically foster religious intolerance and disrespect. The first is that one's own religion is the only true religion and that other religions are categorically false or morally incorrect. The second idea, found in certain forms of fundamentalism, is an extreme intolerance that demands everyone accepts its beliefs, even if people of other worldviews present no direct or indirect challenge to their survival. Compromise is typically a damnable weakness and betrayal, not a virtue, to fundamentalists.

Fourth, and as a corollary to intolerance, fundamentalism tends to be *activist* and often *militant* in promulgating its beliefs. In milder forms, fundamentalists will be unflinchingly active in their efforts to convert the world to their beliefs. A stronger form of militancy attempts to impose legal sanctions and restrictions on others or deny their right to be different. In extreme form, fundamentalists see people who disagree with their doctrine as infidels whose entire heretical religious system, governmental structure, lifestyle, and cultural values must be destroyed. Much like the Christian Crusaders of the medieval era who were offered pardon and salvation if they were willing to bear the sign of the cross and wield the sword, so contemporary Islamic militants are promised instant passage into Paradise if they only sacrifice their lives for the *jihadist* cause. Obviously, religious zeal can move people to violence as easily as greed or land.

The mindset of extreme fundamentalism has been around for centuries. What a deadly combination—ideological blindness, religious certainty, and easy arrogance! Saul of Tarsus might have been viewed as a terrorist by the first generation Christians before the Lord graciously confronted him on the Damascus Highway and then transformed him into a special emissary to the Greco-Roman world Fundamentalist intolerance also fueled the Inquisition that attempted to coerce Jews and Muslims into conversion and also leveled persecution on Christians who held doctrinal beliefs considered heresy. Intolerance and fear also fueled the witchcraft purges of colonial New England. Arrogant intolerance fostered persecution of scientists whose discoveries challenged traditional interpretations of Scripture. In a sense, militant fundamentalists and legalists, whether in religious organizations or the literal battlefield, play the role of emotional terrorists. And all warriors for their version of "the faith" could quote scriptures from sacred texts in defense of their virulent action.

In more recent times, in 1989 many opponents of Salmon Rushdie's *Satanic Verses* reminded the western world that its Muslim citizens abide by values, laws, and a theology very different from its own, and will use violence to insure that they are respected. Religious intolerance fueled the Taliban's dynamiting in April 2001 of two giant, "idolatrous" 140-foot Buddha statues that dominated the valley of Bamiyan, high in the Hindu Kush mountains of Afghanistan. It fueled the killing in 2002 of several hundred Muslims by Hindus in Gujarat, India, with the collaboration of public officials and the police. And militant-fundamentalist Islam has certainly inspired acts of barbarism and savagery against U. S. and European citizens. The beheading of American civilian Nicholas Berg in 2004 sadly served as an opening round for more beheadings by radical Islamic militants to protest American occupation of Iraq; the first beheading came within days after photos of American military abusing Iraqi prisoners at the Abu Ghraib prison were released.

The alleged massacre of innocent Iraqi civilians by U. S. Marines, including women and children, at Haditha in late 2005, though investigated many months later, seemed to announce to the world that fanaticism, carelessness, and excess cannot be confined to any one nation or cause. Radical fundamentalism clearly finds welcome compatibility with educated classes of people. For example, the London train and bus bombings in July 2005 cannot be explained by poverty and disadvantage, for the bombers came from working class, but comfortable backgrounds. And the failed schemes of car bombings on a London street and the Glasgow airport in June 2007 were planned and attempted by several Muslim doctors.

Clearly, fundamentalism will not disappear with the mere passage of time. Fundamentalism may appear a throwback to an allusive past, but, historian Karen Armstrong reminds us that contemporary "fundamentalisms are essentially modern movements that could take root in no other time than our own," and they certainly employ all the modern strategies and technologies at their disposal. The dynamics of this international context—the evolution of western world-Middle Eastern politics (including the western demand for oil and the formation of the modern state of Israel) and the availability of modern electronics such as remotely-controlled explosive devices, computers, and cell phones—all combine to render contemporary expressions of fundamentalism both modern and unique.

The most dangerous people in the world are those who have convinced themselves that they alone have been divinely commissioned to carry out the will of God or that one party represents God and the other does not. Religiously-inspired hatred is the next step. Along the way these radicals with tunnel vision have forgotten what it means to practice compassion and humility. Even in a democracy, a system of government that presupposes negotiation, compromise, and the good sense of a majority of citizens, political leaders can be guilty of claiming that God sanctifies their most partisan public and foreign policy positions. One's faith can be co-opted and wielded by fanatics whose political positions are not shared by the majority and whose intolerance is abhorred. The word "Christian" belongs to no single political party, for, as journalist-social activist Jim Wallis reminds us, "God is not a Republican...nor a Democrat!"

THE INSIGHT OF LINCOLN

Of all American presidents, Abraham Lincoln seemed to possess the most mature religious insight. One could almost see the providence of God in bringing Lincoln to the White House at such a crisis point in American history. Had it not been for Lincoln's divided opposition in the rival Democratic Party and the splitting of votes among three candidates, Lincoln, who had experienced several political defeats earlier in his career, would most surely not have gained enough electoral votes to be elected (he won the U. S. presidency with just less than 40 percent of the popular vote and no support whatever in the Southern states)

The intriguing irony is that Lincoln did not formally hold membership in any religious group or denomination, yet he continually contemplated the great mystery of the Almighty. As Commander-in-Chief, he did not engage Union forces lightly, for the death of fighting men on both sides of the Mason-Dixon line created a source of personal agony. And yet he was determined to uphold his Constitutional duty to maintain the national sovereignty and unity of the relatively young republic.

Lincoln was deeply aware of the unfathomable distance between Almighty God and his erring human beings, and believed for any person to claim perfect knowledge of the divine will and purpose was the unpardonable sin. This wartime president acknowledged that, on the issue of slavery, both sides read the same Bible and came to different conclusions. And both Union and Confederate soldiers and supporters also prayed to the same God, invoking their Father's aid in the fight against the foe. There was no room for arrogance in knowing God's will. Every major decision that involved human life must be made with all the wisdom and humility a political leader can summon.

Lincoln thus waited for providential guidance at critical points in the war. He did not consider himself to be the personal agent of God's will, though others seemed to infer that claim for themselves. Lincoln wrote: "If it were not for my firm belief in an overriding providence it would be difficult for me, in the midst of such complications of affairs, to keep my reason in its seat. But I am confident that the Almighty has his plans and will work them out, and...they will be the wisest and the best for us."

When asked if God was on the side of the North, Lincoln replied: "I am not at all concerned about that, for I know the Lord is always on the side of the right. But it is my constant anxiety and prayer that I and this nation should be on the Lord's side...I am not bound to win but I am bound to be true. I am not bound to succeed, but I am bound to live up to the light I have." "Let us judge not, lest we be judged harshly," Lincoln argued, for "the Almighty has his own purposes."

Devotional Reflection

As Christians, doctrine is important to us. We certainly want to believe the claims and assertions that are true and we want to teach others the truth. We do not want to be wrong or misguided about any major concept that impacts our spiritual lives. And yet, Christians are called more than anything to be faithful, not "right." Faithful not to religious systems or creeds, faithful not to particular religious or political leaders, faithful not to particular institutions or organizations, and faithful certainly not to any religious system that requires us to cast out or persecute those who seem to us in error in their religious beliefs and practices.

There is a fine line for all of us to walk. We must not be naïve and tolerant of blatant evil about us, and we are certainly summoned to use whatever peaceful means at our disposal to influence our community and the world for good, acting as both "light" for the world to see truth and "salt" that preserves moral goodness. We seek to be loyal to our faith and contend for the special vantage point of a Christian worldview on the vast, seemingly intractable, problems of our civilization, yet all the while understanding the limits of human knowledge of God's purpose. A strong dose of humility is totally in order for relating to people of different worldviews, as well as an enormous reluctance to impose our beliefs, through civil law, on other groups or individuals.

Remember that as Christians we are not actually called to a "religion." We have certainly not been commissioned by a prophet to go forth and execute all of God's enemies, as was Israel's ancient King Jehu, who, incidentally, seemed to fulfill that role with the greatest of zeal and glee. We are called to a relationship of trust with the Lord Jesus; we are called to a lifestyle of lovingkindness and humble service to others; and we are challenged by the teaching and example of Jesus to seek nonviolent ways of confronting our enemies. Our goal in life is not to become more "religious," but to become more Christ-like. And there is a dominant Christ-like value that can define who we are and that allows everything else to fall into place: namely, compassion.

Prayer: Holy God! We seek to be healthy and whole in all our relationships. And yet, how clearly we embrace some perversion of your perfect plan when the insecurities and fears of life overwhelm our souls. In those moments of terror we abandon reason. And, worse, we abandon you!

Our unredeemed human nature is to fear, to seek power, to conquer, to violate. Often we can take our most self-serving ambitions and behavior and defend them before others as being your will. Abba, your love sent us Jesus to show us a perfect model of perfect love. Only by Christ your Son may our weaknesses be converted into true strengths, and by your Holy Spirit our hearts and minds are transformed. By the your keeping of your promise not to abandon your children we will gain the courage to believe and surrender our unbelief to the refuge offered to our souls.

Father God, may we find faith enough to believe that your grace will not let us go even in the darkest of hours, and from that faith may we share the truly "good news" with those around us. May we believe and trust ultimately and only in you and follow your light, however it may appear, out of the darkness. May we live as souls resurrected by the power and blood of Jesus. In his name this confession and prayer are offered. Amen.

23

Mountain or Maze?—Do All Religions Lead to God?

T his young man had grown up right before my very eyes. In fact, some 22 years earlier I had visited his parents in the hospital on the day he was born. He was raised in a conservative church and attended a private Christian school until he graduated and began studies at a prestigious private university. His spiritual interests led him to choose world religions as his major. After returning home from his four years of study, I looked forward to dialogue with him about world religions. Obviously, his mind had expanded in many ways. "And do you still think Christianity is the one true religion?" I asked. His reply was simple and forthright: "I believe that any path that leads to God is the right path."

As we have wandered through a wide range of thoughts and meditations in this book, we have now arrived at the most crucially important questions yet to be raised: What is the relationship of Christianity to other world religions? Is salvation found only in Jesus and Christianity or can adherents to other great faiths find spiritual salvation? And how should Christians feel about other religions? Are all religions of equal value? Can any religion lead us to God?

The world is a global village. As Americans, we live in a pluralistic society. We seek to be eminently fair and kind in our thoughts and words about other people, especially people of a different heritage. In our desire to be open-minded, tolerant, and non-judgmental of the faith of others, it is easy to accept the claim that "all religions do lead to God." The analogy of the mountain is often drawn.

Think of a monstrous mountain that reaches a lofty peak in rarefied air. At the broad base of the mountain may be found a variety of roads, perhaps each with different surfaces, different widths, different signs and markings, and all the roads take different routes upward. The roads represent the different religions and differences in the roads may represent the different names, doctrines, ceremonies, and rituals. As the roads move up the mountain, they come closer together as they bring travelers closer to the peak which almost disappears in the mist and clouds. At this high level nearing the peak (translate: nearing God), the differences in the roads at the base of the mountain are no longer relevant. At this high level, hardly anyone notices differences. Each road, though it took a slightly different route, eventually les travelers to the same divine destination.

Could, perhaps, another analogy be more accurate? Imagine: A large number of adventurers seek to find their way through a maze. They know that true spiritual life is at the end of the maze. The maze, however, is vast and highly complicated. There are numerous routes that one can stay on for a great deal of time, but they keep bringing seekers to an abrupt dead end and fail to extricate them from the maze. There is only one way through the maze. Not many will find the correct route to the light of eternal life. In fact, Jesus enters the maze and meets people all along the way. For those who trust him, he is willing to lead people along the one and only proper route to escape the maze.

Now which of these analogies is more compatible both with biblical teaching and with what you know about the nature of God? Or is each analogy faulty? Perhaps you could construct an even better analogy or allegory that explains your conception of God's presence in the world today and how sincere seekers can move toward God.

CHRISTIAN PERSPECTIVES ON WORLD RELIGIONS

Religious diversity and pluralism are not some recently emergent western world phenomena. Christianity was born in the cultural stream of Greek, Roman, Jewish, and even Oriental religious and philosophical currents. Can you imagine how many different religions and worldviews were represented in the apostle Paul's audience during his address on Mars Hill in Athens? We'll offer four categories of interpretation regarding a Christian attitude toward other religions:

First, a widely-held conviction is that Christianity is so clearly superior to all other religions and, in fact, other religions remain devoid of ultimate truth and have precious little to offer seekers. This is the *absolutist* or *exclusivistic* understanding of religion. God has chosen to reveal himself originally through Israel and then specifically and supremely through Jesus, and God's revelation comes today only through reading the Bible. Thus, Christianity is the only true religion. All other religions are considered false, their basic teachings are in error and may be summarily dismissed as examples of human blindness Their adherents are pagans and idol worshipers, all of whom are bound for hell. Nothing in their beliefs, values, teachings, institutions, or ethics has any major insight or significance. Some might even claim other religions are demonic in origin and nature. The main motivation for Christian missions, of course, is to free people from the bondage of these false religions.

A completely opposite perspective emerges in reaction to the "hard-line *restrictivism*" of the first position. This second position is *reductionist*, reducing all religion to mostly human invention and insight. It advocates a phenomenological approach to religion. All religions are considered as basically equal. One need not pass judgment in terms of which is "right" or "wrong" in its teachings, but merely study how a particular religion works in the lives of its followers. In fact, one need not be "religious" in order to study world religions by this historical and phenomenological approach any more than one needs to be a tennis player to study the history and nature of the game of tennis.

A third approach is to consider Christianity as the "highest rung on the ladder" of world religions. Some might call this view *elitist*. Other religions do have significant value and are good "so far as they go," to be sure, but Christianity is clearly superior. Other religions may serve a valuable function in giving direction for the highest aspirations of the human spirit, and they also prepare their followers for the gospel of Jesus. Important doctrines about salvation, life, death, and suffering are given commendable yet only partial and fragmented explanation in other religions, but in Christianity these vital doctrines are explicated in full truth and deepest insight. Christianity is thus the religion which fulfills all other religious aspirations.

A fourth approach that many Christians take toward other religions might be labeled as *pluralism* or *syncretism* or, put simply, "total equality." This generalized view is that there is no real difference in any of the religions in areas of ultimate significance. Christianity is just one among many world religions and its unique claims are not greatly different in kind from unique claims in other religions. Christ is not the only way to salvation. Salvation, however it may be defined, is available through all religions. Each religion produces the same results for its adherents by pointing them to a Supreme Being, by providing moral rules which enable them to become good people, by giving them a hope for something better than the current life, by providing a community of faith for fellowship and encouragement, and by providing rituals and practices that keep them in touch with the sacred. And pluralists do not need to appeal to biblical support for their views, because the Bible is only true for Christians in the same sense that the *Vedas* are true for Hindus, the *Qur'an* true for Muslims, and other sacred literature true for other pious people. The only truth is found in human reason and experience.

This fourth approach has gained widespread acceptance among many spiritual-minded people in our contemporary, pluralistic society. University students generally hold this view by far more than any other. In fact, the basic premise of pluralism underlies Western liberal ideology in general. How tempting to see the broad similarities in major religions as reason enough to accept the proposition that all world religions are equal in doctrine, value, and function. Some leading religious and humanist thinkers have contended that the most dangerous idea in religion today is the notion that any one religion is truer than any other. Obviously, this perspective is the one employing the "mountain analogy." God is far bigger than the biggest mountain and all the religions in the world are like all the different roads up the same mountain or like all the different ways humans have tried to understand God. Another analogy is the experience of symphonic and choral music: the most beautiful music in the world is beautiful because it brings together different notes, different sounds, different parts, and they fit together in perfect harmony. Thus, each religion has a certain part to sing or notes to play that harmonize into the grand song of the universe.

In sum, according to the pluralist view, all religions are basically equal. Any religion can lead a devotee to God. Sure, one religion might fit the individual better than the others, so Christianity is good for Christians in the same way that Buddhism is good for Buddhists and Hinduism is good for Hindus. And Jesus is special for Christians, but he need not be savior for Muslims and Daoists. The unity within all world religions far outweighs the minor historical and cultural differences. Therefore, all religiously devoted people must go their own way free from being targeted by mission efforts, judgment, and criticism of others.

HOW WIDE IS GOD'S MERCY?

Let's proceed with two crucially important axioms. The first is that God's ultimate manifestation of himself is in the person Jesus Christ. The apostle Paul's powerful declaration to the Colossian Christians remains a stumblingblock to Jews, Muslims, and other pious religionists: "He [Christ] is the image of the invisible God....For in Christ all the fullness of the Deity lives in bodily form" (1:15; 2:9). God's plan to reconcile sinners to himself is through Jesus. God's abundant grace is rendered available to all through the voluntary sacrificial death of Jesus on the cross. And Jesus is the one mediator between God the Father and human beings. God is in the process of reconciling the world to himself through Jesus Christ. Jesus came to bring salvation to the entire world. In his farewell dialogue with his disciples, Jesus proclaimed that he was "the way, the truth, and the life" and that no one could access the Father except through him (Jn. 14:6). Early apostles preached that salvation from sin was located exclusively in the name of Jesus (Acts 4:12; see also the stern warning in 1 Jn. 2:23).

When the apostles and missionaries of the early Christian church proclaimed this radically new message, it was often received with great joy and gratitude. First century Christians considered Jesus an asset, not a liability. In modern times, the mention of Jesus among the general population can be potentially divisive. Mel Gibson's 2004 movie about the suffering and death of Jesus, *The Passion of the Christ*, became highly controversial even weeks before its general release. Sadly, some Christians today are somewhat apologetic in claiming that Jesus is truly something more than an inspiring teacher, a great moral example, or a vastly influential character in history—that Jesus is truly the divine Son of God who came to bring salvation to lost souls. Just as the apostle Paul claimed that the gospel of Christ would be foolishness to the intellectual elite and a scandal to traditional religious establishments, so the unique claims of the gospel seem folly and scandalous today to masses of non-Christians. Yet, whether popular or unpopular, persuasive or non-persuasive, Christians must continue boldly proclaiming this claim for the unique role of Jesus as God's Son and Savior for all humanity.

There is a second, equally important axiom: God's mercy is so wide and his grace is so deep that both divine mercy and grace are beyond our deepest imagination. God's compassion and lovingkindness toward the human family are both immeasurable and unfathomable. At this point, we must not cherry-pick certain Scriptures to build a case that God is some elitist, arbitrary, and stingy deity who only wants to save a handful of people who were "lucky enough" to be at the right place at the right time or just "smart enough" to get all the legal technicalities of church doctrine and practice figured out and properly implemented. We must stand back and look in awe at the big picture of the entire biblical narrative when it comes to depicting the true nature of our Father God—a God who seeks a loving relationship with every one of his created human beings. If it has always been God's will that salvation is a gift that will be shared with the many instead of the few, then God has always found a way, and will continue to find a way, to bring women and men into his fold of divine love and fellowship.

THE GOLDEN TEXT OF ALL SCRIPTURE

God has not simply made a few overtures to a few outstanding citizens. He has always sought healing and hope for nations of people. In Christian theology, students speak of both universality and particularity. Big words, for sure, but see how they can be drawn from the Golden Text of all Scripture: "For God so loved the world [that is, God loved all humanity; hence, universality] that he gave his one and only Son [particularity, as salvation is sent through the one Son], that whoever believes in him shall not perish but have eternal life" (Jn. 3:16). Nowhere in Scripture do we find a caricature of a petty, insecure, dictator-God who is sitting around and remaining passive while large numbers perish. And we certainly do not see a sadistic God who takes great pleasure in watching people perish. Yes, we do read of a God who could punish evildoers, but never without providing ample opportunity for sinners to renounce their evil ways and embrace faith-filled righteousness. The point is clearly made by the apostle Peter: "[God] is patient with you, not wanting anyone to perish, but everyone to come to repentance" (2 Pet. 3:9). And Paul echoed the same doctrine when he declared that God wants all people "to be saved and to come to a knowledge of the truth" (1 Tim. 2:4).

The selection of Israel as a special nation in covenant relationship with God was not some petty, arbitrary favoritism. God had a special role for Israel as a "light for the Gentiles" so that his chosen people would facilitate bringing "my salvation to the ends of the earth" (Isa. 49:6). God's election of Israel did bring privileges, but it also brought responsibilities of servanthood. As we look at Old Testament narratives, we see a God who was deeply concerned about the spiritual welfare of men and women outside the covenant community of Israel. Job is a non-Jewish person who is praised in both the Old and New Testaments for righteousness and loyalty to God in the midst of unrelenting personal hardship (note James 5:11). Melchizedek was a Canaanite priest of a god he called *El Elyon*, God Most High, a pagan priest who gave Abraham a special blessing and who received a tithe from Abraham in return (Gen. 14:17-24). Another pagan believer who receives honorable mention in the Old Testament is Abimelech, king of Gerar, described as a man of integrity and respect for God (Gen. 20:1-18). Jethro, father-in-law of Moses, was a priest of Midian who had known and worshiped God outside the family of Israel before he met Moses (Ex. 18:1-12).

The Bible narrates or references episodes of men and women of other traditions being deployed as conveyors of vital truths about life. Jesus himself marshaled examples of pagans who knew little or nothing of the true God or the chosen people of Israel and their mission. Jesus commended a pagan queen, the Queen of Sheba, for having sought the wisdom of Solomon; he even claimed that her example would condemn the stubborn complacency of the Jewish religious establishment of his day (Mt. 12:42; see 2 Chron. 9:1-12 for the original story). The more we learn about the devotion of religious people who are non-Christian, the more we may be either rebuked for lethargic commitment or inspired to deeper devotion. Jesus even spoke of some who served him without even being aware of serving the Christ (Mt. 25:37).

The most powerful Old Testament example of God's love and mercy, perhaps, is the story of Ninevah. Jonah's stubborn resistance to God's call for him to journey to Ninevah and deliver a message of rebuke and call for repentance, along with the famous three-day residence in the belly of a whale, have drawn the biggest headlines from the book of Jonah. The better part of the story, by far, than Jonah's unusual marine trauma is God's compassion for all citizens in a large urban area and his desire to demonstrate mercy and lovingkindness to "outsiders." God is so desirous to save these pagans that he simply seeks their repentance and new righteousness. God does not demand that they become Israelites, engage in certain rites and rituals, or make a special pilgrimage to the Temple in Jerusalem. In the Old Testament there are briefer references to God's acceptance of the righteousness of pagan peoples (see Psalm 87:4; 47:1; Jer. 18:7-8; Isa. 19:25; some might include God's relationship with the patriarchs in this list.). How many others have there been in history like the tax collector in Jesus' story (Lk. 18:13), who recognize their sinfulness and plead to God for mercy? Surely God's mercy and forgiveness are extended in these cases!

When Jesus preached the good news of the kingdom of heaven, he never described the kingdom in terms of only a few experiencing the glory of God. There will be a large, innumerable host of people at the banquet table enjoying a feast in the presence of the risen Lord. "All nations" come and worship before God in the heavenly scene (Rev. 15:4). Countering the attitude and strategy of some of his followers, Jesus was always finding ways to include in the kingdom those whom others rejected. After all, the Jesus of gospel narratives frequently shocked his disciples by associating with people whom they considered outside the pale. Just as the publican who is forgiven simply by asking for mercy (Lk. 18:9-14), so, too, the poor, lame, blind, and all others who are suffering must be invited to God's table. Jesus is quite clear on this point: God's grace is boundless. He commended the faith of a Roman military official (Mt. 8:10); he praised the Good Samaritan (Lk. 10:33-37); he engaged in theological dialogue with a Samaritan woman (Jn. 4:1-26). He included children in his welcome call despite the objection of some disciples. The piety of Cornelius found much favor with God and a reluctant Peter is dispatched to that household to teach everyone there about Jesus so that their faith might be complete (Acts 10).

The point: the Bible paints such a glorious picture of God's immense love for the entire world of people. God's mercy is wide. It extends indeed to amazing lengths. His grace is deep. His outreach, even at times through reluctant servants, is global. God longs for the salvation of all the nations and of all peoples. While human nature is elitist and exclusivist, God's nature finds every reason for being accepting and inclusive. And God is willing to operate outside the box that his orthodox believers have constructed for him. God has made provision for all people to be saved and become righteous before him. He never leaves anyone without at least some witness to his power and glory. What gloriously good news!

Can we bring all these biblical narratives and pictures to bear on the central question with which we began? Jesus spoke of his Father working continuously. Would not God still be working today behind the curtains of the stage of history, drawing people to himself? When we think of the examples of Abel, Enoch, Noah, Rahab, Ruth, Daniel, and Naaman, can we not conclude that God finds favor with spiritual faith that is uplifting and ennobling? Even though we have been commissioned to proclaim the good news of salvation found in the life and death of Jesus, would any of us dare deny the sovereignty and power of God to draw people to himself who have never heard of Jesus? Do we believe the declaration of Jesus that he, when lifted up, would seriously draw all people to himself (Jn. 12:32)? And just as people of biblical history who were outside the boundaries of God's chosen people still could find favor with God on the basis of responding in faith to whatever light from God was available, could not people find favor with God today on the same basis? We must never presume to cordon off people from God's favor on the basis of our own understanding, our own logic, or our own preferences. "Who has known the mind of the Lord?" Paul cautions us, "Or who has been his counselor?" (Rom. 11:34).

True Religion/False Religion

Let's return to our original question: how should Christians regard other religions? In the past, Christians mostly ignored other religions, just as other religions ignored Christians. And too many Christians have approached Hindus, Buddhists, and Muslim (and other non-Christian religionists) with the assumption that their religions are totally false, perhaps even demonic, and that if they accept Jesus as the divine Son of God they must abandon every concept and insight they have ever known about Ultimate Reality.

Let's reject the legalistic, hard-line view that claims Christianity is so superior to all other religions, and that other religions have nothing of value or insight to offer Christians. This view is both arrogant and judgmental. It fails to take seriously the cultures of other people, and, actually, there is a human element in *all* religions. This view also neglects to take into account that all the world's great religious traditions are similar because they help us become better human beings. This exclusivist position also fails to consider the light that Jesus can bring to every person regardless of background (see Jn. 1:9). As we've noted, Jesus himself spoke of people of another religion and culture rising up and condemning hypocritical or apathetic adherents of God's covenant faith.

A healthy respect for others means an understanding and appreciation for the best in their religious traditions. Is it possible that Hindus could teach Christians something valuable about the importance of spirituality and meditation? Might Hindus also teach Christians something of the dignity and value of all living creatures and avoidance of unnecessary harm against them? Is it possible that Buddhists could teach Christians something valuable about renouncing materialist values and pursuing peace? Might Buddhists also teach Christians something about the ideals of selflessness, pacifism, and social action? Is it possible that devout Muslims could teach Christians something valuable about daily spiritual disciplines and reverencing the name of God? Might Native Americans teach Christians something about the intricate web of life that connects all living creatures, the sanctity of all nature, and the inherent value of natural resources?

In humility we must concede that truth for our lives can come from many sources if our hearts and minds are open and receptive. Truth is truth, no matter who brings it. And all truth is God's truth. Along this journey, we Christians could swallow a dose of humility before we criticize other non-Christian religious people and admit that we too have sometimes perpetrated our own injustices, extolled the wrong values, committed terrible sins, endorsed the wrong causes, made embarrassing mistakes, and acted unwittingly even as enemies of the gospel. We might ask ourselves what positive values, other than our claims about Jesus, other religionists might learn from Christians.

Let's also reject the idea that all religions possess equal value. All religions definitely do *not* lead to God. The truth is, despite so much similarity in world religions, there are some crucial differences. False religion has always been a reality in every generation. Error can masquerade as truth. Darkness can masquerade as light. The New Testament teaches that both light and darkness co-exist (Jn. 1:5) and that both Satan and his servants masquerade as servants of light (2 Cor. 11:14-15). There is religion that is positive, healthy, and beneficial to all devoted followers; contrariwise, there is religion that is negative, dysfunctional, and destructive to those who drawn by its influence. Healthy religion can heal divisions and unite brothers and sisters; false religion can divide, harm, and destroy men and women.

Canaanite religion is depicted in the early books of the Old Testament as so wicked and destructive by its idolatry, rank immorality, and degrading worship ritual (sacred prostitution) that God called for its denunciation and destruction. In the first century, apostles and early Christians confronted idolatry and sexual immorality in pagan worship rituals. Can anyone consider the religion of the Aztecs and other Mesoamericans, which countenanced scores of thousands of human sacrifice each year, or the practice of voodoo and sorcery in some Caribbean countries, to have been totally positive and healthy? Today, one might only consider dangerous cults, for example the People's Temple controlled by the late Jim Jones or the Branch Davidians controlled by the late David Koresh, to reach two conclusions: first, while ordinarily a source of blessing, religion can degenerate into a dangerous curse upon people's lives; and, second, no one is immune from becoming "religious" in unhealthy and dangerous ways.

Are the major world religions stepping stones to Christ? Though we might romanticize about the relationship between Jesus and non-Christian religions, there is one realistic answer: very seldom are other religions the preliminary steps to acceptance of the divinity and authority of Christ. True enough, pious and devoted followers of the major world religions may very well develop many of the character traits that the Holy Spirit develops in Christians, but it is phony confidence to believe these people will easily name Jesus as their Savior. How many devout Hindus, Buddhists, or Muslims might you know who have embraced Jesus and Christian doctrine? On the other hand, is it possible that some people through God's common grace, meditation, and spiritual discipline can find the "way, truth, and life" of Jesus without knowing specifically about Jesus? Do all major religions simply provide recognizable variants of the same path, all of which speak of dying to an old identity and being born into a new, much more spiritual identity?

To our central question: do all world religions lead to God? First, let's consider that not all religions accept the existence of a personal, sovereign Supreme Being. For example, Buddhists generally profess no belief in a deity, and their ideas are rooted in empirical observation and evidence and not in personal faith. Jainism is essentially atheistic. Thus, not all religions even attempt to lead followers to God. Also, there are some major religions that have no interest in salvation from sin as evangelical Christians think of salvation and redemption. And, we have noted there are so many unhealthy and evil sides to many religions that many times these religions are paths to hell, either literally or figuratively.

Perhaps the most positive conclusion about various world religions at their best, most healthy, practices would be: all religions may not lead to God, but all great religions offer counsel for becoming better people. They lead their followers to some sense of purpose in life as well as to peace and understanding about dimensions of reality beyond their control. Basically, then, all the major faith and wisdom traditions seek in one way or another to benefit human beings.

THE CRUCIAL ROLE OF FAITH

Now let's return to a final question, one that has confounded thinkers within Christian communities: what will be the plight of people who have never heard of Jesus Christ? As we move toward an answer, let's offer some basic premises.

First, God has always revealed himself in some way to all people everywhere. There is no one who does not have some light from God. To the ecstatic observers at Lystra who had seen Paul and Barnabas heal a crippled man and had sought to worship them, the two missionaries spoke of God: "In the past, he let nations go their own way. Yet he has not left himself without testimony" (Acts 14:17). Paul told the Athenian intellectuals that God created humanity in such a way "so that men would seek him and perhaps reach out for him and find him" (Acts 17:27). So God has revealed himself in nature, in the human conscience, and in sacred Scriptures. Could not the omnipotent and loving God who revealed himself most completely in Jesus also be at work behind the scenes in all the healthy religions of the world? God has not left himself without witness anywhere in the world!

Second, the Bible never condemns the *unbeliever*, the one who does not believe because he has never been blessed with the opportunity to hear the good news. The *disbeliever* is the one who hears clearly and stubbornly rejects the good news. Scripture is clear about those who are lost—those who persistently reject God by rejecting such light as God gives them. God rejects only those who reject him.

Third, those who are saved are saved by faith and not by merely possessing all the right facts or being in the right church or right religion. A major point of Paul's magnificent treatise to the Romans is that Abraham was justified before God by his responsive faith when he surely knew next to nothing about comparative religions and various worldviews. And he certainly could not have known about Jesus. Remember that Abraham's faith is presented by Paul as the modeling ideal faith for all people who desire to be right with God.

And what is the essence of faith? Well, it is not simply a pre-packaged set of correct propositions and doctrinal statements that await our signing the dotted line. Faith is more than the content of one's theology. Faith is more than factual accuracy on our recalling all the sacred stories. A faith that requires every piece of the puzzle of life to fit perfectly just might be factually correct but present an empty, useless picture for ourselves, for others, and for our God. After all, we cannot master all the little facts and details of our faith tradition. Neither is authentic faith pretending to believe something, either to ourselves or others, when deep inside we do not really believe it. Pretended faith is phony and impotent.

By contrast, "heart faith" is being in "sync" with God. Such faith permeates every fiber of our being. This faith is a longing and seeking for God. It is the humble search for, and disciplined response to, the will of God. Faith is a process. It is a journey taken step by step with a certain degree of emotional investment. This journey sometimes means stumbling, taking a few falls, and yet, at certain happy times, breaking into a spontaneous dance of joy and gratitude. The author of Hebrews is clear: "Without faith it is impossible to please God" (11:6).

—•—

Devotional Reflection

God made us as creatures who can reflect on our existence, seek a better world, and search to find ultimate truth, and real life. Truth is crucially important in worldviews and religion. Sincerity of convictions is not enough in the practice of religion any more than it is in the practice of medicine or aeronautics. All Christians should be tolerant and appreciative of other world religions and worldviews, to be certain, if for no other reason than Christian charity and the Golden Rule demand such an attitude. On the other hand, considering any religion just as true and valid as any other religions invalidates the principle of objective, universal truth and would actually insult followers of some major religions.

As Christians we believe. God has revealed himself ultimately and fully in Jesus. The claims Jesus makes for himself are unlike the claims any other moral or religious leader makes. The declarations Jesus makes about God the Father are unlike statements about God from any other teacher. He is reality; he is authentic. Jesus has neither peers nor equals on the world scene nor may we look for any successors to him. As Christians, he is not simply our Savior, but he is Lord of our lives.

One of the great truths Jesus taught us is that God possesses expansive mercy and lovingkindness for all the people of the world and that his Father remains active in the world drawing people to himself. God is the one who begins and ends his redemptive work, and he does this work in his own way and on his own timetable without consulting us or explaining his strategy. We are in no position to predict what God will do in his radical grace and generosity. God is God and we are not! What we can surely know is that if we worship a God who rejects those who sincerely seek after him the best they know how, however stumbling and bumbling may be their effort, we worship the wrong God. And beware especially of any church that writes people off, that seeks ways to exclude people rather than to draw them into fellowship.

How does this translate into our everyday, interpersonal relations? Our initial response in meeting someone for the first time, perhaps a person we perceive to be culturally different, should not be, "I wonder if she knows the Lord Jesus Christ," but, instead, "Here is another human being, a person who, like me, also bears the image of God, someone I have been blessed to encounter in life's journey, and someone who may be receptive to my deeds and my words of service and compassion." So we approach others as human beings, each one as an individual with a personal name and a personal history, rather than as just another person who happens to be a Muslim, a Hindu, a Jew, a Buddhist, or an agnostic. We make clear that we care about others as neighbors before we engage them as subjects of evangelization. This outreach of empathy and acceptance is not a cowardly compromise of Christian discipleship—it is a demonstration of it!

Our task can be understood positively and negatively. In a positive sense, we are commissioned to spread the good news about Jesus. As someone has put it, we can tell others that the good news is that the bad news is not true. Once we have met others as neighbors we care about and with whom we seek a relationship, the purpose in sharing the good news is to take the story of Christ and his cross to those who are willing to believe when they hear it. No one is worse off for hearing the gospel. Stated another way, God has never called us to determine who is going to heaven and who is going to hell. Our challenge is not to prove we are right and all others are wrong. We can genuinely accept Jesus as the way without condemning those who disagree or those who have never heard of our Savior.

Let's draw a simple, yet profound, conclusion: wherever people of any culture or nation seek God, we Christians may genuinely feel a common cause. Wherever they confess Jesus, listen to Jesus, follow Jesus, and serve others in his name, we may feel a family bond of sisters and brothers.

Prayer: Dear God, thank you for your abundant gift of mercy and salvation. Most of all, thank you for Jesus. May we be true to our summons both to live and to share the glorious message of our Son, but be spared the obsession to instruct you on who should be saved and who should be condemned. We do not pretend to know how you work through the various religions and faith traditions of the world or how you may use people very different from us to accomplish your will. So, Lord, keep us humble. May we have proper appreciation for the riches found within various worldviews different from our own, but reject and offer correction for those teachings that we know to be clearly in error. And grant us the wisdom to know the difference. May we always remember we are not called to trust in a religion, but to trust in you. May we grow in faith by the light you have given us. Through your Son, whom we joyfully accept as the light of the world. Amen.

24

Epilogue: Christianity Makes Sense

Our study has not spoken yet about Plato, but one of the most enduring passages in western philosophy, found in book seven of his *Republic*, is his famous allegory of the cave. As typical, Plato uses Socrates as the spokesman. At the back of this cave a group of prisoners has been chained from birth, and they can only see shadows on the wall in front of them that are cast by statues held up before a bright fire behind them. The unfortunate prisoners do not really know what they are seeing. The shadows on the wall are the only reality they have experienced. One of the prisoners breaks free from his chains, sees the fire, and then makes his way through darkness to stand in the bright, blinding of the sun. While tempted to stay in this bright new world, his compassion for the prisoners compels him to return to the cave, tell them about the other world and its glory, and facilitate their release. Alas, the prisoners reject the message, kill the messenger, and remain in the cave to maintain their illusions and sense of security.

The Allegory of the Cave has become a touchstone of western thinking, rich with applications. Aren't the images projected to the back wall of the cave similar to the images we perceive in the movies or on television or in newspapers and magazines? Don't many people confuse appearances with reality? Aren't the perceptions we experience in our daily lives often incomplete, distorted, or inaccurate? Does not the mind of a human being make an ascent from shadowy illusion to enlightenment—from mere feeling and opinion to informed opinion to rationally based knowledge and wisdom? Isn't discarding false beliefs and convictions and then embracing the truth at times a disturbing and painful process? Though Plato certainly predates Christian thought, his allegory clashes mightily with the secular humanist's (or naturalist's) most basic paradigm—that the world perceived through our five senses and the human life experienced in an earthly life span constitute the only world and life that exist.

Clearly all worldviews are not alike. We must not gloss over serious differences in the faith claims of Jews, Christians, Muslims, and any other religious people and then pretend that differences are unimportant. Rather, worldviews should be continually tested and evaluated. Quite likely you as reader have already tested your personal worldview without giving much awareness to the process. Ronald Nash, a Christian philosopher and professor, recommends four tests for worldviews: (1) The test of *reason* is the test of logic. A worldview must have logical consistency; inconsistency or contradiction is a sign of error. (2) The test of *outer experience* means that worldviews should be relevant to what we know about the world and to ourselves; a worldview claim must not conflict with what we know to be true about the physical universe. (3) The test of *inner experience* means that a worldview must fit what we know about ourselves and our inner world. (4) The test of *practice* means that worldviews should be tested not simply in the library or classroom but also in the laboratory of life; in other words, the worldview must actually work to bring harmony, peace, meaning, and fulfillment to the person who espouses it.

While you likely may have received early indoctrination within one religion or faith, you have been confronted with challenges to that system. Perhaps it is a major failure in your life. Perhaps the sudden, accidental death of a classmate. Perhaps the diagnosis of terminal cancer with one of your parents. Or maybe the news of a tidal tsunami that suddenly wipes out the lives and fortunes of thousands of people. Maybe it's having relatives who lose their home and their material possessions in a hurricane. Or maybe news of more suicide bombings, not simply in the Middle East but also in Madrid or London. Or maybe having a dear friend falsely accused of a crime or serious offense that he or she did not commit. The longer we live, the more life seems to hurl such tests our way.

THE INEVITABILITY OF CHOICE

Wouldn't it be nice, some might think, to spend a lifetime of reflecting on various worldviews and crucial political and social issues and never make a choice about any one? Does God exist or not exist? Why commit to some position? After all, God's existence cannot be proved or disproved with absolute scientific certainty. Is there an afterlife? Who can conclusively prove its existence, so why not just live for this life since it is the only life we know for certain? Is Jesus the divine Son of God? Well, how can we say for certain? Aren't there some archaeologists who have claimed recently to have found the family burial tomb of Jesus? The bodily resurrection was the most important, authenticating miracle in the story of Jesus, yet none of us actually witnessed that event. Since we can only depend on the account of biased reporters, why believe?

Lack of sufficient evidence for irrefutable answers does not make these questions any less important. Even if we feel we lack sufficient evidence, we must live our lives as though we believe or disbelieve. If we disbelieve we will not pray, we will not study Scripture, we will not worship, we will not seek spiritual fellowship with other believers, and we will not contemplate the life to come. If we do believe, we will not only do these things, but we will see ourselves as possessing a spiritual dimension, or soul, and believe that the material blessings and advantages of our culture are not nearly as important as spiritual blessings. The existentialist thinkers may have been wrong about the despair and absurdity of human life for most people, but they were correct in their insistence that all humans cannot evade choice about meaning and purpose in their lives. To borrow some language from Sartre: not to decide is to decide—to decide on the status quo in social and political issues and in religion to live by an uninspired, legalistic, paint-by-the-numbers system.

So is it really possible to be an agnostic or uncommitted observer in practice? In the final analysis, must not all of us choose to live as a believer or as a nonbeliever? It may be possible to say to ourselves that intellectually we do not take a position on the existence of God, the divinity of Christ, or the claims of Scripture. But in the end we must choose how we are to live.

THE WAY OF JESUS

We all need a path. We would be lost without a path or without truth. You may be one of a growing throng of people who declares, "I'm not religious, but I am spiritual." To you, this declaration may mean you are totally "turned off" by assembly-line, organized religion and religious services. It may mean that you believe all religions contain truth and you must not judge them. It may be that you enthusiastically embrace a statement attributed to Gandhi: "God has no religion." On the other hand, to say that you are "spiritual" surely means you embrace the idea that there is some force, some power, some reality, some set of values, that transcend yourself and your immediate life situation.

Hopefully you have seen that there is undeniable uniqueness about Jesus. We have contended there are an ultimate mystery, ineffability, and infinity about God beyond human comprehension. We would surely concur with the Apostle Paul's statement to the church in ancient Corinth some two thousand years ago: "We know only a portion

of the truth, and what we say about God is always incomplete" (from Eugene Peterson's
The Message, 1 Corinthians 13).

Despite the inescapable and essential mystery, God has truly revealed himself in
a unique way in Jesus the Christ. There have been many great religious leaders and
teachers, but Jesus makes claims for himself that are not made on behalf of any other
religious teacher. Jesus makes declarations about God and the Kingdom of Heaven not
uttered by any other religious teacher. Jesus was not simply "great" as were Socrates,
Alexander, Michelangelo, da Vinci, Mozart, Napoleon, Shakespeare, Washington,
Jefferson, Lincoln, or Einstein—he was and is unique! And in his unchanging nature,
as claimed by the anonymous author of Hebrews in the New Testament (13:8), he will
always be unique. He has neither peers nor equals.

Jesus offered himself as the way, as truth, and as life (Jn.14:6). Though the rugged
path of Jesus at times cuts radically across mainstream culture, this way is sensible.
The path begins by dying to self, dying to an old identity, and resolving to live a new
life. The essence of the new life is one of unselfish, humble, and relentless servanthood to others. God's Spirit dwells within us as the driving force for our fidelity, love,
compassion, kindness, generosity, peace, and patience toward other people that we
encounter in our journey. We both continue and indwell this grand story of divine
love as we seek to be the voice, the eyes, the hands, and the arms of Jesus for our place
and time. Sometimes our servant acts are grand and magnificent and often inspire
attention and gratitude, but, in most cases, these deeds seem insignificant and unno-
ticed by worldly people. And in this steadfast commitment to live as Jesus lived and
relate to others as Jesus related to others, we find both energy for our burdens and joy
and peace for our inner souls.

The heart of Christianity remains sensible and practical. Yes, the libraries of
Christian institutions are filled with volumes on systematic theology. The Christian
religion and Christian thought through the ages can be studied in great depth and its
subject matter from Abelard to Zwingli and from "adventism" to "worship" may be
carefully analyzed. After all, there are so many deep and profound subjects in theology
to debate and digest. One can earn a Ph. D. in biblical studies or a Th. D. in theological
studies. Always remember, however, there is an essential difference between the religion *about* Jesus and the religion *of* Jesus.

In religious publications and religious programming, much space and time are
devoted to the religion *about* Jesus—having the right doctrine, combating false doctrine, implementing proper *ecclesiology* (the doctrine of the church), knowing all about
the end of time, determining "correct" interpretation of difficult biblical texts, and
taking the "right" position on public policy issues such as welfare, immigration, abortion, euthanasia, stem cell research, and same-sex marriage. But Jesus seemed not

concerned over doctrinal issues, church organization, church growth strategies, parachurch organizations, controversial socio-political issues, or styles of worship. The gospel narratives do not teach us about Jesus as "sound doctrine," but a real person. His "truth" embraced by his disciples resides in right relationships, first with his Father and then with one another.

The religion *of* Jesus, by contrast to religion *about* Jesus, demands a response that is much less academic and argumentative in nature and is much more practical in real life—love your neighbor as yourself, feed the hungry, care for the sick and dying, provide opportunity for the poor, visit those who are in prison, work to bring understanding and peace, reach out to the alienated and disfranchised women and men, demonstrate hospitality to the stranger, care for the homeless, reject the materialistic and self-serving values of the prevailing culture—behavior that Jesus both commanded and modeled.

Regrettably, much of the radical nature and rhetorical force of Jesus' commands have dimmed by frequent repetition and familiarity. Jesus simply commanded, "Follow me!" He did not command, "Explain me," "Compare me," "Defend me," "Analyze me," or "Develop complex doctrines in my name," but simply "Follow me." To follow Jesus is to follow the way of Jesus, that is, to take up his cross, listen to his words, and perform his deeds, and not obsess over what others say. And if we claim that we truly love God, then we must truly love those whom God loves.

Yes, other religions besides Christianity capture some of this way, this truth, and this life. And Jesus was certainly the fullest and most perfect embodiment of this way, but not the only expression of the way. How appropriate to be blessed and inspired by the noble example of courageous and principled people such as Socrates, Francis of Assisi, William Tyndale, Joan of Arc, Martin Luther, Sir Thomas More, William Carey, Anne Hutchinson, William Wilberforce, Harriet Tubman, Susan B. Anthony, Albert Schweitzer, Dietrich Bonhoeffer, Helen Keller, Anne Frank, Mohandas Gandhi, Rosa Parks, Mother Teresa, Martin Luther King, Jr., Nelson Mandela, and the list could continue almost *ad infinitum*! And, undoubtedly, the chief distinction between Christianity and all the other of the world's religions is the cross. Gandhi contended that of all the truths emanating from the Christian religion, the one which emerged supreme and paramount was the cross of Jesus.

The cross of Jesus, a melodramatic story and a stumblingblock to disbelievers, is without parallel in other world religions and worldviews. The cross demonstrated in history the magnanimous gift of God's grace. The cross depicted the depth of evil in humankind and is not a story about any one race, one culture, one nation, or one generation. The cross stands as an indictment of the moral guilt in all of us. This cross was not *for* the benefit of some and *against* all others. The cross is the totally innocent person dying for the totally guilty masses of all humanity. The cross is God's way of showing our real Savior and what he was willing to offer to satisfy God's holy demands of justice.

We can know Jesus in some special way. The Muslim will not typically claim to have a special relationship with Muhammad; nor the Buddhist with Gautama; nor the rationalist with Socrates or Confucius; nor the naturalist with Aristotle; nor the Marxian with Marx; nor the Taoist with Lao-Tzu. These leaders inspired devotion and appreciation in their followers. Their contributions to philosophy and intellectual history cannot be denied. With Jesus and his disciples there is significant difference—in no other religion does the founder offer the blessing of living within the hearts and lives of his followers.

Christians are called to be faithful to Jesus, not "right" on every moral position and every religious technicality. Faithful not to particular religious systems or institutions and certainly not faithful to any custom or tradition that seeks to exclude, marginalize, or discount people who are simply different from us. Being a Christian is not simply a matter of intellectual acceptance of certain faith claims and following the ethics of Jesus. The awesome experience is an earnest quest for the will of God and inviting the Spirit of the Christ into our hearts and lives, thus giving us the hope of glory. Even if we do not fathom the movement of God in history and in our lives, as Christians we can cherish and maintain a relationship with the risen and living Christ. And that relationship is our highest calling and our deepest honor.

Bibliographical Essay

In the writing of this book, I have drawn from a diverse collection of materials—articles, essays, and books, but also from two other important sources: one, a wide range of class lesson materials and lecture notes in religion, philosophy, and history accumulated over the years in teaching and speaking, and, two, informal discussions with a diverse group of students and colleagues. In my classes at Nashville State Community College I have enjoyed interaction with fundamentalist Christians, mainline Christians, evangelicals, Muslims (usually there were several enrolled in every class), a few Hindus, an occasional Buddhist, and, finally, several atheists and agnostics. I've always attempted to learn something new about the worldviews of the brightest of these colleagues and students.

The bibliography lists the books that were consulted during this study and this essay will provide more specific documentation with attribution to publications, including periodicals, and people to which I am indebted for evidence and insight.

Chapter 1 is an introduction to the concept of worldviews. I am indebted to my colleague at Lipscomb, Lee Camp, for explaining the concept that one's worldview determines what questions one asks of God. See his *Mere Discipleship: Radical Christianity in a Rebellious World* (Grand Rapids, MI: Brazos Press, 2003), pp. 20-21; the reference to James Cone is drawn from this source. Author James W. Sire has devoted much of his professional life to explaining worldviews. His *The Universe Next Door: A Basic Worldview Catalogue*, 3rd ed. (Downers Grove, IL: InterVarsity Press, 1997), has served as a standard text on the subject. In his more recent little volume, *Naming the Elephant: Worldview as a Concept* (Downers Grove, IL: InterVarsity Press, 2004), Sire discusses the history of philosophical thinking in terms of worldview. He claims that Wilhelm Dilthey (1833-1911) was the first to use the term, and he discusses its use in the writing of other philosophers and theologians, including Ludwig Wittgenstein, James Orr, Abraham Kuyper, James Olthuis, Albert M. Wolters, and Ronald Nash. Sire contends that worldviews have both an objective referent and a deeply subjective character (p. 47).

Though an older work, I highly recommend Colin Chapman's encyclopedic work, *The Case for Christianity: An Eerdmans Handbook* (Grand Rapids, MI: Eerdmans, 1981). In a highly organized format, Chapman lays out the basic questions a worldview answers and then, employing a large number of quotations from philosophers and theologians, contrasts Christian answers with other worldview answers. Several of the writings of Charles Colson, former Nixon aide who began a prison ministry, are structured in terms of worldview thinking. The best of these books in worldviews seems to be *How Now Shall We Live?* (with Nancy Pearcey; Wheaton, IL: Tyndale House, 1999); Colson, along with Ellen Vaughn, discusses his understanding of the prevailing worldview in America *in The Body: Being Light in Darkness* (Dallas: Word Publishing, 1992); he sees our prevailing worldview as secular, antihistorical, naturalistic, utopian, and pragmatic (pp. 165-82). And finally, I would recommend Arthur F. Holmes, *Contours of a World View* (Grand Rapids, MI: Eerdmans, 1983), a volume rooted deeply in theology and philosophy.

Chapters 2, 3, and 4 deal with the proper use of the mind as a special gift from God to discover truth and think creatively in order to bless others and improve society. I gladly acknowledge my indebtedness to Dallas Willard's *Renovation of the Heart: Putting on the Character of Christ* (Colorado Springs, CO: NavPress, 2002) for his insights about the process of thinking, the development of ideas, and the power inherent within great ideas (idea grip). To his assertion, "The prospering of God's cause on earth depends upon his people thinking well" (p. 105), I could only add a hearty "amen." I am also indebted to John MacArthur (general editor), *Think Biblically: Recovering a Christian Worldview* (Wheaton, IL: Crossway Books, 2003), especially chapter 2, "Cultivating a Biblical Mindset," by Richard L. Mayhue. Statistics on the brain, heartbeats, breaths, *et cetera,* are drawn from this source, p. 38. The brief quotations in these chapters are drawn from my personal file of quotations, many of which were collected from anthologies in books or on-line sources, and some quotations were drawn from Claudia Setzer, *The Quotable Soul: Inspiring Quotations Crossing Time and Culture* (New York: John Wiley and Sons, 1994). The quotation from Stephan Prothero near the end of chapter two is from his book, *Religious Literacy: What Every American Needs to Know—And Doesn't* (New York: HarperCollins, 2007), p. 277. A relatively new book that discusses the theology of thinking and the nature of true wisdom is J. Mark Bertrand's *(Re)Thinking Worldview: Learning to Think, Live, and Speak in This World* (Wheaton, IL: Crossway, 2007).

When teaching a course in the Introduction to Philosophy, I typically offer an assignment early in the semester for each student to write a one-page essay on the greatest idea in human history. The student was free to make one's own selection and great ideas could be drawn from any of the arts, humanities, or sciences. The fun and challenge I enjoyed with that assignment provided the idea for chapter three, which captures the essence of what I attempted to teach my students. As for brief stories of the great inventers and great explorers, I have always been intrigued by two substantial volumes by historian Daniel J. Boorstin: *The Discoverers: A History of Man's Search to Know His World and Himself* (New York: Random House, 1983) and *The Creators: A History of Heroes of the Imagination* (New York: Random House, 1992). The final book in that fascinating series of stories is *The Seekers: The Story of Man's Continuing Quest to Understand His World* (New York: Random House, 1998). And finally, a very colorfully illustrated encyclopedic approach to a wide range of ideas is Felipe Fernandez-Armesto, *Ideas That Changed the World* (New York: DK Publishing, 2003); scores of ideas are presented in brief essays that are placed in categories of major eras of history from "The Mind of the Hunter (30,000 to 10,000 B.C.E.)" to "The Age of Uncertainty (1900 to 2000)."

Chapter 4 presents some fairly traditional material in understanding the nature of truth. One source of this traditional epistemology is Ronald H. Nash, *Life's Ultimate Questions*, chapter 10, pp. 228-51. Pilate's question to Jesus, "What is truth?" is, of course, a crucially important question, perhaps more important than the questioner ever realized. An interesting narrative of Jesus standing before Pilate when that question was asked is offered by Charles Colson in *The Body*; see chapters 12-13, pp. 149-64.

Chapters 5 and 6 discuss the existence and presence of God. Most standard philosophy textbooks will give some detail on the life and arguments for God of Thomas Aquinas. For an historical survey of atheism and skepticism in western world philosophy as well as other ideas for this discussion, I gladly acknowledge the research, analysis, and insights of Alister E. McGrath, *Intellectuals Don't Need God and Other Modern Myths: Building Bridges to Faith Through Apologetics* (Grand Rapids, MI: Zondervan, 1993). Chapter 6 in this book, entitled "Clash of Worldviews," discusses western world philosophy and includes discussion of rationalism, humanism, and postmodernism. A somewhat less traditional, yet very readable, approach to apologetics is Brian McLaren's *Finding Faith: A Self-Discovery Guide For Your Spiritual Quest* (Grand Rapids, MI: Zondervan, 1999). I am indebted to Alistair E. McGrath, *Studies in Doctrine* (Grand Rapids, MI: Zondervan, 1997), especially the section entitled "Understanding the Trinity," pp. 123-218, for insights about the existence of God and the nature of God as revealed in Scripture. For a clear statement of both the theistic and the atheistic position, I recommend the dialogue in J. P. Moreland and Kai Nielsen (with contributions by several outstanding thinkers), *Does God Exist? The Debate Between Theists and Atheists* (Amherst, NY: Prometheus Books, 1993). Readers may enjoy learning of how a famous atheist changed his mind about God in Antony Flew, with Roy Abraham Varghese, *There Is A God: How the World's Most Notorious Atheist Changed His Mind* (New York: Harper One, 2007).

Studies show that Americans believe in God by a margin of 92% to 6% with only 2% saying "don't know;" over 60% of Americans said they would not vote for an atheist for president (*Newsweek*, November 11, 2006, p. 47). The recent books cited in these chapters as authored by three atheists are Sam Harris, *The End of Faith: Religion, Terror, and the Future of Reason* (New York: W. W. Norton, 2004); Richard Dawkins, *The God Delusion* (Boston: Houghton, Mifflin Company, 2006), and Christopher Hitchens, *God Is Not Great: How Religion Poisons Everything* (New York: Twelve [Hatchet Book Group USA], 2007). An interesting dialogue between best-selling Christian author and pastor Rick Warren and atheist and neuroscientist Sam Harris is conducted in *Newsweek*, April 9, 2007, pp. 58-63. Christian scholars Alister and Joanna McGrath have written a review and refutation of Dawkins in *The Dawkins Delusion: Atheistic Fundamentalism and the Denial of the Divine* (Downers Grove, IL: InterVarsity Press, 2007). The statement about a "meta-realm of space-times" and the universe being zillions of times more vast than most ever imagine is drawn from Dennis Overbye, "Zillions of Universes? Or Did Ours Get Lucky?" *New York Times*, October 28, 2003. The statement by C. S. Lewis toward the end of chapter 6 is quoted in a number of sources, one of which is Kumar, *Christianity for Skeptics*, p. 116.

Chapter 7 discusses faith and doubt. The early quotes from Yancey are drawn from his book *Reaching for Invisible God: What Can We Expect to Find?* (Grand Rapids, MI: Zondervan, 2000), pp. 37 and 41. While I have long thought about doubt and its role in my Christian walk, I am especially indebted to Yancey for helping me clarify some thoughts about doubt, especially chapter 3, "Room for Doubt." The Buechner quote is also drawn from this Yancey source, pp. 42-43. The quote from Mother Teresa is taken from her correspondence found in Brian Kolodiefchuk, *Mother Teresa: Come Be My Light* (Doubleday, 2007) and is included in a cover story by David Van Biema, "Her Agony," *Time*, September 3, 2007, pp. 36-43. The quote from Kathleen Norris is drawn from her book of essays, *Amazing Grace: Vocabulary of Faith* (New York: Riverhead Books [Penguin Putnam], 1998), p. 67. The quote by Paul Tillich is drawn from Francis Collins, *The Language of God: A Scientist Presents Evidence for Belief* (New York: Free Press, 2006), p. 33.

Chapter 8 discusses the concept of God as understood in various worldviews. I offer special thanks to my colleague and good friend at Lipscomb University, Dr. Larry Brown, for reading this one chapter and offering several valuable insights. There are so many books written on the nature of God, of course, though many readers may especially be informed and challenged by Karen Armstrong's popular volume, *A History of God: The 4,000-Year Quest of Judaism, Christianity, and Islam* (New York: Ballantine Books, 1993). A scholarly book on the conception of Ultimate Reality in various worldviews and cultures is Aida B. Spencer and William D. Spencer, *The Global God: Multicultural Evangelical Views of God* (Grand Rapids, MI: Baker Books, 1998); I have found this book to be one of the most provocative books on human understanding of God that I have ever read. A more recent significant publication is Rodney

Stark, *Discovering God: The Origins of the Great Religions and the Evolution of Belief* (New York: Harper One, 2007). Sociologist Stark believes truth about God can be discovered through the application of reason; he also contends that Christianity offers the most "complex and nuanced" vision of God and the most "comprehensive doctrine of salvation."

Though most Americans are willing to make a pledge of allegiance to "one nation under God," they do not all have the same image of the Almighty in mind. A 2006 survey of religion in the USA found four very different images of God's personality and engagement in human affairs, and the region in which Americans live may be as much a determining factor as broad denominational affiliation. The survey was written and analyzed by sociologists from Baylor University's Institute for Studies of Religion and conducted by Gallup. The four categories of Americans' perception of God: (1) The Authoritarian God (31.4%) is angry at humanity's sins and fully engaged in every creature's life and world affairs; (2) The Benevolent God (23%) sets absolute standards in the Bible and is primarily a forgiving God, much like the father who embraces the penitent prodigal son; (3) The Critical God (16%) has his judgmental eye on the world, but he is not going to intervene, either to punish or comfort; (4) The Distant God (24.4%) is a cosmic force that launched the world, then left it rotating on its own. Source: *The Tennessean,* September 12, 2006, p. 3A, and *Time,* October 30, 2006, pp. 50-51.

Chapter 9 on free will and determinism certainly raises again a perennial issue and most philosophy texts will discuss the issue. I acknowledge with appreciation and respect my teaching colleague at Lipscomb University, Dr. David Lawrence, professor of history, who read this manuscript and shared his insights on God's election and human response. David counsels me gently that this chapter embraces free will a bit more than he can endorse. Nearly all my material in this chapter is from lecture notes for lessons on the topic in my philosophy classes.

Chapter 10 on Socrates was surely influenced most by my reading of several introductory philosophy textbooks, preparation of class lesson material, and teaching classes in philosophy. One interesting essay entitled "Was Socrates a Christian Before Christ?" may be found in Timothy C. Tennent, *Christianity at the Religious Roundtable* (Grand Rapids, MI: Baker [Academic] Books, 2002), chapter 8, pp. 199-210. The quotation from Jean-Jacques Rousseau toward the end of the chapters is cited in Kumar, *Christianity for Skeptics,* p. 31.

Chapter 11 on Buddha and Buddhism is drawn from my reading over the years in various texts in world religions. Check the bibliography to follow for titles of some of these texts. One of the best briefer pieces on the subject, with the added benefit of colorful photographs, Perry Garfinkel (with photography by Steve McCurry), "Buddha

Rising: Out of the Monastery, into the Living Room," *National Geographic*, December, 2005, 88-109. My thinking on the similarities and differences between the Buddha and Jesus were surely influenced by Ravi Zacharias, *The Lotus and the Cross: Jesus Talks with Buddha* (Sisters, OR: Multnomah, 2001).

Chapter 12 places Gandhi and Jesus side by side. The story of Gandhi is told in many secondary sources in recent world history and in at least one movie. I have found that many university students have as much respect for Gandhi as almost any other character in history. I'm indebted also to a wonderful essay by Philip Yancey on Gandhi in *Soul Survivor* (New York: Doubleday 2001), pp. 147-77.

In **chapter 13** which discusses Judaism and touches on why the Jewish people have rejected the claims for divinity of Jesus, I have benefited and been blessed by professional association with Rabbi Kenneth Kantor, one time chief rabbi at Nashville's Congregation Micah, and Professor Amy-Jill Levine of the Divinity School, Vanderbilt University. Professor Levine specifically read this chapter and offered numerous valuable perspectives and insights. There is such a large body of literature about Judaism. I hope readers will pick up on the simple reality that there are major differences between biblical Judaism and rabbinic Judaism as it has developed over the centuries and that Christians must not stereotype Judaism as simply continuation of the beliefs and practices of the Old Testament. Herman Wouk's book *This Is My God: The Jewish Way of Life* (Boston: Little, Brown, and Company, 1987) is a very straightforward explanation of Judaism. I greatly benefited from a book written for Christians by Rabbi Yechiel Eckstein, *What Christians Should Know About Jews and Judaism* (Waco, TX: Word, 1974). Eckstein deals with sensitivities of Jewish people that are unwittingly trampled on by Christians. He addresses Christian readers forthrightly on points of difference and argues that after the Holocaust "neither Christians nor Jews can ever be quite the same" (p. 186); his discussion of the mystery of the Holocaust was most helpful to me. I benefited also the dialogue between Walter Harrelson and Rabbi Falk, two Nashvillians at the time, in their *Jews and Christians: A Troubled Family* (Nashville, TN: Abingdon, 1990). And from a specifically Jewish perspective, a brief essay by Susannah Heschel, "Nativity of the Jews," *Newsweek*, December 18, 2006, p. 59, explains a Jewish "take" on Jesus. My discussion of the Holocaust in this chapter, as well as the reference to Corrie ten Boom, has been influenced by Rabbi Daniel Lapin's book, *America's Real War* (Sisters, OR: Multnomah, 1999), chapter 49, "Christians and the Holocaust," pp. 325-33.

Finally, I recommend a new book from aforementioned Vanderbilt University (the Divinity School) professor in New Testament, Amy Jill Levine, *The Misunderstood Jew: The Church and the Scandal of the Jewish Jesus* (San Francisco: Harper, 2006). I have heard Professor Levine speak in Nashville's Temple and in Christian churches as guest lecturer on several occasions and continue to marvel at the depth of her knowledge of New Testament documents and Christian teaching. Levine's basic point is that Christians must remember that Jesus was born as a Jew, and his teachings and actions were entirely consistent with first century Jewish belief; furthermore, it is unfair to stereotype Judaism as a religion of oppressive, rigid laws, while Christianity is a religion of grace. Such stereotypes have fostered distrust and contempt between the two faiths, Levine contends.

Chapter 14 discusses Muhammad and the Islamic religion. There is so much source material now available on Islam. I recommend two sources: Colin Chapman, *Cross and Crescent: Responding to the Challenge of Islam,* 2nd ed. (Downers Grove, IL: InterVarsity, 2003) from an author with personal experience of life in the Middle East and George W. Braswell, *What You Need to Know about Islam and Muslims* (Nashville: Broadman and Holman, 2000), also by an author who has lived in the Middle East. Norman L. Geisler and Abdul Saleeb, *Islam: The Crescent in Light of the Cross* (Grand Rapids, MI: Baker Books, 1993), is a substantial study. Christopher Catherwood, *Christians, Muslims and Islamic Rage* (Grand Rapids, MI: Zondervan, 2003), is easily understandable and offers some historical analysis.

There is much background information in Bernard Lewis, *The Middle East: A Brief History of the Last 2,000 Years* (New York: Scribner, 1995). An even more recent study of the U. S. involvement in the Middle East since the time of the Barbary Wars of the 18th century and fought its first foreign war there is Michael B. Oren, *Power, Faith, and Fantasy: America in the Middle East 1776 to the Present* (New York: W. W. Norton, 2007). A succinct statement of the roots of enmity between the Sunnis and Shiites in the Middle East today may be found in a cover story, "Why They Hate Each Other," *Time*, March 5, 2007, pp. 28-40. A special report and cover story on Islam in the USA is offered in Lisa Miller, "American Dreamers: Islam USA," *Newsweek*, July 30, 2007, pp. 24-33. Miller's thesis is that Muslims in the USA are enjoying overwhelming success and are especially blessed in their various opportunities and rights. The quotation from Bruce Feiler in this chapter is drawn from his *Abraham: A Journey to the Heart of Three Faiths* (New York: Harper Collins, 2004), pp. 163-64.

Chapter 15 discusses tragedy, pain, and evil, and the literature on this subject is, of course, vast. Most textbooks in Christian apologetics will include one or more chapters on the subject. Chapter 2, "If There is a God, Why is There Evil?" of Steve Kumar's *Christianity for Skeptics: An Understandable Examination of Christian Belief* (Peabody, MA: Hendrikson, 2000), pp. 38- 57, is a very readable, simple review of arguments reconciling God's presence and love with the reality of moral evil. My analogy of the two wayfarers is adapted from J. Edwin Orr and is found in the above work

(p. 51). I discovered a more sophisticated and challenging discussion of sin and evil in Carter Heywood, *Saving Jesus From Those Who Are Right: Re-thinking What It Means to be Christian* (Minneapolis: Fortress Press, 1999), pp. 84-114. Heywood speaks of the global context in which sin must be considered "our out-of-touchness with the fact that we are in relation—that our lives are connected at the root and that this is the sacred basis of our "creatureliness," our humanity, our lives together on planet Earth. And finally, I was influenced by comments about evil by Philip Yancey in *Rumors: What On Earth Are We Missing?* (Grand Rapids, MI: Zondervan, 2003), chapter 7, pp. 113-25. Readers interested in whether modern neuroscience provides any answers to the enigma of moral evil should benefit from the cover story by Jeffrey Kluger, "What Makes Us Moral?" *Time*, December 1, 2007, pp. 54-60. The author's thesis: "Morality and empathy are writ deep in our genes. Alas, so are savagery and bloodlust. Science is now learning what makes us both noble and terrible—and perhaps what can make us better" (p. 54).

Chapters 16 and 17 deal with two subjects that are very much connected with contemporary New Age religion: pantheism and reincarnation. These topics are discussed in most textbooks on world religions. Pantheism is discussed analytically in Chapman's *The Case for Christianity*, pp. 202-06. Richard Halverson discusses New Age as well as the major Eastern religions in *The Compact Guide to World Religions* (Minneapolis: Bethany House, 1996). "That New Age Religion," chapter 28 in Charles Colson, *How Now Shall We Live?* (Wheaton, IL: Tyndale, 1999), pp. 263-71, offers a perspective on New Age themes from a conservative Christian. The analogy of humans living in a huge art gallery wherein God is the creative artist is one I have heard discussed by Brian McLaren and other teachers. While a huge bibliographic listing could be cited on the issues of environment and global warming, the study cited in chapter 16 is reported in "Raising the Climate Stakes," *Time*, February 19, 2007, p. 18. As for my thinking about any possible biblical insight about reincarnation, I acknowledge indebtedness to a somewhat older lesson presented by Leslie Weatherhead in *The Christian Agnostic* (Nashville, TN: Abingdon, 1965), pp. 293-316. The contrast between the life lived by a Hindu guru and the life of Mother Teresa is drawn from Kent E. Richter, et. al., Understanding Religion in a Global Society (Belmont, CA: Thomson Wadsworth, 2005), p. 294. The contrast in worldviews on the subject of the afterlife are discussed in a cover story by Lisa Miller, "Visions of Heaven: How Views of Paradise Inspire—And Inflame—Christians, Muslims, and Jews," *Newsweek*, August 12, 2002, pp. 44-52.

Chapter 18 deals with the practical wisdom that can be drawn from Eastern religion and philosophy. The thinking of Lao-Tzu and Confucius are discussed in most introductory philosophy and religion texts that include Eastern thought. A valuable anthology of writings across the spectrum of religious traditions is edited by Joel Beversluis, *Sourcebook of the World's Religions* (3rd ed.; Novato, CA: New World Library, 2000). The latest anthology of such wisdom literature of various religions is collected in Raymond Scupin, editor, *Religion and Culture: An Anthropological Focus* (Upper Saddle River, NJ: Prentice-Hall, 2008).

Chapter 19 deals with the power of myths, rituals, and ceremonies in our lives and all texts in the history and/or philosophy of religion discuss this subject, and I have drawn information and insights on tribal and ancient religion from several listed in the bibliography. I acknowledge my indebtedness especially to Clare Gibson, *Sacred Symbols: A Guide to the Timeless Icons of Faith and Worship* (Edison, NJ: Chartwell Books, 2002). The idea about karmic guilt cited in the devotional reflection is drawn from an interview of Ram Gidoomal, a multinational businessman and politician who came from a Hindu background, attended Muslim schools, and became a follower of Jesus. Gidoomal states: "In my cultural context, the biggest religious problem is your karma: your karma debt....You come to earth with a karma account....*Sanatan* is a Sanskrit word meaning 'eternal.' *Sat guru* means 'true living way.' *Guru* is a living way.... So Jesus is a *sanatan sat guru* who paid our karmic debt." The interview, conducted by Andy Crouch, is published in *Christianity Today*, May, 2007, pp. 34-37.

Chapter 20 tackles the fascinating topic of ritual sacrifice. Any reputable Bible encyclopedia can provide information and scriptures dealing with sacrifice in biblical times. I'm indebted to a general overview of religious sacrifice, including human sacrifice, in Roger Schmidt, *et. al., Patterns of Religion* (2nd edition; Belmont, CA: Wadsworth, 2005), pp. 46-49. And there are many textbooks in world history that tell the story of the Aztec and Mayan rituals of human sacrifice. One book that I consulted was Albert M. Craig, *et. al., The Heritage of World Civilizations*, Volume 1 to 1700, 7th edition (Upper Saddle River, N. J., 2006), especially pp. 376-91. Some of my thought about the narrative of Abraham being called to offer his son Isaac was stimulated in what at first seemed like an unlikely source: Alan M. Dershowitz, *The Genesis of Justice* (New York: Warner Books, 2000), chapter 6, pp. 103-31. As the title suggests, Dershowitz, both a Jew and nationally-known attorney, provides his own unique legal interpretation of several stories in the first book in the Bible.

I have also consulted with profit Simon John De Vries' essay, "Human Sacrifice in the Old Testament: In Ritual and Warfare," in Harold Ellens, editor, *The Destructive Power in Religion: Violence in Judaism, Christianity, and Islam* (Westport, CT: Praeger Publishers, 2004), chapter 6, pp. 99-121. And, not surprisingly, Bruce Feilor provides some very interesting insight and possible interpretations of Abraham's command to sacrifice his son in chapter 4, "Isaac," in Abraham: *A Journey to the Heart of Three Faiths*

(New York: HarperCollins, 2004), pp. 82-110. Feilor suggests that Abraham may have been testing God and that forever after this incident that God is referred to as the "God of Abraham."

Chapter 21 discusses in brief form how various worldviews approach the issue of ethics. There are, of course, numerous books on ethics and the issue of how we live and what our duties are toward others and ourselves has been discussed and debated for centuries. I have drawn from my lecture notes of over fifteen years of teaching ethics and from other published material in ethics in two previous books: *Harsh Realities/Agonizing Choices* (Joplin, MO: College Press, 1996) and *Etched in Stone*, 2nd ed. (Brentwood, TN: Welverst, 2004). A good survey is *Ethics of World Religions* by Arnold Hunt, Marie Crotty, and Robert Crotty (San Diego, CA: Greenhaven Press, 1991). I also recommend Dennis P. Hollinger, *Choosing the Good: Christian Ethics in a Complex World* (Grand Rapids, MI: Baker Academic, 2002), chapter 3, "A Christian Worldview Foundation for Ethics," pp. 61-86; the author argues that the foundation for Christian ethics is a Christian worldview and that "our understanding of the moral good, right, wise and just emanate from the nature and actions of God" (p. 64). The emphasis upon compassion in all the great religions is underscored in chapter 10, "The Way Forward," of Karen Armstrong's outstanding study of Axial philosophy and religion, *The Great Transformation: The Beginnings of Our Religious Traditions* (New York: Alfred A. Knopf, 2006), pp. 367-99.

As for **chapter 22** on religious fundamentalism and fanaticism, my thinking about the connection between fanaticism and holy war was stirred by an article by Andrew Curry, "The First Holy War," in a special issue, "Mysteries of the Faith," of U. S. News and World Report (my photocopy n. d.), pp. 68-75. I highly recommend the historical and analytical study by Karen Armstrong, *The Battle for God: A History of Fundamentalism* (New York: Random House, 2000). Armstrong places fundamentalism in historical context, showing it is always a product of its times and that the dynamic of fundamentalism has not changed over the centuries. She argues that all ideologies and theologies are rooted in fear and that drives the desire to define doctrine, establish borders and segregate the faithful in a sacred enclave where the law is stringently observed. The quote from Armstrong about fundamentalism being a modern movement is from the above source, p. viii.

This chapter also references Jim Wallis' writing. Jim is the long-time editor of *Sojourners* magazine and is an evangelical political activist who respects Scripture and gives special attention to Christian peacemaking and concern for the poor, underprivileged, and disadvantaged in America and abroad. I recommend two books by Wallis: *God's Politics: Why the Right Gets It Wrong and the Left Doesn't Get It* (Harper Collins, 2005), and his *Soul of Politics: Beyond "Religious Right" and "Secular Left"* (New

York: Harcourt Brace and Company, 1995). A fairly recent book has gained critical acceptance: Gregory A. Boyd, *The Myth of a Christian Nation: How the Quest for Political Power Is Destroying the American Church* (Grand Rapids, MI: Zondervan, 2005); the title and subtitle of this book succinctly capture its thesis.

An older, but very sound little book is by Richard Wentz entitled *Why Do People Do Bad Things in the Name of Religion?* (Mercer University Press, 1987). Wentz argues that the problem of religious violence and carnage is not the religion itself, for violence has been done in them all, but the problem is the "demon of the absolute, the human craving to worship absolutes of our own making and call them 'god.'" The story of the Crusades has been told in so many history books and the History Channel has also presented a dramatized series on the topic. The quote by Abraham Lincoln near the end of the chapter is drawn from Paul Johnson, *A History of the American People* (New York: Harper Collins, 1997), p. 471. Readers interested in Lincoln—and who isn't?—might enjoy the chapter entitled "God's Man" in J. G. Randall and R. N. Current, *Lincoln the President: Last Full Measure* (New York: Dodd, Mead, 1955). And, finally, I recommend a three-part documentary series entitled "God's Warriors," first telecast over CNN in the fall of 2007 and hosted by Middle East correspondent Christiane Amanpour. Ms. Amanpour was informed of this book's purpose and conveyed personal best wishes for the success of the project.

As for **chapter 2**3: A number of authors have wrestled with this crucially important question of whether all major world religions are simply different roads to God. This is a tough issue to be sure that touches on nature of God's grace and the fate of those who have never heard the gospel. Actually, theologians have wrestled with this issue for centuries. Those who make Scripture teaching authoritative on these related issues fall into two camps: *exclusivist* and *inclusivist*. A scholarly discussion of the differences in these two camps is found in the opening pages of Timothy C. Tennent's *Christianity at the Religious Roundtable*, pp. 16-33, and a more detailed scholarly discussion and dialogue among five Christian scholars is published in *Four Views on Salvation in a Pluralistic World*, edited by Dennis Okholm and Timothy Phillips (Zondervan, 1996). Carl E. Braaten makes a convincing case for the uniqueness of Christ and the Christian faith in his *No Other Gospel!* My own thinking and writing in this chapter were greatly influenced by the excellent analysis of biblical teaching by Clark H. Pinnock in his very readable book, *A Wideness in God's Mercy: The Finality of Jesus Christ in a World of Religions* (Grand Rapids, MI: Zondervan, 1992).

Other works that were consulted for this topic were: Michael Green, *But Don't All Religions Lead to God?* (Grand Rapids, MI: Baker Books, 2002), a very brief, readable volume Ronald H. Nash, *Is Jesus the Only Savior?* (Grand Rapids: Zondervan, 1994); Nash sees a pluralist view as a threat to Christianity and his last chapter is entitled, "Why I Am Not an Inclusivist," pp. 163-75. Millard J. Erickson, *How Shall They Be*

Saved? The Destiny of Those Who Do Not Hear Jesus (Grand Rapids: Baker Books, 1996) analyzes both traditional and non-traditional positions. *What About Those Who Have Never Heard: Three Views on the Destiny of the Unevangelized*, edited by John Sanders, presents the thinking of Ronald H. Nash (arguing the restrictivist position), Gabriel Fackre (advocating divine perseverance with the expectation that those who die unevangelized will have another opportunity for salvation after death), and John Sanders (arguing that the work of Jesus can save people who have not had the chance to know Jesus); (Downers Grove, IL: InterVarsity Press, 1995.) Jesus as the unique Savior is just one of the themes in James R. Edwards' thoughtful volume, *Is Jesus the Only Savior?* (Grand Rapids: Eerdmans, 2005); Edwards also asks other vital questions: Is a Savior from sin meaningful in a day of moral relativism? Does an exclusive Savior threaten world peace? Lesslie Newbigin's *The Gospel in a Pluralist Society* (Grand Rapids, MI: Eerdmans, 1989), is a very thoughtful study, as is John Sanders, *No Other Name: An Investigation into the Destiny of the Unevangelized* (Grand Rapids, MI: Eerdmans, 1992). *Through No Fault of Their Own*, edited by William V. Crockiett and James G. Sigountos (Grand Rapids, MI:: Baker Book House, 1991), presents essays in biblical theology, exegesis, and missiological issues by approximately twenty theologians and Bible scholars. A simple, yet profound statement of God's grace is found in Edward William Fudge's *The Great Rescue: The Story of God's Amazing Grace* (Abilene, TX: Leafwood Publishers, 2002). A briefer statement of Fudge's theology is published in his article, "How Wide Is God's Mercy?" *Christianity Today*, April 27, 1992, 30-33. And, finally, best-selling author Stephen Prothero wrote a brief article entitled, "True or False: The Major Religions Are Essentially Alike," *Newsweek*, July 9, 2007, p. 52, and concludes: "It is a fantasy to imagine that the world's two largest faiths are in any meaningful sense the same."

In the **epilogue**, "Christianity Makes Sense," Ronald Nash's four criteria for testing a worldview have been listed in several of his books, one of which being *Life's Ultimate Questions: An Introduction to Philosophy* (Grand Rapids, MI: Zondervan, 1999), pp. 25-32. Also, Ravi Zacharias discusses criteria for a valid worldview in *The Real Face of Atheism* (Grand Rapids, MI: Baker Books, 2004), Appendix 2, pp. 173-78. Zacharias relies on Arlie J. Hoover, *The Case for Christian Theism* (Grand Rapids, MI: Baker Books, 1976) for the criteria. For readers seeking a much simpler statement of criteria, see "The Criteria for Evaluating Religious Truth Claims" in Halverson, *A Compact Guide to World Religions*, pp. 248-49. Also, Brian McLaren raises practical questions that help us to test a worldview in *Finding Faith*, p. 153. Some understanding of how Christianity has impacted history can be gained by reading Jonathan Hill's colorfully illustrated volume, *What Has Christianity Ever Done for Us? How It Shaped the Modern World* (Downers Grove, IL: InterVarsity Press, 2005).

Bibliography

In addition to periodical literature cited in the previous essay, the following books were consulted in the writing of this volume (and some annotation is added for those readers who choose to continue their search):

Abingdon Dictionary of Living Religions. Keith Crim, general editor; Roger A. Bullard and Larry D. Shinn, associate editors. Nashville: Abingdon, 1981.

Annotated Dictionary of Modern Religious Movements. Benjamin Beit-Hallahmi, editor. Danbury, Conn: Grolier Educational Corporation, 1993.

Albanese, Catherine L. *America: Religion and Religions.* Belmont, CA: Wadsworth, 1999. A text on religion in U. S. history.

Anderson, Gerald H. *Sermons to Men of Other Faiths and Traditions.* Nashville: Abingdon, 1966. An older, but interesting work with several ministers contributing sermons on how Christians may relate to adherents of other faith traditions.

Anderson, Norman. *Christianity and World Religions: The Challenge of Pluralism.* Downers Grove, IL: InterVarsity, 1984.

Armstrong, Karen. *A History of God: The 4,000-Year Quest of Judaism, Christianity and Islam.* New York: Ballantine Books, 1993. A very thoughtful, readable discussion of how the three dominant monotheistic religions—Judaism, Christianity, and Islam—shaped and altered the conception of "the one God." The author traces how people have perceived and experienced God from the time of Abraham to the modern age.

Armstrong, Karen. *Jerusalem: One City, Three Faiths.* New York: Ballantine Books, 1997. Traces the history of how the Jews, Christians, and Muslims have all laid claim to the sacred city, arguably the most important city throughout history. Thousands of years of history are reported about a city that has changed hands so frequently and been the site of both holy war and momentous events.

Armstrong, Karen. *The Battle for God: A History of Fundamentalism.* New York: Random House, 2001 (with a new preface written after 9/11). Explains the mindset of fundamentalists, noting that the most extreme forms of separation and violence from fundamentalists springs from their fear of extinction by secularists.

Armstrong, Karen. *The Great Transformation: The Beginning of Our Religious Traditions.* New York: Alfred A. Knopf, 2006. A very solid examination of great themes of humanity and how various religious traditions from the Axial Age till modern time have contributed insights to our collective understanding.

Aslan, Reza. *No god but God: The Origins, Evolution, and Future of Islam.* New York: Random House, 2000. Contending that Islam is the fastest-growing religion in the world and yet it is still shrouded in ignorance and fear, the author paints a most sympathetic historical and analytical account of Islam's beauty and complexity.

Beckwith, Francis J. and Stephen E. Parrish, *See the Gods Fall: Four Rivals to Christianity.* Joplin, MO: College Press, 1997.

Beckwith, Francis, William Lane Craig, and J. P. Moreland. *To Everyone An Answer: A Case for the Christian Worldview.* Downers Grove, IL: InterVarsity, 2004.

Bertrand, J. Mark. *(Re)Thinking Worldview: Learning to Think, Live, and Speak in This World.* Wheaton, IL: Crossway Books, 2007. Explains in understandable language the nature and functioning of a worldview and provides a theology for Christian thinking, truth, and wisdom.

Bishop, Peter and Michael Darton, general editors. *The Encyclopedia of World Faiths: An Illustrated Survey of the World's Living Religions.* New York: Facts of File Publishers, 1988.

Blamires, Harry. *The Christian Mind: How Should a Christian Think?* Ann Arbor, MI: Servant Books, 1978. The first edition of this book was published in 1963. The author is an English theologian who started writing through the encouragement of C. S. Lewis, his tutor at Oxford University.

Boa, Kenneth and Robert M. Bowman, Jr. *An Unchanging Faith in a Changing World: Understanding and Responding to the Critical Issues that Christians Face Today.* Nashville: Thomas Nelson, 1997. A conservative analysis of different issues.

Boorstin, Daniel J. *The Creators: A History of Heroes of the Imagination.* New York: Random House, 1992.

Boorstin, Daniel J. *The Discoverers: A History of Man's Search to Know His World and Himself.* New York: Random House, 1983.

Boorstin, Daniel J. *The Seekers: The Story of Man's Continuing Quest to Understand His World.* New York: Random House, 1998.

Borg, Marcus, editor. *Jesus and Buddha: The Parallel Sayings.* Berkeley, CA: Ulysses Press, 1997. Places sayings of Jesus and Buddha side-by-side, thus calling attention to some remarkably parallel utterances by two great teachers who were separated by five centuries and three thousand miles.

Borg, Marcus. *The Heart of Christianity.* New York: Harper Collins, 2003.

Bowker, John. *World's Religions: The Great Faiths Explored and Explained.* New York: DK Publishing, 1996. An oversize format for lay readership, this book introduces readers to world religion with brief articles and numerous colorful pictures and illustrations.

Braaten, Carl E. *No Other Gospel: Christianity Among the World Religions.* Minneapolis: Fortress Press, 1992. Makes a strong argument for the uniqueness of Jesus Christ and the Christian faith.

Brasher, Brenda, editor. *Encyclopedia of Fundamentalism.* New York: Routledge, 2001. Contains nearly 200 entries written by a diverse group of scholars, extracts from primary source materials, and numerous pictures and images. Discusses major events, primary beliefs and institutions, major movements, denominations, sects, and individuals who have been central to fundamentalist movements. A valuable resource.

Braswell, George W. *What You Need to Know About Islam and Muslims.* Nashville: Broadman and Holman, 2000. Easy reading and containing a number of facts from someone who has lived in the Middle East.

Braswell, George W. *Understanding World Religions.* Nashville: Broadman and Holman, 1994.

Breuilly, Elizabeth, Joanne O'Brien, and Martin Palmer. *Religions of the World: The Illustrated Guide to Origins, Beliefs, Traditions, and Festivals.* New York: Facts On File, Inc. and Transedition Limited and Fernleigh Books, 1997. Designed as a guide to general readers to lead them through the maze of religions around the world.

Burson, Scott R. and Jerry L. Walls. *C. S. Lewis and Francis Schaeffer: Lessons for a New Century from the Most Influential Apologists of Our Time.* Downers Grove, IL: InterVarsity Press, 1998. A volume of substance.

Campbell, Joseph. *The Masks of God: Primitive Mythology*. New York: Viking Press, 1968.

Carmody, Denise, and Brink, T. L. *Ways to the Center: An Introduction to World Religions*. Belmont, CA: Wadsworth, 2002.

Carson, D. A. *The Gagging of God: Christianity Confronts Pluralism*. Grand Rapids, MI: Zondervan, 1996.

Catherwood, Christopher. *Christians, Muslims, and Islamic Rage*. Grand Rapids, MI: Zondervan, 2003. Offers a simplified historical analysis to explain differences between the western world and Muslims.

Chapman, Colin, editor. *The Case for Christianity: An Eerdman's Handbook*. Grand Rapids: Eerdman's, 1981. Encylopedic, basic, and colorful in illustrations.

Chapman, Colin. *Cross and Crescent: Responding to the Challenge of Islam*. Second edition; Downers Grove, IL: InterVarsity Press, 2003. An excellent volume on Islam.

Clarke, Peter B. *The World's Religions: Understanding the Living Faiths*. Pleasantville, N. Y.: Reader's Digest Association, 1993.

Collins, Francis S. *The Language of God: A Scientist Presents Evidence for Belief*. New York: Free Press, 2006. A leading geneticist presents sound reasons for people to believe there is an all-wise, omnipotent God. The book is written in understandable language.

Colson, Charles and Nancy Pearson. *How Now Shall We Live?* Wheaton, IL: Tyndale, 1999. Brief essays in worldviews.

Crockiett, William V. and James G. Sigountos. *Through No Fault of Their Own*. Grand Rapids, MI: Baker Book House, 1991. Presents essays in biblical theology, exgesis, and missiological issues by approximately twenty theologians and Bible scholars.

Dershowitz, Alan M. *The Genesis of Justice*. New York: Warner Books, 2000.

Dictionary of Contemporary Religion in the Western World. Christopher Partridge, general editor. Downers Grove, IL: InterVarsity Press, 2002. Encyclopedic approach with brief articles written by approximately fifty contributors.

Eerdman's Handbook to the World Religions. Revised edition; Grand Rapids, MI: Eerdman's, 1994. Filled with wide variety of articles and color photos from numerous contributers.

Eckstein, Yechiel. *What Christians Should Know About Jesus and Judaism*. Waco, TX: Word, 1984. An excellent, plain-spoken message from a Jewish rabbi to Christians about Jewish doctrine, history, heritage, and sensitivities.

Edwards, James R. *Is Jesus the Only Savior?* Grand Rapids, MI: Eerdmans, 2005.

Ellens, J. Harold, editor. *The Destructive Power of Religion: Violence in Judaism, Christianity, and Islam*. Four volumes. Westport, CT: Praeger Publishers, 2004. A very specialized and provocative resource. Volume one: "Sacred Scriptures, Ideology, and Violence" and treats "toxic texts;" Volume two: "Religion, Psychology, and Violence" and contains a chapter on the dynamics of prejudice; Volume three: "Models and Cases of Violence in Religion" and treats more "toxic texts;" Volume four: "Contemporary Views on Spirituality and Violence," treats the Crusades, fundamentalism, and Canaanite genocide.

Encyclopedia of Fundamentalism. Edited by Brenda E. Brasher. New York: Routledge, 2001. Contains nearly 200 entries written by a diverse group of scholars, extracts from primary source materials, and images. Discusses major events, primary beliefs and institutions among fundamentalists, major fundamentalist movements, denominations, sects, churches, and individuals who have been central to fundamentalist movements.

Encyclopedia of Religion and War. Edited by Gabriel Palmer-Fernandez. New York: Routledge, 2004. A valuable resource since there is such a complex relationship between religion and war. The reference work contains 130 articles by various scholars and addresses the role of war in the development and spread of major religions; the role of religion in major conflicts, such as the American Revolution or the Civil War; theology and war.

Encyclopedia of World Faiths: An Illustrated Survey of the World's Living Religions. Peter Bishop and Michael Darton, general editors. New York: Facts on File Publishers, 1988.

Erickson, Millard J. *How Shall They Be Saved? The Destiny of Those Who Do Not Hear Jesus.* Grand Rapids, MI: Baker Books, 1996).

Fisher, Mary Pat and Lee W. Bailey. *An Anthology of Living Religions.* Second edition; Upper Saddle River, N. J.: Prentice-Hall, 2008. A representative collection of readings on the major religions and also containing a glossary of terms and a set of discussion questions on each religion.

Friedman, Thomas L. *From Beirut to Jerusalem.* New York: Doubleday, 1989. Explains the Middle Eastern world, especially of the 1980s, shedding light on the Palestinian-Israeli conflict.

Fudge, Edward. *The Great Rescue: The Story of God's Amazing Grace.* Abilene, TX: Leafwood Publishers, 2002. A simple, but profound statement of God's grace.

Geisler, Norman L. and Paul K. Hoffman, editors. *Why I Am a Christian: Leading Thinkers Explain Why They Believe.* Grand Rapids, MI: Baker Books, 2001. Provocative writing by a number of thoughtful evangelicals.

Geisler, Norman L. and Abdul Saleeb, *Islam: The Crescent in Light of the Cross.* Grand Rapids, MI: Baker Books, 1993.

Geisler, Norman L. and William D. Watkins. *Worlds Apart: A Handbook on Worldviews.* Second edition; Grand Rapids, MI: Baker Book House, 1989.

Gibson, Clare. *Sacred Symbols: A Guide to the Timeless Icons of Faith and Worship.* Edison, N. J.: Chartwell Books, 2002. A good overview with many colorful illustrations.

Glaser, Ida. *The Bible and Other Faiths: Christian Responsibility in a World of Religions.* Downers Grove, IL: InterVarsity Press, 2005. Treats the role of biblical teaching as Christians determine their attitude toward people of other faiths.

Green, Michael. *But Don't All Religions Lead to God? Navigating the Multi-Faith Maze.* Grand Rapids, MI: Baker Books, 2002. Brief and intended for mass audience, but sensible and insightful.

Green, William Scott and Jacob Neusner, editors. *The Religion Factor: An Introduction to How Religion Matters.* Louisville, KY: Westminster John Knox Press, 1996.

Hall, Douglas John. *Why Christian? For Those on the Edge of Faith.* Minneapolis: Fortress Press, 1998.

Hanh, Thich Nhat. *Living Buddha, Living Christ.* New York: Riverhead Books, 1995. A popular little volume with the central message: peace, love, and compassion are central to the teachings of Buddha and Christ, and people of both faiths should be tolerant of each other.

Harrelson, Walter and Randall M. Falk, *Jews and Christians: A Troubled Family.* Nashville: Abingdon Press, 1990. Deep and respectful dialogue between a thoughtful Christian scholar and a thoughtful Jewish scholar on how the devout of these faiths view each other and how mutual understanding can be enhanced.

Heywood, Carter. *Saving Jesus From Those Who Are Right: Re-Thinking What It Means to be a Christian.* Minneapolis: Fortress Press, 1999.

Hexham, Irving and Karla Poewe, *Understanding Cults and New Religions.* Grand Rapids, MI: Eerdmans, 1986.

Hill, Jonathan. *What Has Christianity Ever Done for Us? How It Shaped the Modern World.* Downers Grove, IL: InterVarsity Press, 2005. A readable and logical treatment to an important question and containing several color illustrations of leading figures of history who were influenced and motivated by Christian faith.

Hollinger, Dennis P. *Choosing the Good: Christian Ethics in a Complex World.* Grand Rapids: Baker Academic Books, 2002. A thoughtful discussion of ethics, drawing from highly regarded ethicists and emphasizing the Christian worldview.

Holmes, Arthur F. *Contours of a World View.* Grand Rapids, MI: Eerdman's, 1983.

Johnson, Phillip E. *The Wedge of Truth: Splitting the Foundations of Naturalism.* Downers Grove, IL: InterVarsity Press, 2000.

Jones, Milton. *Christ—No More, No Less: How to be a Christian in a Postmodern World.* Abilene, TX: Leafwood Publishers, 2001.

Kreeft, Peter. *Socrates Meets Jesus: History's Great Questioner Confronts the Claims of Christ.* Downers Grove, IL: InterVarsity Press, 1987.

Kreeft, Peter. *Fundamentals of the Faith: Essays in Christian Apologetics.* San Francisco, CA: Ignatius Press, 1988.

Lapin, Daniel. *America's Real War.* Sisters, OR: Multnomah, 1999. An orthodox rabbi makes his case that general Judeo-Christian values are vital for the nation's survival.

Laderman, Gary and Luis Leon, editors. *Religion and American Culture: An Encyclopedia of Traditions, Diversity, and Popular Expressions.* Three Vols.; Santa Barbara: ABC/CLIO, 2003. A great resource of information on all world religions in America.

Levine, Amy-Jill. *The Misunderstood Jew: The Church and the Scandal of the Jewish Jesus.* San Francisco: Harper, 2006. A powerful summons to Christians to re-think Jesus' heritage, teachings, and actions in order to enrich dialogue between Jewish people and themselves.

Levinson, David. *Religion: A Cross-Cultural Encyclopedia.* Santa Barbara, CA: ABC-CLIO, 1996. Concise with good bibliographic citations.

Lewis, James F. and William G. Travis, *Religious Traditions of the World.* Grand Rapids: Zondervan, 1991. A standard survey text on world religions with a theological evaluation of main ideas in the various religions. Contains a few black and white photos.

Livingston, James C. *Anatomy of the Sacred: Introduction to Religion: An Introduction to Religion.* Fifth edition. Upper Saddle River, NJ: Prentice-Hall, 2005.

MacArthur, John, with Master's College Faculty. *Think Biblically: Recovering a Christian Worldview.* Wheaton, IL: Crossway Books, 2003. A conservative position on several worldview issues.

Maguire, Jack. *Essential Buddhism: A Complete Guide to Beliefs and Practices.* New York: Pocket Books, 2001. A readable, interesting book that focuses on the core of Buddhism as a uniquely practical faith with a small body of basic beliefs.

Mather, George A. and Larry A. Nichols. *Dictionary of Cults, Sects, Religions, and the Occult.* Grand Rapids, MI: Zondervan, 1993.

Matthews, Warren. *World Religions*. 4th edition. Belmont CA: Wadsworth, 2004.

McDermott, Gerald R. *Can Evangelicals Learn from World Religions?: Jesus, Revelation, and Religious Traditions*. Downers Grove, IL: InterVarsity Press, 2000. The author contends that we must not dismiss lessons which can be learned from other world religions.

McGrath, Alister E. *Intellectuals Don't Need God and Other Modern Myths: Building Bridges to Faith Through Apologetics*. Grand Rapids, MI: Zondervan, 1993.

McLaren, Brian D. *Finding Faith: A Self-Discovery Guide for Your Spiritual Quest*. Grand Rapids, MI: Zondervan, 1999. In this easily read and less traditional approach to apologetics, McLaren differentiates the doctrine of God in various worldviews.

Marsden, George M. *Fundamentalism and American Culture: The Shaping of Twentieth-Century Evangelicalism, 1870-1925*. New York: Oxford University Press, 1980.

Moore, Peter C. *Disarming the Secular Gods: How to Talk So Skeptics Will Listen*. Downers Grove, IL: InterVarsity Press, 1989.

Moreland, J. P. and William Lane Craig. *Philosophical Foundations for a Christian Worldview*. Downers Grove, IL: InterVarsity Press, 2003. A major philosophy textbook for serious students.

Nash, Ronald H. *Faith and Reason: Searching for a Rational Faith*. Grand Rapids, MI: Zondervan, 1988. This work begins with a discussion of worldviews and then moves to a discussion of the rationality of religious belief, God's existence, the problem of evil, and miracles.

Nash, Ronald H. *Is Jesus the Only Savior?* Grand Rapids, MI: Zondervan, 1994.

Nash, Ronald H. *Worldviews in Conflict: Choosing Christianity in a World of Ideas*. Grand Rapids, MI: Zondervan, 1992. Repeats the material on worldviews in the above volume and elaborates on choosing a worldview; also discusses the New Age movement.

Neill, Stephen. *Christian Faith and Other Faiths*. Downers Grove, IL: InterVarsity Press, 1984.

Newbigin, Lesslie. *The Gospel in a Pluralistic Society*. Grand Rapids, MI: Eerdmans, 1989.

Newport, John P. *Life's Ultimate Questions: A Contemporary Philosophy of Religion*. Dallas, TX: Word, 1989. An extensive discussion of the most important questions in life from a biblical worldview; a volume of significant substance.

Newport, John P. *The New Age Movement and Biblical Worldview*. Grand Rapids, MI: Eerdman's, 1998. Another extensive discussion from a biblical perspective.

Noebel, David A. *Understanding the Times: The Religious Worldviews of Our Day and the Search for Truth*. Eugene, OR: Harvest House, 1991. A large volume with much information and a strong biblical orientation from a conservative perspective.

Okholm, Dennis and Timothy Phillips, editors. *Four Views on Salvation in a Pluralistic World*. Grand Rapids, MI: Zondervan, 1996.

Oxtoby, Willard G. and Alan F. Segal. *A Concise Introduction to World Religions*. New York: Oxford University Press, 2007. A standard university textbook.

Palmer-Fernandez, Gabriel, editor. *Encyclopedia of Religion and War*. New York: Routledge, 2004. Some of the worst wars have been fought over religious ideology; this valuable resource offers valuable articles on the connection between religion, wars, and nationality.

Pinnock, Clark H. *A Wideness in God's Mercy: The Finality of Jesus Christ in a World of Religions*. Grand Rapids, MI: Zondervan, 1992.

Prothero, Stephen. *Religious Literacy: What Every American Needs to Know—and Doesn't*. New York: HarperCollins, 2007. The author laments the basic ignorance of most Americans not only about world religions, especially Islam, but about the Bible. He refers to the USA as "a nation of biblical illiterates," and contends that "religious illiteracy is at least as pervasive as cultural illiteracy, and certainly more dangerous...because religion is the most volatile constituent of culture, because religion has been, in addition to one of the greatest forces for good in world history, one of the greatest forces for evil." (pp. 7-8, 10). Nearly one-third of this book is composed of "A Dictionary of Religious Literacy" (Section 6, pp. 283-450).

Pye, Michael, editor. *The Continuum Dictionary of Religion.* New York: Continuum Publishing, 1994. Very inclusive with brief explanations and definitions.

Religions of the World: A Comprehensive Encyclopedia of Beliefs and Practices. J. Gordon Melton and Martin Baumann, editors. Four Volumes. Santa Barbara, CA: ABC-CLIO, 2002. A wealth of articles, statistics, maps, and pictures.

Religions of the World: The Illustrated Guide to Origins, Beliefs, Traditions, and Festivals. Martin E. Marty, consultant editor; Elizabeth Breuilly, *et. al.,* general editors. New York: Facts on File, Inc., 1997. Designed as a guide for general readers to lead them through the maze of religions around the world.

Rhodes, Ron. *The Challenge of the Cults and New Religions.* Grand Rapids, MI: Zondervan, 2001.

Rideout, N. Kenneth. *The Truth You Know You Know: Jesus Verified in Our Global Culture.* Nashville, TN: NDX Press, 2005. The author draws insights on sharing Christianity with Asian cultures from many years of missions in the Far East.

Russell, Bertrand. *Why I Am Not a Christian.* New York: Simon and Schuster (Touchstone Books), 1957. A "classic" in agnostic literature by a noted philosopher. Russell speaks of harm done by religions and contends that major religions are both untrue and harmful.

Sanders, John. *No Other Name: An Investigation into the Destiny of the Unevangelized.* Grand Rapids, MI: Eerdmans, 1989.

Scupin, Raymond, editor. *Religion and Culture: An Anthropological Focus.* Second edition; Upper Saddle River, NJ: Pearson/Prentice-Hall, 2008. Twenty essays in world religions by various contributors.

Setzer, Claudia. *The Quotable Soul: Inspiring Quotations Crossing Time and Culture.* New York: John Wiley and Sons, 1994. The collector of these brief quotes sees religion as a crucial element in global affairs. This work contains quotes from a diversity of worldviews.

Sire, James W. *Naming the Elephant: Worldview as a Concept.* Downers Grove, IL: InterVarsity Press, 2004. Reviews history of worldview studies and seeks clarification of definitions.

Sire, James W. *The Universe Next Door: A Basic Worldview Catalogue.* Third ed. Downers Grove, IL: InterVarsity Press, 1997. A basic text in worldviews.

Sire, James W. *Why Should Anyone Believe Anything at All?* Downers Grove, IL: InterVarsity Press, 1994.

Smart, Ninian. *Worldviews: Crosscultural Explorations of Human Beliefs.* 2nd ed. Englewood Cliffs, N.J.: Prentice-Hall, 1995.

Smith, Huston. *The World's Religions: A Guide to our Wisdom Traditions.* San Francisco: Harper, 1994. A best-selling classic on world religions.

Smith, Huston. *Why Religion Matters: The Fate of the Human Spirit in an Age of Disbelief.* San Francisco: Harper Collins, 2001. Smith's concern is that a dominant materialistic worldview in our time threatens the health of the human spirit and that religion must once again be treasured and practiced as a vital source of human wisdom.

Spencer, Aida Besancon, and William David Spencer, editors. *The Global God: Multicultural Evangelical Views of God*. Grand Rapids, MI: Baker Books, 1998. A scholarly collection of essays.

Tennett, Timothy C. *Christianity at the Religious Roundtable: Evangelicalism in Conversation with Hinduism, Buddhism, and Islam*. Grand Rapids, MI: Baker Academic, 2002. A scholarly, detailed dialogue between advocates of various world religions highlighting distinctions in major world religions..

Webber, Robert E. *Secular Humanism: Threat and Challenge*. Grand Rapids, MI: Zondervan, 1982.

Willard, Dallas. *Renovation of the Heart: Putting on the Character of Christ*. Colorado Springs, CO: NavPress, 2002.

Wilson, Colin. *The Atlas of Holy Places and Sacred Sites*. New York: DK Publishing, 1996. An excellent encyclopedic resource with colorful pictures and brief narratives.

Woodfin, Yandell. *With All Your Mind: A Christian Philosophy*. Nashville, TN: Abingdon, 1980.

Yancey, Philip. *Rumors of Another World: What on Earth Are We Missing?* Grand Rapids, MI: Zondervan, 2003. Yancey speaks of the clashing of worldviews, mainly the secular and the Christian worldviews, on the subject of the invisible world.

Yandell, Keith E. *Christianity and Philosophy*. Grand Rapids, MI: Eerdman's, 1984.

Zacharias, Ravi. *Can Man Live Without God?* Nashville, TN: W Publishing Group, 1994.

Zacharias, Ravi. *Jesus Among Other Gods: The Absolute Claims of the Christian Message*. Nashville, TN: W Publishing Group, 2000.

Zacharias, Ravi. *The Lotus and the Cross: Jesus Talks with Buddha*. Sisters, OR: Multnomah, 2001.